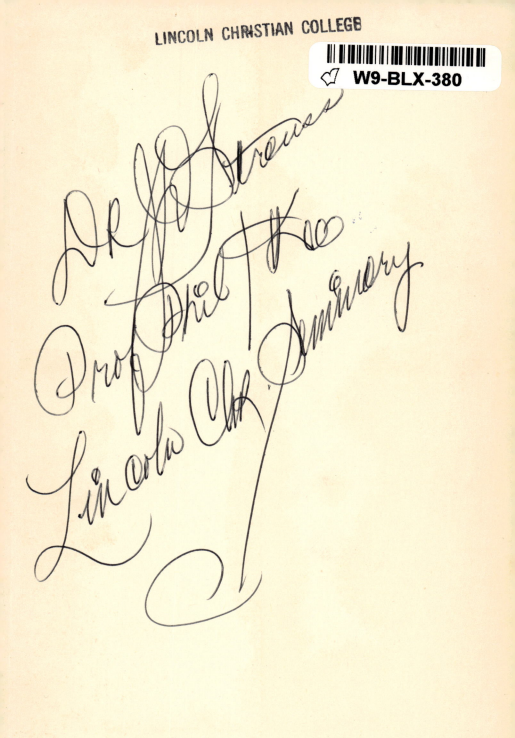

Dr. J. J. Strauss
Prof Phil + Rel
Lincoln Chr. Seminary

SIN AND SCIENCE

SIN AND SCIENCE

Reinhold Niebuhr as Political Theologian

by

HOLTAN P. ODEGARD

The Antioch Press · Yellow Springs, Ohio

Printed in U.S.A.

Contents

Preface

This book owes an immoderate debt to generous people. Its organization and coherence rely heavily on the early help and criticism of Professor Leon D. Epstein. Chapter 6 has been much enriched by the full and faithful notes of Mr. Martin S. Stanford. Professor Max Otto, Dr. Alfred Stiernotte, Mrs. Margaret Bond Odegard and, again, Mr. Stanford have provoked many important revisions, corrections, and improvements by their penetrating and detailed criticisms of the manuscript. I am especially grateful to Professor Sidney Hook for his excellent critical suggestions.

Much of my point of view stems from the teaching of the late Professor Horace S. Fries. Unfortunately his valuable essay "Social Planning" (posthumously published in *The Cleavage in Our Culture,* edited by Frederick Burkhardt) was not yet available at the time the manuscript for this book was written and rewritten. Had it been, it would have received frequent specific references in the footnotes. I am very pleased to be able now to designate this fundamental indebtedness.

H. P. O.

SIN AND SCIENCE

CHAPTER ONE

Introduction: Retreat from Reason

> . . . If past history teaches anything, it is that with in-
> tellectual order we have the surest possible promise
> of advancement to practical order.
>
> JOHN DEWEY

Uprooted in their expectations by repeated outcrop-
pings of evil in proportions of which they had come to
think human nature incapable, two generations of men
have been tragically unnerved. Disillusioned, they have
lost confidence, security, direction among the confused
disorders of the day. The searing tragedy of human impotence, of minds distraught as a result of human failure,
drives men to doubt traditional human methods. Indeed,
the loss of human control over human concerns has been
so dramatically demonstrated by the vivid cruelty of two
Great Wars and a Great Depression that even the most
hardened optimists are awakening to a distrust of the ways
and beliefs they had come to rely upon.

Out of this hell of human ineffectiveness has arisen the
phoenix of irrationalism, a bird of seasonal brilliance —
bedraggled, dusty, and unnoticed through periods of human achievement, but groomed and seductive in resurrection during times of trouble.

The current retreat from reason finds its precursors as
far back as Kierkegaard, but its direct impetus was the
eruption of unprecedented warfare. As one might expect,
the first apostles of the new movement sprang from the

tortured soul of Europe, from the heartland of tragic experiences. Thus the so-called neo-orthodox school came into being under the lead of such men as Karl Barth, Eduard Thurneysen, and Friedrich Gogarten, as a Protestant variant of the larger world mood. It is an aggressively reactionary movement looking back into tradition to biblical myth for security in the present. It is a form of pessimistic escapism which prematurely gives up the task of inquiry, turning instead to an emotional distrust of critical thinking and analysis because recent formulas have proved faulty.

Neo-orthodoxy tells the story of the world by means of beguiling paradoxes, in terms of the complete otherness of God and the complete necessity of accepting His Plan by faith. It offers a serious appeal, given the temper of today's events. There is something contagious, thrilling, and defiant in commitment to unresolved paradox and to supernatural-natural dualism. In Dean Sperry's words,

. . . No one can read these neo-orthodox works without a certain feeling of excitement and exhilaration. To put it on no other ground, the pattern of the paradox automatically gives to the structure of the sentences, paragraphs and chapters an intellectual and emotional tension, which communicates itself to the reader. Beyond all this the reader feels that he is witnessing the one drama above all others which really matters. Its grand strategy unfolds over aeons of time, through its tragedy to its triumph. Its movement is, of course, the old, familiar Plan of Salvation, but in its most recent statement new vitality has been given to it.[1]

By inviting men to be in things instead of observing things, neo-orthodoxy appeals to the active social part of their nature. By revitalizing the concept of original sin, it proclaims itself the advance guard of a crusade against sin and evil. By speaking with the unwavering conviction of final authority, the quality of its certainty appeals beyond measure, taking utmost advantage of the contemporary exhaustion of human hope and resources; there is a kind of excitement or agitation in making a life commitment contrary to reason.

By now neo-orthodoxy has spread beyond the Continent to take up a dominant position in Protestant England. And it has struck a responsive chord in America — the erstwhile citadel of optimism, where men once confidently believed that they could devise humane methods for the control of human affairs. Indeed neo-orthodoxy has found in America its most progressive, persuasive, and able leader: Reinhold Niebuhr, one of the exceptionally brilliant men of our time.

Niebuhr, as an American variant of an essentially German movement, is as important in American life for his political philosophy as for his theology. While other leaders of the neo-orthodox movement have turned otherworldly, Niebuhr has become an active and radical participant in politics. He has been a genuine inspiration toward the improvement of our social and political institutions. The influence of his personal good will, his sensitive social conscience, and his drive for social betterment has been great. He brings to the cause of human welfare a deep fund of learning and a great wealth of high moral intent, providing us with penetrating analyses and valuable new insights. His political views have gained wide respect — even among people who consider his theology mere obscurantism.

A part of the " neo " in Niebuhr's orthodoxy attempts to renovate the old by adapting it to the findings of science, the scientific method, and the experimental treatment of morals. Although " orthodoxy " has been in some respects politically conservative, and although we have become so accustomed to seeing orthodox Christianity oppose democratic aspirations and social achievements as almost to assume that such is the necessary course of events, this conservatism has been an indirect effect of a more basic apolitical, ascetic, other-worldly tendency. It has resulted from a feeling of defeatism before the problems of establishing as rules in this world the precepts of perfection advocated by Christ.[2] The particular importance of Niebuhr's adaptation of orthodoxy is that his work charts an avenue for the possible re-entrance of " orthodox " religion into politics. Many people steeped in traditional religion are eager for authority to help them hold liberal or radical views of politics or believe in the latest achievements of science. And many are the disillusioned who welcome a scapegoat — even if it must be the taint of original sin in human nature — upon which to cast the blame for failure of nerve and by means of which to avoid the duty of arduous thought. The net effect of Niebuhr's teaching, of his novel combination of orthodoxy and radicalism, is a more realistic attitude toward present-day problems of social reconstruction.[3]

The wedding of orthodoxy and radicalism has received competent descriptive treatment at the hands of D. R. Davies,[4] who interprets the growth of Niebuhr's thought as a movement to the right followed by a movement to the left. Niebuhr first revolted against modern liberal theology, finding his inspiration in Augustine, Paul, and the prophets, and returning to the supernatural dualism of orthodoxy. He then revolted against modern liberalism, building his political theory on the foundations of neo-orthodoxy under the influence of Marxism. From the teachings of romantic realism he turned to a new and improved form of orthodoxy; from the perfectionism of the social gospel he turned to a form of realistic socialism. He has been found preaching sin in the lecture hall and supporting the Socialist party ticket at elections.

What is important here, however, is the order of events: orthodoxy first and radicalism following. In so far, then, as the total body of Niebuhr's thought is integrated, it should be possible to say that his interpretations in politics are founded in his religious and philosophical neo-orthodoxy; his basic beliefs are not, strictly speaking, an outgrowth of his radical political observations.

Niebuhr's drift down the rapids of radicalism in a neo-orthodox canoe has stranded him finally on an island between two main streams of American thought. He has been drenched in each stream and has emerged with a synthesis that is startling indeed. On one shore he speaks of progress, of the relativity of democratic structure, organization, values, actions, and solutions to historical context, and of the need to " approach the facts of life experimentally and scientifically, rather than traditio ily." [5] On the other he talks about the " permanent factors in the human situation," [6] about the immutable in human nature, and about a permanent element in man's historic situation. Over all he maintains that " it ought not to be impossible to preserve the poetic with the scientific attitude, the mystical with the analytical, to have both worship and instruction." [7]

Niebuhr's political theory is empiric, but limited by a dogmatic theory of the nature of man and a semi-dogmatic theory of history. He tries to span experimentalism and absolutism (by dialectic). He looks for an empiric democracy and expects citizens to maintain an experimental attitude toward it while they are " under the criticism " of

a divine, unchanging, and perfect standard or "norm."
His neo-orthodoxy seems thus to occupy an intermediate
position between the two most conspicuous philosophies
in America today — neo-Thomism and pragmatism. Like
neo-Thomism it looks to the past for a key to the present,
like neo-Thomism it relies ultimately on supernaturalism,
like neo-Thomism it inserts the unchanging into human
nature. Like pragmatism it denies a prescriptive role
to natural law,[8] distrusts the absolutes of man's churches,
adopts an experimental attitude toward values. Niebuhr
himself notes that he has occupied a position between
" legalism " and " relativism." His position is more novel
than the first and more permanent than the last. For him
the structure of man is immutable, but not under the fixed
norms of Christian legalism because the freedom of man
can create new configurations of freedom and necessity.[9]
If the parts of Niebuhr's philosophy were separable and
independent it might be possible to say that he is both
dogmatist and pragmatist — but that is not the case.
His over-all philosophy is well integrated, and its parts
are interwoven.

Today, under challenge from the left and the right,
democracy finds itself in urgent need of a strong theoretical basis to help stem the incursions of dangerous ideologies, and to strengthen it for the task of world reconstruction and world leadership. Democracy seems at times
to be faltering for lack of basic self-assurance, for lack of
an accepted creed. It persists in habit and in stereotype
but falls into inept factions for theoretical or philosophical
self-justification. In a cold age characterized by the fear,
anxiety, and powerlessness of the individual, democracy
does not respond with soul-warming inspiration or heart-

warming social purpose. Even legislatures, the bulwarks of democracy, are showing signs of bankruptcy and are reaping rich harvests of scorn or ridicule. While Communism trumpets its challenge and its triumphs, the voice of democracy, the Voice of America, succumbs to confusion. A new understanding of democracy is needed for democracy's own internal support and for its support in the respect of the nations of the world.

One possible direction for the reconstruction of democratic theory is through revitalizing and strengthening the concept of natural law. This has been undertaken and largely pre-empted by the Catholic resurrection of St. Thomas under the spadework of Jacques Maritain and Etienne Gilson. Another possibility lies in the enthronement of the scientific attitude and in the vision of democracy as a scientific method for the control of social affairs. This is the legacy left to experimental pragmatists by John Dewey. Niebuhr offers a third alternative — what might be called his dialectical democracy. Unsatisfied with the traditional defense of democracy, he constructs a new theoretical vindication, a democracy based largely on one determined absolute — original sin — and vindicated by an irrational, pessimistic rationale.

Despite the wide renown he has received as a radical, Niebuhr is essentially conservative — the basis of conservatism being the attitude, "This has always been, therefore it always will be." At the core of his thought is the revitalized Augustinian doctrine of sin, postulated not as a problem to be dealt with but as an inevitable (except for momentary deliverance by "grace" or "rebirth"), an inherent, and a dominating factor of human nature — almost a thing of worship in itself. The question, then, is whether Niebuhr can support democracy

on a foundation of sin and irrationalism. Does he for-
mulate adequate alternatives to the discredited assumptions of nineteenth-century liberalism (e.g., free trade,
the individual as a political unit, the rule of reason)?
Will he produce habits of mind at odds with attitudes
required for the maintenance of democracy? Is his irrational dialectico-paradoxical method indeed compatible with the methods of democracy? In more general
terms, what are the results of overdoing one quality or
aspect of the human situation? What is the promise or
the danger to American democracy — to the whole of
the human enterprise, for that matter — of over-empha-
sizing one factor, sin?

As participant in the world movement of distrust of critical thinking, of disillusion with the provisional character of
hypotheses, and of impatience with the specific, Niebuhr
presents a clear challenge to democracy. But, at the same
time, he becomes a formidable problem for critical analysis. His philosophy, incorporating as it does a technique
of systematic paradox, comes close to making a virtue of
inconsistency. What possibility, then, is there for the
mediation of consistent thinking? Furthermore, he has advanced some cogent arguments against unlimited reliance
on reason alone, some of which, in their context, are not
to be denied.[10] He has not delivered us, however, from
the duty of arduous thought or exempted himself from the
consequences of his thinking. The most telling and, at
the same time, the fairest analysis of his work remains a
practical consideration in terms of results.

CHAPTER TWO

The Chains of Dogma

" We all have our flaws," he said, " and mine is being wicked."

JAMES THURBER

To present a simple review of Reinhold Niebuhr's philosophy one logically should start with what seem to be his first premises: his faith and his sources of truth and " meaning." Niebuhr does, in the final analysis, ground his whole system of thought in faith; correspondingly, all his contentions ultimately rely on his sources of truth and meaning. This would be a customary way of looking at it. But unfortunately first premises cannot always be definitively sorted and ranked for precedence. Thus it may be that a fundamental belief about man is also a first principle and is either the precursor of faith or the significant reason for retention of a dogma picked up in childhood.

Niebuhr does not present himself as a logician. As a matter of fact, as will be shown later, he entertains a certain amount of distrust for the reasoning process itself. Few philosophers, indeed, start from a single basic concept; they rather have a basic set of concepts, more or less interdependent. Only occasionally is one found to maintain that " from this principle everything is deduced in an inevitable manner."

The presentation of Niebuhr's philosophy may be somewhat distorted by proceeding in the order adopted here.

Nevertheless, the importance assumed in his thought by his understanding of human nature and of the place of sin in human nature, is sufficient to give it standing over what might be regarded as more basic factors. In view of this consideration, and of the fact that this study is not intended to be simply a review of a philosophy, faith and meaning will accordingly be discussed later, to be interpreted in the light of Niebuhr's concept of human nature.

A fundamental, central idea, when loudly proclaimed and implicitly and explicitly believed, becomes a conditioner of thought, embodied in habitual will as attitude, warping the non-conscious part of man so that interpretations and observations do not derive from the observed but are predetermined in the observer. Methods of observation, reflection, and test are predetermined. Alternative methods are automatically ruled out. Imagination may be deadened in some directions and sensitized in others.

The central, overwhelming idea for Reinhold Niebuhr is sin. Before following it through to an analysis of its pervasive effect on his strictly political thought, it will be necessary to place sin in its setting in human nature, to determine its character, and to note the coloring it casts over faith, meaning, and method.

Although the printed formulation of Niebuhr's theory of man did not appear until after he had delivered the Gifford Lectures (1939), by which time much of his political thought was already published, his emphasis on sin has been a constant feature of his writings. Sin seems to have changed its locus to a small extent during the development of his full-blown theory of human nature — at least in the terms used to place it. As will be seen, such changes as have taken place in the locating of sin are not great enough to require separate consideration of his earlier and later thought in relation to sin. The theory as here presented is that of the more recent and elaborate formulation.

"I SEE A LAW IN MY MEMBERS . . ."

According to Niebuhr, the Christian interpretation of the stature of man is determined by the basic assumptions postulated by the Christian faith. God is the object of the Christian faith and thus exists as the first principle, that from which all comes and that to which all proceeds, the beginning, the end, and the meaning. Man, on the other hand, is — on the authority of the Bible — a created, finite being. The Christian view of man, then, depends upon an assumption which is beyond our experience, ultrarational, and therefore in danger of distortion as a consequence of rational attempts at precise explanation. Obviously, the creature of God, in the image of God, can be fully understood only from the viewpoint of God.[1] In this tremendous task of understanding man, Christianity has the great resource of biblical myths, in which are contained disclosures of the nature of man. Niebuhr tries to unravel myth far enough so that glimpses of human nature may be available to man's rationality.

Niebuhr maintains that the *true* nature of man is to be found in the life of Christ. Christ is the portrait of essential man without the irrelevancy of sin.[2] Man is part nature and part spirit. Romanticism falsely over-emphasizes the natural in man; idealism deceives because it gives undue place to man's spirit. Christianity emphasizes that nature and spirit are unity, that man is a whole and that he acts as a whole — symbolized in the Resurrection (not only the soul being saved, but the body as well being resurrected). The two realms of spirit and nature are not distinct; they are not separable. This saves Christianity from the error of attributing evil to the finite part of man.

Man as spirit participates in creation. The essential character of man is his freedom, his capacity for self-tran-scendence, which means that he is free, within limits, to determine his own character. He is " a spirit who stands outside of nature, life, himself, his reason and the world." [3] The freedom of his spirit, his self-transcendence, is limited to a degree by the forms of nature (e.g., will to live, sex) ; but, within limits, his spirit is free to transcend the forms and to redirect the vitalities of nature. It also has a capacity for forming or creating " a new realm of coher-ence and order." [4] This is the essential man as seen in Christ, what man *truly* is. Precise limits of man's creativ-ity are not known nor can they be known.[5]

The *actual* nature of man may also be seen in the life of Christ — in the story of the cross. Man is *truly* expressed by Christ, the norm; man is *actually* seen as " the cruci-fier of Christ, despite his conscious efforts to approximate to the perfection of Christ." [6] In actuality man is a sinner. He is not under the necessity of sinning because sin is not part of his essential character; it is a part of his actual character and is thus inevitable.[7]

The highest self-realization for the self is the subjection, the conformance, of its particular will to the universal will — i.e., attainment of the perfection of Christ. " But the self lacks the faith and trust to subject itself to God." [8] This lack of faith is the first sin and the basis of all sin. The self then proceeds to set itself up as the center of life, committing the sin of pride *(hybris)*, pretension to divinity, inordinate self-love, will to power, and disturb-ing the original harmonies of nature. This is the sin that primarily interests Niebuhr; and the preoccupation with this sin makes Niebuhr a political philosopher worth observing.[9]

Man's ambiguous situation of finiteness and freedom is the temptation to *hybris,* but it is not operative until sin (lack of faith) has entered into life. In his ambiguous position man feels insecure without a faith in God. A state of anxiety is thus engendered, an anxiety of unbelief, which man tries to overcome by setting up false gods — himself or projections of himself. He inevitably strives for power to fulfill his need for security.

" Sin is to be regarded as neither a necessity of man's nature nor yet as a pure caprice of his will. It proceeds rather from a defect of the will for which reason it is not completely deliberate; but since it is the will in which the defect is found and the will presupposes freedom, the defect cannot be attributed to a taint in man's nature." [10] Sin arises from man's creativity, from his freedom; it is possible only because he is free.

Formerly Niebuhr had located sin (*hybris*) " at the juncture of spirit and nature." [11] Its later relocation can be considered a refinement of his theory, but it is not a fundamental alteration. The change should be looked at as a process of sharpening the concept of sin. Sin has always been closely tied with freedom; the bond has only been more clearly stated. The conceptual knot has been retied more firmly.

The importance to Niebuhr's thought of the situation of *hybris* in human nature cannot be over-emphasized. He has transplanted sin from the gardens of nature, embedding it firmly in the soil of the spiritual, in the humus of freedom. This maneuver has revivified evil by forcibly extracting it from flux and heightening man's responsi-

bility for it. It has brought attention to Niebuhr as a
political philosopher (and as a theologian), for without
it his theories would have been but a slight revision of
what has many times been said.

Returning to Niebuhr's theory, sin and its attendant
evil accompany every creative act, since they are so organically part of freedom. The will to power is the perversion
in man of the will to live, created by the application of
man's freedom to that vitality of nature in him. Niebuhr
places great emphasis on the fact that sin is not attributable to man's finiteness, to nature, but is found in his
spirit paradoxically attendant upon his every free creative
act.

The human situation is that, while we have some knowledge of the law of life which the example of Christ may clarify
and perfect, there is also " a law in our members which wars
against the law that is in our minds." The human situation
is, that while I revere schemes of impartial justice in the abstract I am never impartially just in my actions.[12]

Pride, he contends, destroys life's harmony.

Man commits another kind of sin which Niebuhr calls
" negative " in contrast to the " positive " sin of egoism.
Positive sins are Promethean; negative sins, Dionysian. In
these negative sins the spirit, the free will, sharpens up the
natural impulses or vitalities, and centers life around them,
setting them at war with the ideal of virtue. Thus, for instance, the sexual and possessive impulses become distorted into lust and avarice.[13] Sensuality destroys harmony within the self.

One particular difficulty in Niebuhr's theory of man
should be pointed out here. Niebuhr has obviously relied
heavily on Augustine for his doctrines of sin and evil.
For Augustine, sin is " self-willed pride " or " loving more

our own private good, than Thee, the Good of all," [14] and evil is found in disharmony.[15] Augustine prefers the unchangeable to the changeable; the inferior is evil because it is constantly subject to disharmony (change, flux) ; and sin is setting the inferior, the changeable, the evil, in place of God the Unchangeable[16] — the greatest possible disharmony. Niebuhr uses approximately the same definition for sin (i.e., *hybris*) , and evil is the consequence of sin and of sin only. The evil of sin in general is that it has destroyed the original harmonies of nature; more specifically, Promethean sin destroys life's harmony while Dionysian sin destroys harmony within the self. Behind Augustinian thought there is an assumption of a fixed standard to which man should conform. Logically the same assumption would be expected behind Niebuhr's thought. But, as will be shown later, he has discovered such a thing as progress — something Augustine knew nothing of and made no provision for with his fixed standard.

As the spirit looks back in contemplation of its previous actions, it recognizes, Niebuhr maintains, that it has invariably confused ultimate realities and values with the self. It may also realize that it will continue inevitably to sin. Niebuhr sums up the paradox in this way: " The ultimate proof of the freedom of the spirit is its own recognition that its will is not free to choose between good and evil." [17] " Man is most free in the discovery that he is not free." [18] And man is responsible for his sins because they are committed in freedom.[19]

The spiritual part of man is a unity of vitality and reason. Sin has its root in freedom, not in reason; reason is morally neutral. Moral resources are found only in the vitalities of the spirit. If reason is defined as the ability to make general concepts, it cannot be identical with the

capacity for infinite self-transcendence; self-transcendence
is a further capacity, an ability to stand outside oneself and
survey oneself as object.[20]   Reason is the forming capacity
of the spirit, the ability of the spirit to create new realms
of order.   The vitalities of the spirit enable man to break
up the forms, the harmonies regulating the vitalities of
animal life and his natural part, and to redirect his natural
harmonies into new channels.[21]   The universalities of reason do not automatically guide his actions when the necessities of nature are transcended.   Man is not under the
discipline of reason until placed there by the impulses of
the spirit, by some urge or stimulus that does not lie in
reason but in the vitalities.[22]   " If [reason] is supported by
some moral standard, it is able to use such a criterion to
determine the relation of various lesser values to the supreme value, and to prompt the choice of the most effective means to reach the desired end. . . .   Reason can
operate only after certain ultrarational presuppositions
have been made." [23]

Reason may function to support spiritual impulses, but
in itself it cannot direct them. It may support impulses
which carry life beyond itself, it may support the freedom
that permits man to look back at himself, to be self-con-
scious — but reason cannot carry man to the realms of the
infinite; it soon deceives when it tries to explain God or
man in too great detail.[24]

Moreover, reason is subject to the taint of sin.   It can
support misdirected freedom, defective will.   It may err
deliberately as rationalization for defective will, but it
also may err sincerely, in the sense that man is not always
aware of his sins but is truly deceived.   There is no fine
line between deliberate error and sincere rational effort;
indeed, in the final analysis, man is always more or less

conscious of his failings and always more or less perverse in his use of reason. To weigh the importance of rational faculties is a task of something more than reason, requiring the capacity to transcend the ability to form general concepts.[25]

Niebuhr's greatest emphasis is on the doctrine of sin; however, this must not obscure the fact that men also do good. Sin is the transformation of the animal survival impulse, by man's freedom, into the will to power; good is the product when the same impulse is spiritualized into self-realization and self-giving. Good and evil are irretrievably intertwined. Though standing in contradiction to each other they cannot be simply distinguished. As man lives and strives, as individual or group, each new creation, each genuine achievement of good, is attended by its parallel evil; the highest achievements of man will ever be attended with his greatest destructiveness.

Briefly, Niebuhrian human nature may be summarized as follows. Man is composed of two parts, one natural, one spiritual. The natural part is made up of vitalities and forms; the spiritual is made up of vitality (freedom, will) and forming capacity or reason. Niebuhr further emphasizes that man acts as a whole; the parts are interdependent; both creativity and destructiveness involve all four factors. Offhand it would seem that in his philosophy the parts of man are only *distinguished,* to enable conceptual handling of his subject. In actuality, he *separates* the parts of man, only superficially uniting them by requiring that they act together. The difference is that he sees these parts not as manifestations of man but as factors which when aggregated make man.

The *separation* can perhaps best be shown by an example, and the obvious example is sin. If man were a unity of *distinguished* parts, sin, or goodness, or evil would be found in man as a whole, for the subdivisions would only be artificial rational tools superimposed on man for conceptual convenience. As man is a unity of *separated* parts, sin can be established as a phenomenon proper to one of the subdivisions, for the subdivisions are recognizable, discrete actualities. In effect Niebuhr's *separation* of man into distinct parts sets human nature into a fixed and eternal pattern. The nature of man is dogmatically established.

Continuing with his dogmatic nature of man, Niebuhr proceeds to separate the vitalities of nature. " Vitalities " in this connection is a generic term to cover instincts, drives, impulses, and such. As the terms " instinct " and " drive " denote concrete, separate factors, so does " vitalities." Among the vitalities he refers to a drive for unity, a drive for consistency, the sex impulse, self-preservation.

As a rule, vitalities and forms are referred to in a cursory fashion and for the purposes of illustration. Niebuhr does not make an exhaustive listing of them; he is not the one to delimit and define them with care. In fact, he does not think man can or ever will fully understand himself, though with the use of science he can make closer approximations. One of his loudest criticisms of Christian legalism is that in trying to deduce from first precepts it invariably errs by favoring its own interests (institutional). And he doubts the efficacy of social science because, he says, disinterestedness will always be corrupted by self-interest.

Self-preservation is the exception to the rule. Self-preservation is singled out and placed at the vortex of Niebuhr's spiraling warning to the world. The vitalities of the spirit clutch at it (this innocent impulse of the animal world) and blow it up to self-interest, a will to power. Thence they carry it higher and higher, swirling it to wider and ever-wider sweeps of destructiveness. Both creativity and destructiveness are the result of complex interactions of natural and spiritual vitalities and forms. But Niebuhr early became preoccupied with one aspect of the whole, which soon became his comprehensive touch-stone of interpretation. While sin does not eclipse free-dom but rather accompanies it like a dogged shadow on a sunny day, Niebuhr treats sin much more systematically and in much greater detail, to the effect that it becomes the fundamental principle upon which his interpretations are based. And he chooses one particular sin as far out-distancing the others in importance. This is the sin that attempts to set man in place of God, the one erected on what might be considered the most fundamental natural vitality — the instinct for self-preservation.

Two things, then, conspire to enhance the importance of sin in Niebuhr's theory. The first is its situation in the self-transcendence or freedom of man and the fact that as the parts of human nature are immutable so is the fact of sin. The second is that Niebuhr pays disproportionate attention to sin.

In terms of Niebuhr's concepts, sin is not, strictly speak-ing, a factor in human nature. It is a " defect in man's freedom." But in effect Niebuhr's sin becomes a self-acting essence, a rather complicated independent factor in the human situation. The distinction that sin is not found in essential man but in " actual " man is irrelevant. Sin appears as a recognizable force inherent in man and independent of physical-cultural surroundings. It is a dogmatic assertion that there is something in the human situation that affects (taints) all actions, thoughts, or aspirations, something that circumscribes all other factors

and lays down conditions for their operation (without itself being subject to serious alteration). It is auspi-
ciously enthroned high above the tumultuous equality of
the other thronging and interacting factors in the human
situation.

Returning to orthodoxy in theology with his resurrection of sin, Niebuhr has reverted as well to the antique
view of a world beset with self-acting agents — a view essentially magical in its postulation of atomistic forces,
although it sophistically hides them within human nature.
All of the vitalities he finds in man, together with *hybris,*
are such forces of a Newtonian or pre-Newtonian character.
Modern physics has, with its field theory, decidedly discarded this essentially animistic view, as have the more advanced thinkers in biological theory. In an attempt to
standardize terminology for a more adequate understanding of man, Dewey and Bentley have suggested the concept of *trans*action, meaning by *trans* not " beyond " but
" across," back and forth from one to the other. To say
that man is " transactive," then, is to recognize the way he
has been found to act, the role he has been found to play
in the existential matrix. It is to say that both self-acting
agents and inter-acting forces (the pool-table picture of
the world) are not to be detected either in the physical
world or within man himself. Indeed, from the transactional approach it is only loosely that we can speak of man
and environment as clearly distinct one from the other,
for otherwise we treat them as separate things merely inter-acting with each other.

In *trans*action the total situation is the main referent,
organism-and-environment-as-a-whole. The parties to a
transaction are only aspects of the " field," so to speak;
they are not atomic actors but parts of a whole in action.

A fairly close analogy can be seen in any economic transaction where it becomes senseless to speak of either the
seller or the buyer by himself without reference to the
other or to the commodity or to the " market." [26] For
particular and small-scale occurrences, where the context
is simple and the relevant factors few — as, say, a description of a tennis match — the old inter-actional way of
analysis is adequate, as Newtonian physics is sufficient to
problems of automechanics. But when social problems of
far-reaching importance are encountered — even when an
exhaustive psychological and sociological explanation of
why the favorite tennis star lost is desired — it is necessary
to go beyond the limitations set by thought in terms of
fictional forces, to a transactional analysis based on man-
and-culture-as-a-whole.[27]

Niebuhr's error, then, is that he takes what are nothing
more than qualities, identifiable qualities, of the total
moving human situation and hypostatizes them into
sources of motion, self-actional or interactional agents. He
calls them vitalities and puts them within a human nature
that is also extrapolated from the transactional whole of
life. And, his *hybris,* in a little more complex fashion,
heads the list of offenders.

Of course love of power, self-interest, egoism, pride, and
so on, are human traits. But they are not explained or
clarified by being lumped together under a general heading (i.e., *hybris*) .[28] And they are lifted out of the realm of
understanding by being set apart as an intractable force
with a supernatural basis.

Acquired nature is stronger than original nature. Whatever nature the human organism might have had at time
of birth is fundamentally altered by surroundings — social
organizations, language, other persons, economics, beliefs,

pursuits: in general, by culture. Indeed prenatal cultural
influence is not without importance. Love of power (the
essential meaning of *hybris*), for example, should be ap-
proached as a complex phenomenon, the product of many
(external) factors transacting with the human organism.
Love of power is an aspect of organism-in-environment-as-
a-whole, and is a trait that becomes intensified or mini-
mized in different cultural milieus.[29]

The correlation — or, rather, *co*-incidence — of the ap-
pearance of Niebuhr's school of sin and the contemporary
crescendo of irresponsible power (political, economic,
moral, and ideological) is apparent. Niebuhr suggests
that the modern creed of progress was made plausible by
momentary historic circumstances.[30] The same charge can
be aimed, with equal justice, at his own school of thought.
It is interesting to note that utilitarianism and laissez-
faireism were erected on the same " self-interest " as is
Niebuhr's *hybris*. In the hands of the former, self-interest
was built into a system of automatic adjustment of human
problems (so long as it was not interfered with) and it
looked to indefinite progress. This occurred at a time
when industry and opportunity were expanding. Niebuhr
builds upon self-interest a creed of pessimism wherein self-
interest leads to conflict and agglomeration of arbitrary
power — this at a time when individual opportunities are
curtailed and powerful interests have grown to dominate
the scene.

In one particular instance and for one particular man
(Niebuhr), it may be unfair to insist that a theory is nothing but a product of the times. But, on the other hand, a
school or popular following may well be due more to the
situation than to its leading philosopher's intellectual,
emotional, or moral persuasiveness. John Dewey puts it

very strongly: ". . . any movement purporting to discover the psychological causes and sources of social phenomena is in fact a reverse movement, in which current social tendencies are read back into the structure of human nature; and are then used to explain the very things from which they are deduced." [31]

Putting it another way, Niebuhr's concept of *hybris* may be said to derive from observation of the present prevalence of anxiety. The reasoning follows that the anxiety of man is due to his guilt — the most apparent cause of which today is self-interest — and a feeling of responsibility for his sin (or for causing this evil) now labeled "*hybris.*" In any case, it is apparent that Niebuhr's *hybris* has been assumed, not found. As Dean Sperry says, "To deal with life in shades of grey is far less satisfying than to damn it with deepest black or celebrate it with purest white, but the white and black antithesis is always a dogma and not an inference from the actual facts." [32]

Niebuhr not only fails to realize that *all* psychological or inner character traits are more imposed than they are indigenous, but also fails to see that the significance of an impulse (to sin) is never exclusively intrinsic. The goodness or badness of an impulse is dependent upon the conditions under which it acts, upon the culture or environment in which it is acting. Its value can be assessed only in connection with the transaction in which other factors are concerned — that is, in terms of results. An isolated impulse, like a bee in a bottle, is morally irrelevant. The maleficence of a love of power varies with all the factors interacting at the moment. Under proper conditions a love of power may even culminate in valuable creation. [33] When, however, a supernatural factor is added to the environment, as it is by Niebuhr, the situation is impossibly complicated. For the supernatural is inscrutable and so then is the meaning of man's impulses. We can no longer ascertain their value except through revelation.

Unless divine pretensions of *men* (not *man*) are tied with non-psychological factors, nothing in particular is explained. The very fact that the abstraction — *hybris* — is generalized indiscriminately, applied without differentiation to *man,* displays it as an irresponsible absolute. It is asserted, for instance, that *man* is anxious because of his sin and guilt. How much more effectively the problem could be attacked if it were seen that not *man* is anxious but *men,* who are not so much troubled by *hybris* as by a myriad of complicated problems, difficulties, conflicts. The theologian is short-circuited by his abstraction of sin and generalization of it in respect to *man,* to the effect that all pride, self-love, and self-interest are read rigidly as attempts of human beings to set themselves up as God. He fails to see that they can also be human beings' attempts to rise up from their knees as men.

Hybris is postulated as something that cannot be manipulated — as inherent in *man* and independent of external factors. It conceals lack of understanding because understanding is found in transaction, and *hybris* acts; it does not *trans*act. It is set as a postulate to explain other things, but it fails because it only postpones the explanation. It cannot be understood itself because it is prior to knowledge: it can only be recognized.

Being prior to knowledge, sin cannot be treated as a problem. Since it is settled in advance that everything is infected by sin, we can do nothing about it. Similarly it might be expected that since Niebuhr knows beforehand the cause of such phenomena as a lust for power or a selfish interest, they are not problems to him and he will be prevented from critically examining and distinguishing the facts actually involved. In the development of Niebuhr's theory, this is true, but to a certain extent only. For example, *hybris* in power politics cannot be altered, but the opportunity to express it may be restricted. Furthermore, Niebuhr has incorporated in the heart of his theory a logic of systematic inconsistency — a dialectic — which enables him to maintain positions which more unfortunate absolutists are unable to support.

FAITH, DIALECTIC, AND MEANING

Besides the fact of sin and its centrality and pervasiveness in human nature, there are three concepts that must be interwoven to make a fairly clear tapestry of the absolutist side of Niebuhr's thought. Faith, dialectic, and meaning form an essential contrast, support, and background for the scarlet dragon of sin. But that is all. They are not woven in counterpoint with sin. They enrich the masterpiece but they do not fundamentally detract from its monolithic scarlet character.

Faith

Faith has been described as the acceptance of a truth on the credit of the object in which the faith is entrusted. Ignoring its capitalistic overtones, this approximate definition has the advantage of showing the intimate relationship obtaining between faith and truth. It has the further virtue of simulating Niebuhr's interpretation of faith when he says, " The truth of the Christian faith must, in fact, be apprehended in any age by repentance and faith." [34] For Niebuhr, religion is the ultimate principle of meaning, the principle of interpretation used in observation of the facts and in trying to give them meanings,

in trying to fit them into a total unity.[35]　It is in the light
of this ultimate principle of meaning that he is able to test
whether or not any particular faith conforms to experience.

But Niebuhr is not satisfied just to accept Christianity
on faith. " All forms of religious faith are principles of interpretation which we use to organize our experience.
Some religions may be adequate principles of interpretation at certain levels of experience, but they break down at
deeper levels.　No religious faith can maintain itself in
defiance of the experience which it supposedly interprets." [36]　Thus Niebuhr's interpretations are in terms of
the Christian faith, a faith which does not defy experience.
That it can maintain itself because it does not defy experience seems, outwardly, a means of verification, an experiential test.　It is certainly true that Niebuhr spends
much time either fitting historical developments into the
meaning he finds in the Bible or rewording Christianity
to fit the patterns of history.　In support of his philosophy
of history, for example, he gives empirical data which he
contends should lead men to anticipate transcendental
fulfillment.　However, as N. P. Jacobson points out, all
of these data are as simply or more simply interpreted
naturalistically.[37]　But Niebuhr would deny manipulations except in so far as he has been subject to error; he
is merely showing how the Christian faith, which has always been true, fits the facts and interprets them.[38]

From this we might presume that even the Christian
faith would prove untenable should it arrive at irrecon-
cilable contradiction with experience.　If the Christian
faith does not prove to be a resource for co-ordinating experience into a deeper and wider system of coherence,
what then?　Is faith in faith to be discarded?　Shall men
give their God a blood test to see if he is indeed the father

of all meaning?   Obviously no theologian would descend to such absurdity.[39]

It would be a serious charge to suggest that Reinhold Niebuhr, a professional philosopher, has indulged in circular reasoning.   Nevertheless, appearances strongly support such a conclusion when it is pointed out that " experience " in turn is not something without all systems of thought but is determined by the system of meaning accepted by the experiencer.   That the " experience " of a Christian is more coherent when interpreted in terms of the Christian faith is then axiomatic.[40]   The circle has come round.

Niebuhr maintains that in the realm of truth " the revelation of Christ is foolishness, in the sense that experience does not lead us to expect or anticipate the answer which it makes." [41]   His view is essentially the view of Anselm (even to the detail of so insisting on rational explanation as to give the false impression that he believes unassisted intelligence can penetrate the mysteries of faith) : that it is not possible to arrive at the truth by an analytic procedure, but that, once accepted, the Christian faith becomes an adequate principle of interpretation. Clearly, the " experience " of those who have accepted the faith on faith will find coherent interpretation in and will " validate " that faith.   But what of the experience of those who have not accepted the faith, and what of the experiences of the faithful before conversion? [42]   Will these experiences find unity and co-ordination in the Christian faith?   And if they do not, is that faith then untenable? Niebuhr does not in this connection differentiate between experiences.

One would be ill-advised to point out internal errors in Niebuhr's system, for they could only be apprehended upon the basis of acceptance of faith. Before accusing him of inconsistency (which is not a vice, considering the frailty of human reasoning and the corruption by sin of human logic), before charging him with an error of circular reasoning (which to him is not circular because the actuality he sees corresponds with his reasoning), we may indict him for obscurantism. Any particular instance where Niebuhr is confusing or contradictory *may* be intentionally so. It may be the instance of a paradox. The previous discussion might be resolved, for instance, by the paradox: Man has and yet does not have the truth.

Dialectic

D. R. Davies says that Niebuhr's " awareness of the depths beneath the depths makes it impossible for him to comprehend man's tragic history in a neat formula, without torn and ragged edges." [43] As a realist Niebuhr senses the fact of complexity and the failure of simple formulas.

Accordingly, Niebuhr has resorted to formulas appropriate to the complexity he sees. He has found it possible to " comprehend " the totality of existence and non-existence by the use of paradoxes, contradictions, ambiguities, antinomies, and a dialectic of a sort.

Paradox is found in the fact that man is a child of nature, yet is a spirit who stands outside nature, life, himself, his reason, and the world. [44] Man is creature *and* image of God; in man is found freedom *and* finiteness. Man has unlimited possibilities of creativity, but attendant thereupon increasing destructiveness. [45] Evil rises from freedom not as a necessary consequence but as an alogical fact, inevitably. [46] "Who loseth his life shall find it." Self-realization is attained through self-giving. [47] Man has and yet does not have the truth or justice. [48] Man must

strive for justice, yet the ultimate truth is love with which
justice is in contradiction.[49]

Paradox is, for Niebuhr, essentially an affirmation of
opposites. Yet at times he succeeds remarkably well in explaining paradoxes by taking one term in one sense and
the other in another. Thus he also uses paradox to cover
cases of seeming contradiction. Characteristically Niebuhr
shows more interest in the phenomena he describes than
in the rigorous use of descriptive tools.

Niebuhr's dialectic is central to his theology and consequently to his philosophy and politics, which latter are
not fully comprehensible apart from his theology. Dialectical relations are found between such things as history
and super-history; [50] *agape* (sacrificial love) and *eros* (mutual love) ; [51] divine judgment and mercy; God and the
world; eternity and time; grace and nature; the ultimate
goal of love and realistic social ethics; [52] inevitable sin and
responsibility for sin.[53] This dialectic is a concept frequently difficult to distinguish from paradox, and indeed
perhaps not unambiguously displaced by the term " paradox " in some of his writings.

The confusion of paradox and dialectic is easily explainable if Niebuhr's dialectic merely affirms the existence of
a thesis and an antithesis which are resolved in divine
synthesis " beyond history." In that case, the only part of
the process apparent to historic man would be the juxta-
position and affirmation of opposites — which is paradox.
Paradox, in this respect, is an element of the dialectic.
However, Niebuhr, through faith, does know something
about the synthesis. He uses dialectic in a rather Hegelian
sense. It is clear that the antithesis rises out of the thesis
and the synthesis resolves the opposition by combining
the two: history (time) springs from eternity and in the

resolution history is not denied nor totally affirmed; *eros* is a reflection of *agape* and in the divine synthesis it is both affirmed and denied. On the other hand the paradox of evil arising from freedom is solved by divine destruction of evil through grace.[54]

Meaning

Since the relation between the temporal and the eternal is dialectical, the relation of time and eternity cannot, Niebuhr believes, be expressed in simple rational terms — the synthesis is at some point without or beyond time, of which we cannot rationally conceive, and it is a resolution with eternity which is incomprehensible to us.[55] It can be expressed only symbolically. Niebuhr arrives at the truth by picking up clues to the meaning of things without being able to make an analytic description of detailed facts. By over-simplifying and by painting things as they seem rather than as they are, he expects to approach the eternal. The analogy is to the artist, who, by the use of deceptive (in one sense) symbols, is able to portray three dimensions of space on a two-dimensional surface.[56]

Unfortunately, thinks Niebuhr, symbolism is deceptive. But, since it is not translatable, there is no possible substitute. We can only be cautious of the surface meaning and try to accept symbolic explanation in all its entirety and all its depth. Biblical myth is the source of Christian truth, but it must not be blithely interpreted. Jesus was wrong in his expectation of returning during the lifetime of some of his contemporaries. In the same way, any interpretation that reads too literally, too simply, the accounts of the Creation, the law of love, the Tower of Babel, the Last Judgment, and so on, will inevitably deceive. The analogy of the arts carries even further into myth: as the artist must over-simplify, must select particular features for emphasis, must distort a face to portray the character of a man, so religion must over-simplify, over-emphasize, and distort the facts to portray the relation of time and eternity, God and essential man.

For example, the myth of the Creation does not deny the truth of evolution. Nor does it " regard the relation of each fact and event in history to a divine Creator as obviating the possibility of an organic relation to other facts and events according to natural order." [57] But the myth is true in a symbolic sense. The myth of the Fall does not mean that men once lived innocent of sin. Nor does it mean that sin is a consequence of natural impulses. " The perfection before the fall is, in a sense, the perfection before the act. Thus we are able to conceive of a perfectly disinterested Justice; but when we act our own achievements will fall short of this standard." [58]

The essential message of myth is available to those who are wise enough to cull out the true insights expressed in it by primitive imagination. This is the over-all chore that Niebuhr sets himself. He is, in fact, such a highly capable interpreter that a reader is likely to forget at times that symbolism is irreducible to rational sense. Reduction of symbolism by means of paradox and dialectic as a logical system succeeds at times in appearing sensible. In the final analysis, however, the task is impossible; it is like trying to rewrite a Schubert quartet in prose. Niebuhr recognizes the impossibility (" we have and yet do not have the truth ") and refuses to pretend that it is otherwise. The dialectic that he finds as the logical structure of myth is ideally suited to the task of " clarifying " the unexplainable. It does not conceal the ineffable quality of the truth but rather serves to emphasize the impossibility of making rational sense of it; the dialectic is itself irrational.[59]

What then, according to Niebuhr, is the meaning, the coherence that Christianity gives to experience? It is only partially rational, for the complete truth is not available to rational man and the parts of truth that he may rationally grasp are in contradiction with each other. For the rest it is esthetic or spiritual persuasion as accepted intuitively from myth, and it is faith that the jumbled truths of Christianity " ultimately explain " self-transcendent man.

Essentially, Niebuhr's search for meaning in the past — in the past as interpreted through dogmatism, it turns out — is based on the same inspiration as that impelling the wanderings of the other neo-orthodox theologians and the neo-Thomists. Meaning is a cultural phenomenon, a quality of man-in-culture-as-a-whole. It is a function of the cultural crosscurrents and coherences of the day. The present time being one of disjunction (primarily because the disruptions brought about by the scientific revolution in things physical have not been alleviated by corresponding developments in social or moral science) , these men have mistakenly assumed that meaning is to be recaptured by retreat in part or in whole to moral harmonies of the past or to ancient prescriptions for harmony.

The character of Niebuhrian meaning may be brought out more clearly by a consideration of causation — a subject intimately dependent on meaning (coherence). Causation participates in the dialectic-logic of myth. The myth of the Creation points out that the temporal process is not self-explanatory. It contradicts what Niebuhr says is the modern understanding in which the antecedent cause tends to become the sufficient cause of a subsequent event. Natural causation is read correctly as long as this error is not made.   But to it must be added the antithetic Christian concept of creation *ex nihilo*.[60]

To go back to sin: the dominant position of human nature and sin in Niebuhr's thought was suggested at the beginning of this chapter.   It has yet to be demonstrated in relation to the other dogmatic or a priori aspects of his thought treated immediately above.   In a sense it cannot be rigidly demonstrated because neither human nature nor sin is the starting point from which the rest of Niebuhr's philosophy is derived in a logical or a necessary fashion. This for two reasons: first, a theologian (and there is no doubt that Niebuhr is a theologian before he is anything else) would be a contradiction in terms and, by Niebuhr's own testimony, the greatest of hypocritical sinners if he did not postulate God and derive man therefrom.   Second, a philosophy built of the strings of dialectic and the straws of paradox is not a simple, step-by-step construction.

In another and more fundamental sense — that is, in the sense of warping, limiting, conditioning, necessitating, and influencing — the dominant centrality of human nature, and particularly of the sin in human nature, can be shown. This may be seen in the interrelations obtaining between human nature and sin, and the other a priori assumptions.

There is a possibility that *hybris* and human nature were read *in toto* out of biblical symbolism.   But they were more probably read into myth. If after thousands of years the true character of man finally has been extracted from the basic literature of Christianity, the interpreter must demonstrate superhuman poetic penetration or an act of grace. The very nature of myth as an artistic medium precludes the possibility of reading anything in detail out of it.   The things men communicate by means of art are put into the art medium precisely because they are ineffable. In so far as writing is poetic or artistic, what it communicates cannot be said in words, even dialectically; it is non-rational expression. What is said in a piece of literature is available to anyone who can understand the words and sequences of words used; what is " said " through the same piece of literature as an artistic medium cannot be told. A somewhat middle ground is held by the symbolic in literature. This is presumably available only to those individuals who are able to " catch on." However, symbolism is not so obscure but what the ordinary person can understand and acclaim it when it is shown to him. After all, it was introduced into the writing to be noticed.

The " symbolism " Niebuhr is interpreting out of myth is not of the order of that used by Jonathan Swift, James Joyce, or Chinese ceremonial. It is indistinctly intermediate or vacillating between artistic expression and symbolism. It is now " poetic truth," [61] now simple metaphor. When he is supposedly articulating artistic communication it is a disguise of direct intuition. When he is supposedly disengaging the truth from the shackles of symbolism, he is in reality reading into the symbol its meaning. No one can recognize symbol except as he knows by other means of the material symbolized. *Erewhon* does not satirize England except when England is previously known; the dove does not symbolize peace except as tradition has carried this special information. If Niebuhr has found the character of man in symbolic myth it is only by virtue of the fact that he has independently observed or assumed this character and has found that it can be nicely fitted into myth. The remarkable coincidence (previously mentioned) of the picture of the *hybris*-ridden man and times of manifest irresponsible power politics is not to be lightly cast aside.

Furthermore it is difficult to see how a detailed theory of human nature could be read *out* of the simple biblical tales. A twofold character of man may be seen in the life of Christ and in the story of the Crucifixion, but the fine points of a full theory of man can scarcely be ferreted *out* of humble narrative.

On the contrary, with truth allegedly found in the interstices of biblical symbolism, the possibilities of domination by a central concept are heightened. The myth can be conveniently viewed (not necessarily " rationalized ") in a new light since symbolism is a non-precise and highly malleable medium. The lack of specific criteria for selection and interpretation of myth leaves the field, by default, to an overweening concept — in Niebuhr's instance, to sin.

It is significant that human nature is tied with ancient statements, with early formulations of the human mind. Only on the assumption that human nature is static (in part) and forever fixed (in part) can a theologian hope to find the key to human character in literature depicting the problems and events of two thousand years ago. To this extent at least the use of biblical myth is dependent on prior assumption in human nature. Any artistic or rational attempts at formulating difficulties into problems are relevant only to their particular historical settings. Problems are particular and they change with the times, with the rise of new, the disappearance of old, and the transformation of other factors in the situation. So far then as " truths " are abstracted from the Bible they can only be generalized, applied to the present, with great attention to relevant similarities of situation. And whosoever indiscriminately generalizes has beforehand assumed that there are truths which are independent of time and place, that difficulties or conflicts (at least those to which the truths of the Bible are applied) are eternal and not affected by or made up of changing factors. Such for Niebuhr is *hybris*. It is an eternal evil (difficulty) in a field of immutable factors. If man's nature were not assumed to be static (in part), biblical truths would have to be accepted in context of the culture in which they were written.[62]

Niebuhr runs into constant criticism for his handling of the Bible, chiefly because of his lack of criteria. C. C. McCown points out that few leading biblical scholars in the well-known theological faculties of either Germany, England, France, or America have taken up with neo-orthodoxy.[63] He finds it inconsistent with a sound method of biblical criticism. Bernard Loomer contends that the philosophical framework involved in a theological statement of faith should be made as explicit as possible and that neo-orthodox transcendentalism erects philosophical predilections in "guise of being part of the content of Christian faith."[64] Andrew Banning points out that neo-orthodoxy not only lacks biblical criticism as a basis for judgment but finds no grounding in the traditions of the Christian Church, in "the historic landmarks of Christianity."[65] He believes neo-orthodoxy's "return to biblical doctrine and the 'theology of the Word of God' shows unmistakable evidence of being rooted in neo-Kantianism and existentialism"[66] — the influence of contemporary perspectives.

Even Karl Barth, one of the German founders of the neo-orthodox school, accuses Niebuhr and his group of quoting "the Bible according to choice, that is to say, according as it appeared to them to strengthen their own view, and without feeling any need to ask whether the words quoted really have in their context the meaning attributed to them."[67]

This seems reminiscent of the old battle of authorities, showing even more the need for criteria. Niebuhr's justified retort is that " literalism " is even more hazardous than the Christ-myth theory because echoes and accents of the period appear in the Scriptures. Thus, he says, literalism " may indeed emancipate us from the prejudices of our own age, but at the price of binding us to the prejudices of bygone ages." [68]

Niebuhr, however, is still left with only " the mind of Christ " as standard. And that is vague indeed. As Dean Sperry says, " We are living in an age when dogmatism is the order of the day." [69] Under the searching scrutiny of biblical criticism, Christianity has been forced to give up, one by one, its cherished beliefs. While accepting the latest in criticism, " the theory of the Christ-myth is intended to defend the spiritual essence of Christianity and to free our religion from its precarious dependence upon dubious historical data." [70] It is, then, an attempt at reassurance in the presence of the insecurity brought about by free inquiry. Nevertheless, Sperry re-emphasizes, " historically, the Christian religion is supposed to rest upon the rock of fact, not upon the shifting sands of pious speculation." [71] Neo-orthodoxy's " cavalier neglect of the words and deeds of Jesus . . . is as partisan an account of Christianity as the critical and historical study of the Gospels may have been at an earlier time." [72]

This opinion is reinforced by the assertion of Paul Tillich (himself a participant in the neo-orthodox movement) that " any dogmatic interference with [philological-historical criticism of the biblical literature] would drive us into new or old superstitions — myths and symbols not understood as myths and symbols — and, since this cannot be done without the unconscious suppression of sounder knowledge, to fanaticism. The power of this neo-biblicism is obvious in continental Europe, but it can already be felt in this country also." [73]   It then becomes a nice question whether or not Niebuhr's group will be able to maintain the purity of their myths as myths and their symbols as symbols.

As usual the idea of sin is dominant in Niebuhr's thinking about the meaning of the Bible.   However, for what it is worth and so far as it goes, he has a subordinate general criterion for biblical interpretation: to avoid conflict with the natural sciences, to incorporate the various sciences into his system of meaning while taking their disciplines, as he sees them, seriously.   " The accumulated evidence of the natural sciences " has convinced him " that the realm of natural causation is more closed, and less subject to divine intervention, than the biblical world view assumes." [74]   So he does not believe that " revelatory events validate themselves by a divine break-through in the natural order," [75] and accepts, for example, the healing miracles which are in accord with psychosomatic medicine.

The limitations set, by Niebuhr's dogmatic presuppositions, on this outwardly liberal gesture toward a criterion are quickly apparent.   On the basis of these concessions to science he expects to be able to " engage in a debate with psychologists on the question of what level of human selfhood is adequately illumined by psychiatric techniques and what level of the self as subject and free spirit evades these analyses " and " with social scientists on the possibilities and the limits of a rational justice in human society." [76] Note that it is not an inquiry for determining the truth, but a debate between truth and error.

With a system of meaning that transcends reason, Niebuhr finds himself in a position from which he cannot accept the standards other men have relied upon. Literalism is out because " scientific " criticism has reduced the Bible to probability. Christian tradition is out because human institutions succumb to the temptation of divine pretension just as do individuals, only, as we shall see,[77] in an aggravated form. As a matter of fact, any standard is out by the simple reason, if by no other, of the limitations on human reason resulting from sin.

Niebuhr sounds a four-bell warning against trying to establish a simple system of coherence, particularly a system that identifies meaning with rationality. " 1. Things and events may be too unique to fit into any system of meaning. . . . 2. Realms of coherence and meaning may stand in rational contradiction to each other. . . . 3. There are configurations and structures which stand athwart every rationally conceived system of meaning. . . . 4. Genuine freedom, with the implied possibility of violating the natural and rational structures of the world, cannot be conceived in any natural or rational scheme of coherence."[78] Thus, he entrenches himself behind ambiguity, paradox, and the dialectic.

As many of his critics have observed, this treatment of reason verges on obscurantism. It may be that Niebuhr's pyrotechnic display of paradox is a subtle way of elevating absurdities to a more worthy level.[79] Perhaps Niebuhr is close to making a virtue of being non-rational.[80] It may be that under Niebuhr's attack upon reason, theology will degenerate into a process of weaving intricate contradictions and paradoxes.[81] These possibilities seem even more grimly ominous when it is pointed out that Niebuhr believes a rational validation of the Christian faith would entail loss of redemptive power.[82] As Klausner says, " there is much [redemptive] power in rational comprehension."[83]

The point is that reason does accomplish a lot and can accomplish we know not how much more.

It is unnecessary to claim infallibility for reason, or yet to expect ultimate rational comprehension of man by man. It is unnecessary even to insist that reason is a divine instrument given to man to use for his betterment.[84] It is unnecessary to pretend that reason can proceed to understanding apart from the other, non-rational aspects of human nature. Indeed, reason is fallible; it proceeds by methods of successive approximation and it depends intimately not just on the non-rational in man but on man-in-culture-as-a-whole. Niebuhr is right to say that reason doesn't work by itself. But he is wrong to separate it out as a thing in itself and then put " limits " to it. He cannot possibly know the line of limitation by any but dogmatic means. And constant reiteration of the supposed fact of limitation must tend prematurely to discourage creative thought. Separating reason from the vitalities of the spirit too absolutely, he belittles the participation of thought (reason) in the freedom of man (as he calls it), in creativity.[85]

While we may agree that the " total of reality is more complex than any scheme of rational meaning which may be invented to comprehend it," [86] we do not find ourselves compelled to an early abdication of thoughtful effort or to an aggravation of the labors of thought by spinning paradoxes in justification of faith. If the latter is to be the alternative abuse of reason, we rather agree with A. E. Murphy that although we welcome it as an aid to reason " we shall have to ask . . . faith to identify itself and present its credentials "; [87] or we half suspect with Sperry " that this anti-intellectual brief for revealed religion is a sign of doubt rather than a sign of faith." [88]

SUMMARY

A case could be drawn up to show that Niebuhr's quest for " meaning " is an elaboration of the observed or postulated (perhaps half and half) vitality in human nature — a drive for unity. It would not be incongruous with his tendency to find (and to explain things by) forces instead of transactions. Man being creature and creator, being in nature and transcendent, being finite and spiritual, is naturally anxious by reason of his ambiguous position, and naturally conceives an impulse to find unity or meaning above and beyond himself. *Hybris* is, in a sense, a misdirected search for this unity.

Hybris is also the reason why " meaning " is above and beyond man. As long as sin perverts reason, the truth cannot be fully known. " Meaning," far from being a function of culture, is thrown outside of reason into the realm of the supernatural. On the other hand, simply because man is (in part) transcendent, coherence for him is also transcendent. (Moreover there is a limited proof of Christianity in its capacity for integrating human experience.) Meaning for the transcendent must transcend. The center of " meaning " must be without history — or man is committing idolatry.

Causation was used above to illustrate meaning. It also illustrates the bonds connecting meaning with human nature and sin. Niebuhr finds causation in sequence *and* in creation *ex nihilo* because man is ambiguously finite *and* transcendent. Because his horizon is clouded with absolutes, Niebuhr does not see that time is a genuine factor in causation and thus that creation *ex nihilo* is unnecessary to an understanding of the world. Furthermore, he does not even consider the possibility of cotemporal causation found in transaction [89] because he thinks in terms of forces: *hybris* is a force and it acts unilaterally to cause subsequent effects.

Even faith, the *sine qua non* of Niebuhr's meaning (and of his Christianity), is not independent of human nature. (I am tempted to say it is tainted by sin — for if it were not, why should it be so elaborately justified with partial proofs?)   Faith is necessitated by man's paradoxical position, part free and part natural.   Being ambiguously transcendent and not transcendent, man cannot view the firmament in all its depths of truth without the grace of God.   The grace of God cannot take the form of enduring communication to the reasoning half of spiritual man on account of the wounds inflicted on the latter by sin.   It must act through the transitory medium of faith. [90]

Niebuhr's dialectic is likewise a function of human ambiguity and sin.   As long as man is composed of opposites — of transcendence and finiteness, of freedom and sin — unity can be achieved only through dialectic and paradox, unless there is some other form of logic suited to the mystical embrace of incompatibles. [91]   Dialectic is a useful way of superficially uniting separated parts.   To anyone not temperamentally suited to paradox and antinomy, reversion to dialectic indicates that new assumptions must be tried, that an attempt must be made to reformulate the problem, that in so far as these ambiguities tie up with human nature the possibilities of a new interpretation of human nature must be sounded.

The dialectic-paradox method embodies the further convenience of adaptability to the whims of the philosopher. It can be turned on and off at will and thus can conform to any capricious interpretation of human nature.   It is an appropriate tool for a man whose reason is stultified by the stale air of sin, because it is found indigenous to the meanings (biblical and later) revealed through the saving grace of faith.[92]

Given the uncompromising, absolute, inevitable fact of sin, a dialectic is an essential tool to facilitate insistence upon responsibility for sin. To a man not versed in the subtleties of the dialectic, inevitable sin and responsibility for sin is of the same order as insistence, for example, that the unemployed during times of industrial world-wide depression are personally responsible and guilty for being unable to get a job. The uninitiated would normally feel that men are responsible for the evils of the world so long as they can set about eliminating them. But Niebuhr postulates a sin that man cannot begin to eliminate. To maintain an attitude of responsibility he must then resort to a mystical technique which recognizes the incompatibility of the two yet affirms them both.[93] It is interesting to notice, in passing, how Niebuhr seeks to temper the strangeness to reason of this irrational procedure. Without at the same time concealing the dialectical relation of sin and responsibility, he pauses to pay tribute to the way men think, making the situation only seemingly rational by the use of general words. Thus the meaningless distinction is made that sin is not " necessary " but is " inevitable." [94]

Not content with abstract responsibility, Niebuhr proceeds to empower man to alter the inevitable and treat the intractable. The dialectic is necessary because otherwise everything would come to a halt under the dead weight of sin. Dialectic is a technique resorted to in order to make it possible to do something about *hybris,* about which nothing can be done (by man), and in order to enable the philosopher to accept change, development, or progress while holding man fixed and unchanging in his nature. The

particular terms of dialectic conjured with in this connection are *agape* (sacrificial love) — the ultimate goal — and
" a realistic social ethic." *Agape* is eternal, fitted to the
eternal in man, but unattainable by man because of his
sinful condition.   Nevertheless, man may somehow work
toward the goal of " a realistic social ethic " in spite of the
" irrelevance " of sin.   Thus in a dialectic way Niebuhr
leaves man an incentive to strive and to overcome evil.[95]
This aspect of Niebuhrian thought will be examined in
greater detail in the next chapter.

The present chapter has been an attempt to deal with
the absolutes of Niebuhr's system.   While the various elements of his a-priori-ism are interconnected and interdependent, sin and its position in the static human nature
(which varies within limits) are seen to be chief among
them.   And it is of great importance to observe that sin
emerges as an abstract force — a " corruption of vitality,"
if you want — not as a concrete phenomenon brought
about within the transactive situation.

Subsequent chapters will endeavor to explain the influence of Niebuhr's dogmatism and of his predominant preoccupation with sin on the more down-to-earth portions of
his thought.   They will be, in a way, an investigation of
Niebuhr's contention, discussed above, that " Christianity " is the greatest resource for bringing coherence into
the world.   Does his theory explain, or explain more fully,
things unexplained or poorly explained by the theories of
others?   How useful, how productive, is it?   In broad outline, however, these questions are settled in advance by the
recognition of men as aspects of a transactional world.[96]
This transactional understanding of the character of man
contradicts any belief that constructs a final statement of

man or of man-in-part. A theory or set of concepts is tested for its usefulness, partially at least, by its seeming promise of development and self-correction. There is little promise of either in a theory that postulates impossibles, unchangeables, and intractables.

CHAPTER THREE

Experimentalism Between Two Christs

Faith is a fine invention
For gentlemen who see;
But microscopes are prudent
In an emergency!

EMILY DICKINSON

The present chapter will endeavor to place what Niebuhr considers his "experimentalism" in its proper position with respect to the absolutes of his philosophy. Niebuhr "comes down to earth" in a dialectic fog. As it lifts, we see man struggling with two antitheses. He is contending with history, time, or finiteness, which sprang from super-history, eternity, or infinity; and he is striving toward "a realistic social ethic," which has emerged from sacrificial love. Niebuhr's "experimentalism" is located in time or history, is illumined by the dialectic of sin and responsibility, and is directed toward the proximate (not ultimate) end of a realistic social ethic.

HISTORY AND THE PARADOX OF GRACE

History, or time, is the stage upon which men must play the drama of existence. The stage as constructed by the architect-philosopher may aid or impede the actions of the players. Before the show begins we must investigate what boards are loose, what trap doors are open, how cramped the space is, what obstacles the actors will encounter.

Niebuhr contends that " the difference in the attitude of various cultures toward history is determined by contradictory estimates of man's transcendence over historical process, including his final transcendence over himself." [1] The true conception of history must then come from the interpretation Niebuhr has given of man's position. Man is ambiguously within and yet transcending history. " In so far as he transcends history the source of life's meaning must transcend history." [2]

There are, Niebuhr believes, two particular characteristics of the Christian view of history. (1) Without an expectation of Christ there can be no Christ. (2) The true Christ cannot be the Christ who is expected. These are the unique features of the Christian view. They indicate that history is potentially meaningful and that potential meaning has been fulfilled in Christianity. But they also insist that the Messiah must disappoint as well as fulfill expectation because man's expectations are invariably tainted with egoism. [3]

The relation (as found in the symbolism of the Bible) of history to super-history is dialectic. History points beyond itself by reason of the freedom and transcendence of the human spirit. Niebuhr thinks this is clearly revealed even from a rational and experiential interpretation of the possibilities and limits of history. [4] That history is fulfilled and negated in eternity leads Niebuhr to an interpretation of history as an " interim " between the first and second comings of Christ. That Christ conceived the " interim " to be short, symbolically expresses the idea that the condition of freedom and finiteness is not normative for man. And, because man can never be completely in contradiction with his own true nature, history also attains realizations of meaning. Final synthesis (at the second coming) is symbolized in the Atonement. Justice and forgiveness of God are one as Father and Son are One. Yet they are not one as Father and Son are two. History is " disappointed " and fulfilled.[5]

The truth of God must be a self-disclosure or we would know nothing of His character. The situation is similar to our lack of understanding of other persons. We may observe a man's behavior, scientifically study his reactions and habits, but, purely in these terms, we cannot understand him. Moreover we falsify his uniqueness by trying to understand him in terms of our own selves and of knowledge we have drawn from ourselves. We assume that his desires conform to our own hopes and desires and ambitions. The other person can be understood only after he speaks to us. So we can understand God only through His Word.

In terms of Christ the meaning of God and the Christian interpretation of history are revealed in three main principles: (1) innocency — the beginning of history — harmony of life without freedom — actually a prehistoric state since man in history has always had freedom; (2) *eros* — the substance of history — harmony within terms of freedom — finite and infinite man; (3) eternal fulfillment or *agape* — the end of history — harmony of the soul with God beyond limitations of sinful and finite self.[6]

Fulfillment of history is accomplished on two levels: by new life within history, and beyond history. Through repentance and faith and grace man may attain new life, a rebirth in Christ.[7] Likewise realizations of meaning which can only be seen from the perspective of the end or faith are possible between Christs.[8] Through grace history is fulfilled at the paradoxical point beyond and at the end of history.

Both types of fulfillment of history come about by grace — yet not by grace alone (for that would be determinism), but by the paradoxical relation of grace and free will or repentance. Niebuhr rejects Aquinas' metaphor of the light of the sun and the seeing eye because it is too precise and because it places the two " too much on the same level." [9] Typically, he retains the logical contradiction: " The real situation is that both affirmations — that only God in Christ can break and reconstruct the sinful self, and that the self must ' open the door ' and is capable of doing so — are equally true; and they are both unqualifiedly true, each on its own level. Yet either affirmation becomes false if it is made without reference to the other." [10]

More light is thrown on fulfillments of history (revelations of meaning in history) by Niebuhr's further discussion of grace. Grace operates in bringing about new life (within history) to redeem man from egoism in that he sees egoism as sin, thereby achieving genuine renewal. " In fact " sin is not destroyed until the end of history because the basic drive of egoism operates again on " whatever new level grace has pitched the new life." [11] The renewal is genuine enough in itself, but it is only momentary because *hybris* sets to work again immediately.

The medieval Catholic synthesis of the paradox of grace asserts that " man has freedom from necessity in the state of nature, freedom from sin in the state of grace and freedom from misery in the state of glory . . . that the difference between the consummation of life in history and the consummation of life beyond history is merely that the former is still subject to the conditions of finiteness." [12] The Reformation and the Renaissance, according to Niebuhr, destroyed the Catholic synthesis; each championed one side of the paradox of grace. The result of the ensuing struggle, however, was false.   The Renaissance was not as right and the Reformation was not as wrong as the qualified victory of the Renaissance would seem to indicate.[13]

The Renaissance emphasized the limitless possibilities of human existence, the meaningfulness of history, and the fulfillment of life in history.   (The " idea of progress " is the current expression.)   Modern ideas of progress agree with Christian concepts in conceiving history dynamically; but for the modern world this progress is without grace and assumes that every development is a step toward the good, that progress inevitably leads toward fulfillment.   It does not see that, as history moves forward to good and order, it also develops possibilities of evil and chaos.[14]

The Reformation (Lutheran) maintained that final peace, fulfillment, could not be achieved by the power of man, that any attempt at perfection was futile and any pretension of finality dangerous.   In its understanding of the ultimate problem (*agape*) it lost sight of proximate problems of human striving.   Calvinism was most nearly right in understanding the paradox of justification and sanctification, but it made the error of legalism — of trying to define too precisely the doctrine of sanctification and feeling too secure in the sanctification of the Christian.[15]

Niebuhr, with due humility, hazards a new synthesis. His position is that modern history has validated the dynamic in Renaissance thought but refuted the optimistic, has validated the basic truth of the Reformation but refuted its pessimism and obscurantism.   In some way or other the biblical truth has been expanded by the insights that modern history, the Renaissance, and the Reformation have added to the basic paradox of grace.[16]   Niebuhr is trying to define the two conceptions in the light of modern history so that they will not contradict or defeat each other, on the theory that " if this were possible a philosophy of human nature and destiny could emerge which would reach farther into the heights and depths of life than the medieval synthesis; and would yet be immune to the alternate moods of pessimism and optimism, of cynicism and of sentimentality to which modern culture is now so prone." [17] The twofold emphasis of grace " upon the obligation to fulfill the possibilities of life and upon the limitations and corruptions in all historic realizations, implies that history is a meaningful process but is incapable of fulfilling itself and therefore points beyond itself to the judgment and mercy of God for its fulfillment." [18] Thus Niebuhr finds the final key to his historical interpretation in the doctrine of the Atonement, the paradox of the judgment and mercy of God. Judgment symbolizes that history is significant and that man's distinctions between good and evil are important; mercy symbolizes that evil corrupts all historic achievements and that man is finally incapable of fulfilling historic meaning. Man ought to be good but he cannot; he has obligations but he cannot fulfill them; his decisions and achievements are important but insignificant in the end. He cannot conquer evil without the grace of God.

The end is a dialectic synthesis of time in eternity, of history in super-history. The end is *finis,* a point where what exists ceases to be; and *telos,* the purpose and goal of life and work. Human strivings are completed by divine act, and human sin and guilt are subjected to divine judgment and mercy.

The character of the end is revealed by the great biblical myths. Parousia — that the consummation of history lies beyond time — negates the historical process. The Last Judgment: that man is judged signifies that there is a meaningful distinction between good and evil in history; that man is judged by Christ, his own norm, means that his sin, not his finiteness, is judged; that judgment is at the end of time means that history is not its own redeemer.[19] The Resurrection means that " eternity will fulfill and not annul the richness and variety which the temporal process has elaborated . . . that the condition of finiteness and freedom, which lies at the basis of historical existence, is a problem for which there is no solution by any human power." [20]

Niebuhr's philosophy of history boils down to a fundamental pessimism upon which is dialectically erected a superstructure of hope and optimism. In essence it seeks to avoid alternate moods of cynicism and sentimentality by embracing them simultaneously.

The stage of history is set in a valley called " interim " between two mountainous Events. Having left the transmountainous regions of off-stage innocence and having seen one great Event, men, the actors, are picking their way through finiteness and freedom under the burden of sin to the promised heights beyond. But the actors are not aimlessly strolling. They are partially informed by the partial revelations of the Event they encountered at the valley's entrance. And they know that should they repent of the burden they carry they may be thrown — as they have been thrown in the past — bouquets of fresh revelation. They know, further, that as they proceed they find greater freedom, but that their burden grows larger and heavier; they know that the mountain in the distant haze seems to get no closer, but that they will approach it without aid when they are helped. All these things the player knows — yet he is expected to act the role of experimentalist while on stage.

The importance of the " interim " interpretation is that it makes history finally unimportant. The human condition of finiteness and freedom is transitory. The importance of the dialectic of grace is that it imbues history, the " interim," with significance. Despite the ineffectiveness and the final unimportance of his strivings, the dialectic assures man that his struggles are meaningful. And as long as history is meaningful man is responsible. Though sin is inevitable, man is responsible for it and must work to eliminate it and its attendant evil. The social scientist has his work mapped out for him.

The two-Christs theory of history establishes a dualism between the natural and the transcendental and then endeavors to overcome the dualism by setting the interval of human history in an intermediate position. Under this theory, human history may be based in the natural world, but it is radically distinct from that world. And it contains within itself divine-human encounters. Niebuhr tries to temper the falling-rock-from-above character of supernaturalistic revelation by insisting that certain aspects of the temporal process point beyond themselves. N. P. Jacobson has culled from Niebuhr's writings eight such empirical data:

1. Man can look before and after and dream of what is not.
2. Man realizes his own finiteness.
3. Man can extricate himself from the causal forces in history enough to achieve freedom.
4. All the meanings of history are fragmentary and frustrated in time.

5. Man has a sense of failure to fulfill the absolute demands of God; this sense issues from the image of God in him.
6. Man looks forward with anxiety to the end of history and to death.
7. History is involved in conflicts which appear on each successive cultural level and are never escaped.
8. The sacrificial love which was manifested in Christ points to super-history.[21]

However, most of these can also be — and have been — just as simply interpreted naturalistically, as cultural traits. To use an example from Jacobson, language, itself a natural phenomenon, is a simple illustration of why men can retain the past and project the future. Further, almost no religious, philosophic, or common-sense explanation pretends that men are *not* finite, frustrated, or anxious (though many men, far from being anxious, have truly welcomed death, having already lost the social ties that would have made them reluctant to die).

Thus, containing no necessary indication of the transcendental, these data cannot be expected to bridge the gap completely. Niebuhr, despite his insistence on this empirical justification, admits that only faith can provide the connecting link. In other words, the natural-supernatural dualism remains finally unspanned.

Ever since the Greek philosophers set the real order of existence apart in a world of Forms, dualists have been having trouble establishing contact. It must be admitted that Niebuhr's paradoxical arrangement is an ingenious device. But it must be just as firmly asserted that his courageous attempt is a failure. The gap between the strivings of men and the actions of God is not eliminated by paradox.

The gap is such a one as we find in electronic behavior. With the addition of a definite quantity of energy, an electron will leap from one " ring " round the nucleus of the atom to another — without traversing the intermediate space. It vanishes from one position and appears in another. And, further, its reappearance may be in the next adjacent " ring " or it may be two " rings " away. Similarly, under the paradox of grace, men may devote energy (quantity unspecified, this time) to their historical strivings — but final achievement is an uncharted course. There is the great difference that in this case we are not only uncertain which realm we shall attain but whether the jump will even be granted by grace. And the important difference in treatment is that in the case of the paradox of grace we are forbidden to investigate the possibilities of higher-level coherence of a field theory. The paradox is an irrational closure to further thought. In particular it stubbornly insists that the assumptions that have led to the rational impasse of contradiction are all unconditionally valid and unquestionable. They are not to be tampered with by way of attempt to resolve the paradox.[22] Thus the division of history from super-history is in effect reinforced.

The triumph of dualism in Niebuhr's thought is glory to the supernatural and tragedy to the world. The human enterprise is sold short to struggle through history under crippling handicaps.

(1) Knowledge becomes by implication twofold. A different knowledge is demanded for each historical series — one, the ordinary knowledge we use in relation to other people and sensible objects; the other, a knowledge of

superior claim, divinely given for purposes of the transcendent in man and "beyond history"; science and
faith. Such division, of course, drastically limits the sphère
of ordinary knowledge. Criticism from the higher realms
of the second handicaps free inquiry by the first. We may
well ask with Neal W. Klausner where this will lead.
"Ultimate mystery? And acknowledgment of faith as the
fulfillment and negation of reason?" [23]

(2) If supernaturalism is to be accepted we quite naturally begin to wonder how we are to distinguish revelations from the welter of confusions in the world. This is
a difficult problem in any case — no scientific criterion has
yet been found. But in Niebuhr's position it is enhanced
because he sees important additions to biblical revelation
in the events of history. Is there any way we can decide
which were revelatory events? Is there any way of telling
whether or not the French Revolution, the election of
Truman, or the circumnavigation of the globe were revelatory events — other than by asking Niebuhr himself? And
then, once the event is isolated and labeled, how is the content of its revelation determined?

Niebuhr cannot even have recourse to miraculousness
because revelations, according to him, do not break the
natural order. They can be apprehended by faith, of
course. But this may quickly degenerate to belief because
of psychological certainty, in spite of the paradoxical definition Niebuhr gives to faith as, independently, both an
act of grace and an effort of man. And simple psychological certainty is equivalent to if not identical with dogmatism. Even the assertion of a world view focused in the
Bible cannot relieve revelation from the arbitrariness of
dogmatism. A world view found in a partial revelation
(the Bible) could not provide criteria for determining

what additional meaning the supernatural intends to make known. The most that can be said in behalf of Niebuhr is that the revelations that he finds serve to reinforce the " meaning " of which he dreams.

The self-contradictory and incoherent character of history together with the ideological taint, the blighted reason of man, would almost suggest that we might as well forget about revelation altogether until the point of " beyond history " is reached. Or would this, by fiat, be sinful?

(3) If the channel from God to man has been silted up with obscurities from the human point of view, the channel from man to God has been even more effectively blocked. The irrationality, super-rationality, or inscrutability of God is itself a block when juxtaposed to man's persistent efforts at thinking. Those who hold " the Christian faith in the impartiality and reasonableness of God " would be justifiably disturbed by this interference. For " if we must hold that creative intervention is God's way, or one of God's ways of counteracting or eradicating evil in the world, our scientific, religious and philosophical interests combine to support the surmise that experience will show such divinely functioning creativity to be universally dependent upon the existence or fulfillment of certain definite conditions, natural or human." [24]

Niebuhr tries to retain redemptions in history in order to keep up the good relations of man and God and avoid the error of the Reformation in allocating God too exclusively to the transcendental. But unless men realize the redemption, unless they see life differently as a result, no change in the character of history has taken place so far as they are concerned. D. D. Williams warns us: " Unless history is seen ultimately as sharing in the dynamic life of God, men will accept a history without God, not so much

because they believe history is redemptive, but because
they believe that nothing of consequence is happening any-
where else." [25]

A naturalist such as N. P. Jacobson discards the " cosmic
mind " because he cannot operate experimentally with it
and it is not open to investigation. Finding it dubious that
the universe is one harmonious whole, he wonders whether
a " cosmic mind " would make any difference to the individual, anyway.[26] If God, then, is known only through
the growth of meaning that we experience, Niebuhr's God,
who is found through the meaning given by mystery
(" The mystery of Divine Providence gives meaning to
history and the mystery of creation gives meaning to
time ") , is at the end of a ruptured channel.[27]

(4) Niebuhr is anti-historical. D. D. Williams thinks
" he has a tendency to reduce theological questions to
the one issue of what the moral effects of certain positions
may be." [28] On the other hand C. C. McCown concludes
that " in spite of his preoccupation with present ethical
problems, [Niebuhr] fixes his gaze chiefly on eternity, rather than on history." [29] I suppose it all depends on which
side of the paradox of grace the reader is looking from.
These contradictory statements at least show that it is not
easy to maintain the purity of paradox.

However, they also illustrate the confusion that arises
when history is defined and judged from a purely arbitrary, dogmatic point of view. It then becomes difficult to
decide whether dogma is being fitted to the exigencies of
earthy ethics or to eternity. At any event the confusion
stems from an anti-historical approach to history wherein
the historian, overwhelmed by the world's present distress,
is prompted to a pessimism toward human achievement

and a denial of human progress and turns from a study of facts or data to the manipulation of myth.[30]

Neo-orthodoxy looks to the Bible not primarily for disclosures of ideal human conduct but for insights into the nature of the world and the meaning of human existence.[31] Thus it quite naturally disappoints those who seek ethical direction from the character of Jesus.[32] But then neo-orthodoxy proceeds to take fright at the idea that history, including the Scriptures, can be dealt with only on a basis of probability. While accepting this idea in a spirit of liberalism, neo-orthodoxy announces its certainty of the existence of God and entrenches its certainty behind the battlements of myths where it can be secure from the sniping of historical and biblical criticism.[33] As a result neo-orthodoxy neglects most of the discoveries of biblical criticism. It seems to make " no effort to distinguish in the scriptures the reliable from the less reliable, no attempt to use the results of ' higher ' and ' lower ' criticism as a means for deriving the core of early Christian teaching and belief. "[34]

Coupled with disreliance on Christian tradition, avoidance of biblical criticism amounts, for many liberals, to reading history without reference to facts or data. In McIntyre's words, " Scripture provides us with the data for constructing theological dogma, and in this process we are not, or should not be, inventing merely arbitrary interpretations, any one of which is as good as any other. In constructing dogma, if we conceive our task aright, we are seeking to determine *fact*. Quarrels about dogma are quarrels about fact and not just about equally valid theories woven around unquestionable data. "[35] Or, in the more colorful words of Dean Sperry: " Historically, the Christian religion is supposed to rest upon the rock of fact, not upon the shifting sands of pious speculation." [36]

There really is no occasion to be surprised at the anti-historicism seen in Niebuhr. How can a dualistic universe with an autonomous realm of the supernatural and a corrupted human understanding merge in Christ other than by doing violence to empirical facts, or to theological prescriptions — or to both?

At the risk of tedium, it seems important to re-emphasize the centrality of sin in connection with Niebuhr's view of history. History's dependence on an estimate of man's transcendence was indicated at the outset in a quotation showing Niebuhr's own agreement.[37]   Since man is transcendent and not transcendent — since he is free and finite — meaning and fulfillment (progress) are not wholly up to him.   The locating of sin within the freedom of man necessitates interpretation of history as resolvable only by an outside Creator, since the creations of man are then ever attended by *hybris*.   And it requires a dialectic of grace, of inevitable sin and responsibility for sin, because sin cannot then be blamed on the finiteness of man.[38]

We have previously noticed that for Niebuhr human nature is not completely static.   Man has freedom to alter the forms *within limits* — for, after all, he is self-transcendent and semi-creator.   As a result Niebuhr is in a position to add to the biblical statements of man's character.   In other words, not only is the Bible an incomplete revelation but it is incomplete because man changes.   (We must remember, however, that the Bible does not require amendment — only supplementation.   Man is chiefly static.)   Later revelations are available to those who, with the aid of faith, can discern the symbolic significance of events in history. Thus Niebuhr has added to the Bible the liberal's concept of " progress " — slightly altered.

The world of Niebuhr's experimentalists is only unlimited within limits. Progress (meaning fulfillments of history) is not in their hands. Niebuhr is unquestionably tilting at windmills on a spent warhorse when he implies that liberalism and naturalism either implicitly or explicitly believe progress to be inevitable. The doctrine of inevitable progress has been in the discard for the last twenty years. There may be isolated and sporadic outbreaks, but liberals long ago accepted this criticism and accommodated themselves to it. After all, they are not blind; the most sanguine of optimists have been forced by events of the last few decades to moderate their joyousness. Niebuhr, of course, has done well to criticize facile confidence in inevitable progress; but he should not impute it as still existent throughout all the ranks of liberalism and naturalism. In particular when this charge is launched at John Dewey,[39] it is apparent that Niebuhr has misconstrued Dewey's philosophy. Dewey comments:

It is probably " natural " for those who engage in sweeping rationalistic generalizations to match their own pessimism by attributing an equally unrestrained optimism to their opponents. But since naturalists are committed to basing conclusions upon evidence, they give equal weight to observed facts that point in the direction of both non-social behavior and that of amity and cooperation. In neither case, however, are facts now existing taken to be final and fixed. They are treated as indications of things to be done.[40]

. . . humanistic naturalism . . . calls for observation of concrete natural causal conditions, and for projection of aims and methods that are consonant with the social conditions disclosed in inquiry.[41]

Though he has a positive faith in the methods of democracy — and is to that extent optimistic — Dewey does not think that progress is inevitable. He views it as possible and unlimited *if* men want it badly enough and will work for it hard enough.[42] Niebuhr finds progress not inevitable, but he further makes it contingent upon other factors than want and work. An experimental-minded individual informed by Niebuhr's way of thought learns that his labor may be in vain. He cannot successfully combat the sin in man. But while fighting it (and evil), he may be helped to strike a blow for progress by the supernatural hand of grace. History has become, in the hands of Niebuhr, a place or state where man can create progress — and yet where he cannot, because progress is also dependent upon divine intervention. History has become a haunt filled with mystery in which human problems cannot be solved by men.

The discussion so far has not clearly shown the position reserved for experimentalism or social science in Niebuhr's thought or its derivation from his basic assumptions. His view of what history is — together with a few remarks as to its inadequacies and its limitations on the social scientist — have been presented first. Since man must work within the bounds of time and history, it was considered important to show the setting — between two Christs — wherein man is expected to operate. Following a résumé of Niebuhr's theory of ethics (the dialectic of *agape* and " a realistic social ethic "), which presents the essentials or the framework for a social science, some consideration will be given to the possibility of genuinely scientific actions and operations within Niebuhrian history and under the terms of Niebuhrian ethical theory.

THE LAW OF JESUS AND MAN'S IDEAL

You shall love your crooked neighbor
With your crooked heart.

W. H. AUDEN

Niebuhr's first three books on politics — *Moral Man and Immoral Society* (1932), *Reflections on the End of an Era* (1934), and *An Interpretation of Christian Ethics* (1935) — are concerned primarily with ethics.[43] He had been bothered during World War I by the problem of applying Christianity and of explaining to soldiers how religion could support them when it clearly maintained, "Thou shalt not kill." As a minister in Detroit during the Great Depression, he was greatly preoccupied with the ineffectiveness of Christianity in dealing with the injustices of capitalism.

The ethic of Jesus is clearly inapplicable, Niebuhr thinks. "Resist not evil," "love your enemies," "if ye love them that love you what thanks have you?" "forgive, not seven times seven but seventy times seven," "to resist evil turn the other cheek," "be not anxious for your life," "be therefore perfect even as your father in heaven is perfect," "worry not about the morrow": all of these are uncompromising injunctions. They are much too absolute to be followed even on rare occasions — to say nothing of being followed consistently. If you resist not evil it will overwhelm you; if you love your enemy and turn the other cheek he is just as likely as not to sneer and smite it; if you are not anxious for your life and do not plan for the morrow you starve. And if you obey not all these commands you are far from the perfection of your

Father. Even an attempt to love without an expectation of return breaks down; it is seemingly against the nature of man to love by himself. In short, man is sinful and must strive to achieve a harmony with others on a level below the highest. He must find means of adjusting the relative claims of family, class, community, nation. He may, for example, recognize that the criminal is not so guilty as we pretend; but he also sees that the criminal cannot be freed just because the community, an environment, was largely the cause of his falling into sin. Man must work on the level of mutual love (*eros*) under perpetual criticism of perfection, complete selflessness, sacrificial love (*agape*).

The ethic of Jesus is a religious ethic too uncompromising to fit the ambiguous position of man in nature and man as sinner. Jesus' ethic was tailored to fit his expectation of an imminent day of judgment when he would return, and to fit the kingdom he would set up here on earth. Thus Christianity was left by him without a code that men could hope to apply. This gap was later filled — so far as it could be filled — by borrowing from the Stoics their *jus naturale* and *jus gentium*.[44]

Christian orthodoxy's ideals of political morality were based chiefly on (1) Romans 13 — Paul's theory of divine ordination of government, and (2) Stoic natural law — a universal standard of conduct arrived at by reason and equally as valid as the laws of God. Orthodoxy, however, Niebuhr thinks, erred in that it placed too great emphasis on the relative rather than on the absolute natural law it appropriated. As a consequence it provided and provides religious sanctification for political order without taking advantage of the higher moral law needed as corrective and perpetual judgment over the lower standards of politics in action.[45] The result has been, if not outward support of tyranny, at least toleration of and failure to challenge either tyranny or anarchy.[46]

Christian liberalism, in Niebuhr's view, has erred in the other direction. It has been mistaken in its over-optimism and sentimentality while orthodoxy has veered to the pole of pessimism and defeatism. Liberalism has taken seriously the law of love and has thought that human egoism could be overcome if only the ethic of Jesus were preached loudly and persuasively. Consequently it has taken too little interest in the actual working of social justice to be effective.[47] Agitation for love in a situation of great inequality (especially economic) inevitably results in philanthropy. "No degree of good will alone can cure a deficiency in glandular secretions; and no moral idealism can overcome a basic mechanical defect in the social structure."[48] In the end liberalism has found itself a justification for capitalism (which can then condemn "politics" while ruling indirectly); it is "really a religio-moral version of *laissez-faire* economics."[49]

According to Niebuhr government *is* divinely ordained, not because God set it up to enforce a natural law, but because it is the restraints of the state that prevent the sinful world from capitulating to lust and anarchy.[50] Not only is it impossible to erect a social ethic out of pure Christian *agape,* but even in simple relationships there is no moral value that can be considered absolute. Moral values must be constantly reanalyzed; those that are considered intrinsically good must be reconsidered in instrumental terms. The problems of morality "cannot be resolved on *a priori* grounds but only by observing the social consequences of various types of punishment."[51]

The Stoics and Christian orthodoxy, according to Niebuhr, were right in conceiving moral law (natural law) as a rational construct. The application of critical intelligence is a prerequisite of justice, and in so far as religions are hostile to a critical use of reason they are a hazard to justice.[52] Reason, despite the corruptions it suffers, and the serious taint it receives from the sins of the spirit, is propelled by an impulse for consistency. To be consistent in claiming for the self what is truly value, reason can, for the self, claim value only in what is valuable to others. In a sense, reason forces a leveling, in that, by its standards, privilege must be shared except where it is necessarily attached to the exercise of special function for benefit of the whole. Reason finds that ideally larger harmonies than actually exist are demanded by life.[53] Since reason is able, within limits, to view the whole of life, it inevitably seeks to affirm life in its most inclusive terms.[54] Every moralist uses reason in the function of supporting impulses that carry life beyond itself to the support of other life. Thus reason is a powerful force for the extension of sociality. And it would also be right to expect morality to grow as rationality is extended. " A growing rationality in society destroys the uncritical acceptance of injustice." [55]

But there are limits to the use of reason for the furthering of morality. Man will never be sufficiently intelligent to see the needs and desires of others in the same light in which he sees his own. His intelligence is corrupted by his sin. He may be able to extend the range of effective sympathy, but again there are limits.[56] Reason can provide standards for criticism, and such contributions of reason are necessary, but it is helpless by itself without impulse to proceed toward the goal; its " norms do not contain a dynamic for their realization." [57] Reason does not completely transcend impulse and impulse does not naturally obey the ideals set up by reason.[58] " Because reason is something more than a weapon of self-interest it can be an instrument of justice; but since reason is never dissociated from the vitalities of life, individual and collective, it cannot be a pure instrument of justice." [59]

In Niebuhr's scheme, science, in order to make coherence out of the world, can only analyze, measure, and classify details on the surface of nature and history and relate them to each other in terms of sequence. It can avoid a too mechanistic view of life only when it accepts a philosophical correction of its philosohical assumptions. It has to treat sequence in history on a basis of strict causality, each new development being explainable in light of its antecedents. From Niebuhr's standpoint this is " committing the logical fallacy, *Post hoc, ergo propter hoc.*" [60]

For Niebuhr, simple causation is out of the question. God is not merely first cause, but Creator. He has a vital, creative relation with the world that would be lost by any acceptance of the mechanistic explanation of " unmoved mover "; he can create out of nothing. " Creator " is, of course, a suprarational concept. It forces Niebuhr to take a stand on the old problem of free will versus determinism. He answers the time-worn question characteristically, and consistently with his picture of human nature. Man is self-transcendent. While, in relation to God, his will is paradoxically both free and determined, it is free within limits to insert new elements into history, to create, thus invalidating analyses founded strictly on cause and effect.[61]

On the whole, thinks Niebuhr, the political theories of rationalists from Aristotle to the present have contributed more to a solution of ethical problems than has Christianity either orthodox or liberal — with the obvious exceptions of Thomist Catholicism and Calvinism. Unfortunately, rationalism, at the same time, has destroyed the profound and true mythological insight of original Christianity — " the idea that the conflict between spirit and nature is a real conflict, that no complete victory of spirit in history is possible, but that defeat is turned into victory when the unachieved perfection is discovered to be a forgiving love which justifies (understands) man's imperfection." [62]

In order to rationalize Christian myths, Christianity " ran upon the rocks either of the Scylla of a too optimistic pantheism or the Charybdis of a too pessimistic and otherworldly dualism." [63] Niebuhr's course through the perilous channel is more skillful; he does not perish on either coast; nor does he sail smoothly between. His modest ship, much smaller than the strait is wide, at once bounds along against the rocks on one side and slips in and out of the whirlpool on the other. The too purely religious reefs to the left save him from the peril of the too political maelstrom on the right. Knowing that there is no perfection for human ethics, he " reinstates " mythical religion by championing the eternal and affirming the political.

This is the dialectical resolution for man, the dialectic of *agape* and a " realistic social ethic." Thesis and antithesis must both be embraced until the grace of God furnishes a synthesis. Meanwhile the vision of perfect love as preserved in myth may help man see his imperfection, and thus eternal criticism may mitigate the imperfections of historic ethic. As social justice contains a religious element, so religion will " leaven the idea of justice with the ideal of love." [64] ". . . perhaps the most essential genius of myth [is] that it points to the timeless in time, to the ideal in the actual, but does not lift the temporal to the category of the eternal (as pantheism does), nor deny the significant glimpses of the eternal and the ideal in the temporal (as dualism does)." [65]

Niebuhr metaphorically sums up this dialectic relation as follows:

Historic Christianity is in the position of having the materials for the foundation and the roof of the structure of an adequate morality. But it is unable to complete the structure. Its faith in a meaningful world, having a source beyond itself, is the foundation. Its faith in the end and fulfillment is the roof. The walls, the uprights and diagonals which complete the building are the moral actions and ideals which are fashioned by the application of religion's ultimate insights to all specific situations. [66]

Niebuhr derives his natural law in two ways: rationally and from religious belief. By the first, the greatest good is freedom to develop essential personality, to fulfill the potentialities of human nature. Since this is impossible, since one man's erratic path rolls over the toes of his neighbor, since all men are competing for the opportunity to develop fully their lives, equality, the second best, must be pursued. There is no principle for final arbitration between the claims of individuals for freedom. Ideally, freedom of the individual must be under self-imposed discipline or else under an externally imposed discipline motivated to encourage his development toward ultimate values. But no such pure motivation can be found in others. The ideal of equality is operative even though men may not be equal in actuality; it is always possible that they are potentially equal and that actual inequality is but the product of environment, heredity, accident. [67]

By Niebuhr's second derivation of natural law — that from religious belief — equality is simply drawn from the Christian doctrine of the transcendent worth of all human personality. If before God all men, all souls, are important, how is man to gage echelons of importance? Niebuhr, in this connection, notes that the religious sense of the height of eternal transcendence usually nullifies this derivation of equality by the fallacious implication that equality before God does not necessarily require equality in history.[68] Equality is " the approximation of brotherhood under the conditions of sin." [69]

Equality holds a position between love and justice. It is not an absolute as is *agape,* but rather a guiding principle — " love in terms of logic." It is set off from justice by the factor of reason or logic. Justice, the " realistic " ethic, should result from social wisdom more than from pure logic.[70]

The ethical panorama created by Niebuhr may be brought into focus through the medium of a comparison with Jacques Maritain, the outstanding Catholic philosopher. Maritain's natural law assumes human nature to be constant and human persons to be identical except for minor " practical " variations. What is good for one, in the higher realm, is then good for all. With fixed subjects it is no trick at all to deduce binding rules from eternal law. The rights and duties of the human person are deduced " in a necessary manner " from the first principle, " do good and avoid evil," and " from the simple fact that man is man." [71] Similarly the less perfect law of nations and positive or civil law, deriving their force from natural law, embody corresponding rights and duties for nations and civic persons respectively.

While Maritain finds human nature to be a constant, Niebuhr finds it constant and changing. He is therefore unable to deduce binding rules in a necessary manner from his first principle — sacrificial love. Furthermore,

he would be committing the sin of egoism if he under-
took such a task, and would inevitably fail because of the
limitations of his reason. On the contrary he develops a
scale of ethics paralleling his own human nature. To his
human being, existing as a dialectico-paradoxical unity of
separated distinct parts (though fuzzy in delineation as
presented by Niebuhr), accrues a corresponding hierarchy
of laws. *Agape,* equality, and justice parallel transcendence or freedom, reason, and sin respectively. Experimental social justice is precisely the by-product of the fact that
man is not completely set and, in particular, it is a by-
product of the fact of sin. And the dialectic of *agape* and
justice emerges from the fact that human nature is and is
not a constant.

Unquestionably Maritain's derivation of binding rules
is a simple assertion of what men *ought* to value. It is not
so clear in Niebuhr's case. His divine law (*agape*) and
his natural law (equality) clearly *ought* to be valued.
However, his norms of conduct (justice) are allegedly to
be held tentatively and validated by experience or experiment. In this essential category of ethics he seems to
contrast radically with his theological counterpart. He
seems to be talking the language of the pragmatists. He
seems to be actually asserting that morals should be determined not by what men ought to value but in terms of
what men do value and do want to value and what they
do find most satisfaction in valuing.[72]

Maritain frankly admits that morals are given, not made
— are deduced, not induced. Niebuhr tries to avoid a
deduction of moral rules from his system of absolutes. By
way of the dialectic he hopes to preserve the absolute and
at the same time provide a relativistic, scientific treatment
of morals. Unfortunately, he does not succeed. His fail-

ure may be accounted for in the terms he himself once used to criticize Communism. Communism had failed, he reasoned, because it had been unable to maintain antithetic purity. The antithesis (proletariat) had been tainted by bourgeois (the thesis) corruptions. The hovering wings of sin, as they are inevitably wont to do, had cast a darkening shadow over the birth of antithesis out of thesis. The iniquities of the parent were visited on the son. Some of the evil of capitalism was inevitably transferred to Communism.[73]

The antithesis of *agape* has similarly been perverted. Everyday norms of conduct have retained some of the evil of *agape*. They are not long left in their scientific or relativistic purity by the scientist-theologian. Moral precepts, says Niebuhr, must " be held with some degree of tentativity and be finally subordinated to the law of love. Otherwise the norm of yesterday becomes the false standard of today; and lawlessness is generated among those who are most conscious of, or most affected by, the historical changes in the human situation." [74] Observe what has happened to Niebuhr's vaunted radicalism. It has evaporated. He is actually afraid of experiment because of lawlessness. His basically conservative assumption of eternals shines through the thin veneer of radicalism.[75] Values are to be held tentatively in tribute to change and progress in history. But they are to be " under criticism of the divine," paying homage to the unchanging. The antithesis is not pure and completely independent of the thesis, but rather, so to speak, under perpetual threat of congressional investigation by the eternal. The moral scientist, as long as he can be checked by " criticism " based on absolutes, is only free by illusion and to that extent is not a scientist.

John Herman Randall, Jr., takes Niebuhr's dialectic of *agape* and a " realistic social ethic " at its face value. His summary evaluation of Niebuhr is as follows:

. . . divorce of the practical moral life from religious salvation is . . . the heart of the present-day revival of Reformation theology. . . . For Mr. Niebuhr, salvation is once more a purely religious problem. It is indeed a personal and psychological problem, of overcoming *Angst* and an uneasy conscience (the pathological vacillation between despair and false hope which only good German Romanticists seem really to feel nowadays) — of achieving an integrated personality. . . . But [man] realizes that through divine mercy and forgiveness his " sinful nature " does not matter; he can stop worrying about it, for it does not really make any difference. With salvation thus disposed of, in practical action Mr. Niebuhr is thus freed to follow a mixture of wisdom and shortsightedness — like *any* [italics added] other socially sensitive and exceptionally intelligent man.[76]

My primary disagreement with this summation concerns the italicized word in the last quoted sentence. On the practical level, Niebuhr may operate like a good many other intelligent men; but he is inimical to the attempt of practical men to develop a working science of morals — and this precisely because his salvation ethics continually intrude upon the workaday world. This point will be elaborated subsequently; it is one of the chief contentions of the present book.

In other respects, Randall's statement is an over-simplification. Niebuhr very deliberately insists on a detachment of religion from the historical relativities in behalf of the moral effectiveness of religion, and on the maintenance of a " certain tension " between religion and civilization in behalf of the health and vitality of religion. This certainly does not sound like a man trying to dispose of religion in order to contend with the practical world on a purely practical level. The confusion here probably is due largely to the vagueness of "final subordination" to the law of love, values being held tentatively "under criticism" of the divine within context of a "certain tension" between religion and civilization. As B. E. Meland says,

. . . neither tension nor detachment of this sort serves a religious purpose unless it proceeds from a source of judgment that is intelligible enough to men to provide them with a criterion for their moral judgments concerning culture. That is why, to declare the judgment of God upon culture without recourse to Divine Criterion, is to enthrone impassioned zeal and to give it the authority of objective right.[77]

Absence of an explicit criterion permits the superficial impression that there is no relationship at all.

An important negative relationship deserves to be singled out for comment. In his anxiety to detach religion from the flux of relativity (in order to permit the proper sort of tension), Niebuhr has over-zealously tried to purify Christian love (*agape*) by claiming its complete otherness from the "mutual" love of the world. As a result, the loving achievements of earthly men, subjected to the dazzling third-degree spotlight "criticism" of an impossible perfection, are seen as cracked, sinful masks of calculation. In the pure light all the gray and black of imperfection are brought into candid relief while the brighter spots of beauty are drowned in the brilliance. The world of relativities is really not so bad. The "mutual loves" of ambiguous men are not so prone to calculate the use of others as Niebuhr presumes. We can say with D. D. Williams that "surely such a calculation deserves the name neither of mutuality nor of love. Mutuality means a love which seeks the common good as two can share it together. It means willingness to be transformed for the sake of the larger good in which both can share." [78]   Furthermore, for the intimate organic level of love that is imaginative, sacrifice is an outmoded, primitive, and unneeded concept. This is the place par excellence where a higher synthesis of opposed interests described below [79] as " creative bargaining " is most possible.   In the words of A. E. Murphy:

It is true, indeed, it is a truism, that the only interests a man can reasonably be concerned about are his own.   But it is no less true, and just as important, to add that he can reasonably be concerned about the interests of others and the claim they make upon him, and can prefer such claims to interests which, if he had had only himself to consider, he would have preferred to satisfy.[80]

This is the aspect of life that Niebuhr's heavenly vision of *agape* and his earthly groveling with sin largely cover over.

Niebuhr's scheme for sin and salvation contains significant hazards for the process of daily morals.   These have been ably pointed out by H. D. Lewis.

The upshot of Niebuhr's doctrine is the presentation of sin . . . as some mysterious cosmic disaster, some vague blot upon the universe which we just cannot conjure away, something also on account of which we must all bow our heads in shame, and, in particular, something towards which we should adopt certain religious attitudes and about which theological doctrines have to be formed.   The preacher must stand in his pulpit at appointed times to pronounce himself " agin it," and to announce the way of salvation.   But none of this appears to touch the individual in the conduct of his life, and however much he may be induced to give formal assent to his own involvement in the sins of the world, he remains fundamentally serene in the assurance that it does not really concern him for the simple reason that there was nothing he could have done about it.[81]

But this is disastrous to ethics. Its result is " to divorce the consciousness of sin and the ' uneasy conscience ' altogether from the business of living." [82]   Lewis's complaint is that Niebuhr fails " to distinguish between ethical and religious truth and to relate the former effectively to the religious life as a whole." [83]   He uses the term " sin " to cover both the concept of " marred " human nature (a religious idea) , and abuse of freedom of choice (an ethical concept). The moral " sense of ought " which normally bears the assumption that I can, not that I cannot, is attached to *hybris* by the paradox of grace; and thus the appeal to remorse, repentance, and responsibility for *hybris* tends to obscure the difference between this religious concept and specific earthly variety in moral worth.   Lewis is convinced that the paradox of grace cannot stand and fears that both types of sin will receive superficial " formal " treatment.

In Lewis' opinion, *hybris* such as Niebuhr presents is " devoid of relevance to the conduct of individual lives." [84]   And, unfortunately, the properly moral sins of wrongful choice are crusted over by refusal to distinguish them from religious sin.   The literal sameness, the universality of the sinfulness in which men generally are steeped, obscures the individuality of life.   By hiding the variation in the sinful acts of individual persons and the variability in people's moral worth, it not only contradicts the presumptions of ordinary ethical thinking but also conceals the springs of individualism; ". . . it leaves the individual impotent and insignificant while the great cosmic forces run their play through to its appointed end." [85]

In so far as Niebuhr minimizes the importance of individual choice, he is indeed a " menace . . . to living morality." [86] " There is danger . . . that the word ' sin ' may become an incantation, lacking solid warrant in the common conscience . . . at least, the word should be kept close to the moral fact . . . we should think twice before allowing the doctrine of grace to cut the nerve of honest moral effort." [87] But further indictment of Niebuhr for not separating extrinsic and intrinsic aspects of ethics I find hard to accept. Lewis condemns Niebuhr because he " really proceeds on the entirely misleading assumption that there are no variations of ethical judgment to be considered besides variations in the outward ' more or less ' of justice that we produce." [88] Lewis divides ethics by actions which are good (1) in their effects (outward action) and (2) by themselves, morally (moral worth), and interprets Niebuhr as dealing only with the " less and more " of the former (on the " relative social ethic " level) while in respect to the latter seeing not " a big sinner and a little sinner " but all involved in the sins of all (on the *agape*-universal guilt level) .[89]

Lewis' attitude is understandable. He postulates absolute standards of good which " have a finality and self-sufficiency not fundamentally different from the principles of arithmetic," [90] (albeit they are independent of religious principles). So he is naturally distressed when an attempt is made to give morals a relative treatment, either empirical or scientific. His ethic confronts " the individual by a duty not constituted in any way by his own nature or inclination, a demand altogether outside himself which burns inexorably into his consciousness." [91] Any attempt to erect human, changeable standards for morality pro-

duces an inward aspect not at all separable from effects
and less agonizing than this inner immolation to (from
Niebuhr's stand and from my own) false gods.[92]

If Niebuhr does tend to ignore the psychological aspects
of his relative social ethic, it is not so much because he
has separated morals into two distinct sorts and works only
with the " outward," but because his concern is chiefly
with the macroscopic, with cultures, civilizations, nations,
and classes — that is, with the operation of relative
standards.

However, true to his paradoxical fashion, we do find
Niebuhr torturing himself with an intrinsic ethic, of a
sort — disconnected from outward considerations at the
agape-hybris crossroads.   That he finds here an equality of
sin should not completely prevent him from treating with
little and bigger sinners in the relativities of the world.
At the most it confuses the issue and leads to the neglect of
relative morality by preoccupation with the disconnected
intrinsic ethic.   This in itself is dangerous and indicates
an important fault in Niebuhr's over-all philosophical effect; but the prime danger is due to the intrinsic ethic's
not being eliminated altogether, for it interferes with an
instrumental handling of relative morality.

Ethics is an instrument for social control.   As Geiger has
observed, " there can be no divorce, as has been customary
in moral theory, between ends which are intrinsic — or
moral, and those which are ' merely ' instrumental — that
is, social.   The effect of that divorce upon ethical concepts
has been too often either to remove them from affairs here
below and make them inhabitants of some other intellectual world of ends and goals, or to transform them into
an elaborate system of apologetics." [93]   Under Niebuhr's
guidance practical moral theories tend to become

" merely " instrumental. Though he is greatly interested in them, they have nevertheless a subsidiary role to the strictly intrinsic ethic up above. They cannot be taken simply and seriously as a means of social control because higher " criticism " depreciates their " ultimate " standing. To transform them for the purposes of more effective and more desirable control we must not only " hold them tentatively" but treat them experimentally, scientifically.

For Niebuhr, " science " seems to be a haphazard affair of trial and error. Historical changes are somewhat external to man; he transcends them. The " social knowledge " upon which, in preference to reason, Niebuhr bases justice appears to be an arbitrary agglomeration of historical facts. He is concerned lest the norm of yesterday become sterile because the tide of history has moved out, leaving it exposed to dry. So he will transpose it back into the ocean of life where it will not become a dry, brittle, change-resistant encouragement to lawlessness. His procedure of makeshift expedients is preferable to blind insistence on outmoded norms. It is empirical but it is not scientific.

A social scientist operating under the auspices of a transactive approach does not feel that he will stray to dangerous extremes without final subordination to a perfect law, for he does not have Niebuhr's restricted view of nature; he retains values, ideals, purposes, ambitions, and all other elevating aspects of human behavior as parts of the experimental world without need of transcendental power. And he is not primarily endeavoring to change morals, to bring them in tune with the times of historical change (except in so far as the two are kept apart by a separation between morals and actions). He finds morals to be an integral, organic part of historical change, and he finds his own function to be that of discovering how to change things to provide greater satisfactions. He observes how things are interconnected by introducing elements to change them. He treats the historical situation and norms of conduct together because they are not separable. He is not afraid of a wrong hypothesis (or of a hypothesis not finally subordinated to the law of love) because even it brings to light significant phenomena permitting improved experimentation. Niebuhr finds morals to fit the new situation; a social scientist develops them within the developing situation. He changes both situation and morals; he finds better morals by introducing change and noting results in terms of greater satisfactions. He works with human problems which are compounded of interests, desires, hopes, values, achieving resolution of them by bringing about changes in their elements; he indulges in fact-changing, not in indiscriminate fact-finding.[94]

By means of an experimental technique, the social scientist creates new configurations which are deemed more or less preferable as they provide more or less satisfaction of interests. They are tested by experience. Niebuhr, too, believes that norms of conduct are " validated by experience." However, not only are his norms found without any process deliberately inducing change, but (as previously suggested [95]) his validating " experience " is not a scientific or experimental experience. Pragmatic experience is not submissive sensory reception. It is a phenomenon of man the actor. A man has an experience when he performs some act *and* the consequences of his action rebound upon him. He has no experience when he does nothing or when the consequences of his doings do not come home to him. Grace isn't even experience; it hits from the void, obviating any circular reflex at all. Its use in a philosophy serves to prevent valid experience.

One of the fundamental difficulties of the present age is this precise dearth of true experience. Personal experience has become to a great extent impossible, because in our widely technological world the consequences of men's actions, their doings, no longer rebound; they are so remotely channelized by complicated mechanisms and conditions that the effects of a man's behavior are indeed frequently undetermined. And on the other hand the individual suffers the effects of the acts of others without being able to detect the source of his woes or intelligently to defend himself. " The intervals in time and space are so extensive that the larger number of factors that decide the final outcome cannot be foreseen." [96] The result is a widely scattered sense of irresponsibility that blossoms into feelings of frustration and anxiety.

In such a context, what is needed is a transactive approach, an approach attempting to bring experience again full circle within the present culture, tying man to man and both together to their environment, thus heightening the sense of meaning carried within culture. But Niebuhr will be of no assistance here. His " experience " is corrupted by his theology; it is the same " experience " that partially proves Christianity because it is within Christianity. It is not man acting and suffering the effects of his actions; it is sensory perception as warped by religious preconceptions.[97]

Experimentation in social affairs is not the technique of laboratory test tube or cyclotron. Unfortunately, many social scientists continue to hold some such arrangement as the ideal for all sciences and correspondingly despair of the possibility of a " real " social science. They seem almost to lament that they cannot institute experiments *over* social specimens. Niebuhr, without the lamentation, has the same limited stimulus-response view of what social science is. And it is this faulty understanding that he criticizes. He is on the right track when he insists that a science that sets the experimenter apart from the experimented — like an alchemist over his potions — needs philosophical correction. His grave error is that he naively accepts this truncated form as science. An experimental social science does not require discrete social chemicals upon which an external operator can perform intricate manipulations, nor does it require a disinterested outside experimenter, nor must it want a pure reason dissociated from the " vitalities of life," nor is it concerned with prediction of what social chemicals will produce when variously juxtaposed. On the contrary, social experimentation is carried on within a transactional situation; the scientist works in close collaboration with the social group (in a sense all the people involved being experimenters) ; the specialist is vitally and intimately, emotionally, artistically, and intellectually concerned; thinking starts from the existential context and takes advantage of all aids, rational or otherwise; and with time considered to be a genuine factor prediction is incidental — the aim being social control.[98]

One additional difficulty is found for a social scientist in his struggle between Niebuhr's Christs. He is forced to treat means and ends unscientifically. There are for him two kinds of ends in history — proximate ends and the ultimate goal, *eros* and *agape*. *Agape* will not, of course, be reached in history, but proximate ends or solutions may be attained. Little difficulty is encountered in agreeing with Niebuhr's decision that the imagined (though not understood) possibility is an impossible possibility. On the other hand the impossibility of the ultimate ideal need not be blamed on the sin of man.[99] It may more simply be seen as the normal expectation when an ideal end is set up divorced from means of attainment. An end that is not an operative, contingent, and alterable goal is not to be attained by human methods. Ends are a part of the means. They function as directives, as operative conditioners of choice and use of means. If they are uncompromisingly absolute, they prevent sensitive selection and use of means and to that extent prevent, instead of facilitating or encouraging, the alteration or adaptation of means, as progress ever more and more begins to deviate from the path to the end.[100] A moral problem or dilemma is resolved not by dialectically shuttling back and forth between horns, nor by blindly groping for new and untried means, but by creatively altering the conflicting " ends." Satisfaction of incompatible interests, of " ends," is brought about by altering both ends and means.

Niebuhr's ideal realm is not a collection of imagined possibilities that stimulates men to new efforts and realizations, but something separated, something gained through grace. Thus it is not an operative ideal that we can work toward (except perhaps as we work at faith to obtain forgiveness).

On a lower level, Niebuhr thinks, proximate solutions to our problems may be found. Proximate ends *(eros)* may be achieved. The very use of the word " proximate " suggests that the ultimates of which these lower ends are adaptations have not been discarded. The superior end persists as " criticism " or directive. Dialectical purity has

again been besmirched. The antithesis, the contingent
end, has not been left completely separate and independent.

Disregarding the taint of the eternal because it is impossible to tell whether its "criticism" consists of snide
remarks or of constructive (that is, positive) influence,
the low-level relationship between means and ends may be
ascertained by a brief inspection of Niebuhr's attitudes
toward revolutionary change. As a "radical," Niebuhr
was early influenced by Marxist ideas; the element of
equality in proletariat philosophy particularly appealed to
him. When he wrote *Moral Man and Immoral Society* in
1932, he was sufficiently enthusiastic to attempt a provisional justification of the revolutionary means that had
been used in Russia toward the end of equality. He reasoned that, in view of the special circumstances of the case,
violence might prove an effective means. By 1935, however, in *An Interpretation of Christian Ethics*, he began to
doubt the efficacy of violence as a method of social change
because of the intricacy of the processes of social change
and the "stubborn vitality" of tradition and cultural in-
heritance.[101] He has gradually been converted to the democratic way of change — but for the reason that the social
world is so complex that hasty action, sweeping action,
cannot but create more chaos and injustice than it quells,
not for the reason that means and ends are conjugate and
interacting parts of one process and cannot be effective if
either is held uncompromisingly. Niebuhr never arrives
at an understanding of how ideals are connected with men,
how they can be operative in life, how they tie with actions,
spring out of the existential situation and put or push
back into it.

SUMMARY

Niebuhr's failure to set the stage for a genuine social science may be traced back to his fundamental assumptions and to his basic explanation of concrete phenomena. It is because he thinks in terms of force instead of in terms of interconnection. He explains actual phenomena by giving them the status of forces. Nowhere is this more evident than in the prototype, his basic postulate of sin, where the phenomenal abuse of power and quest for power are translated into a psychic force — love of power, egoism, *hybris,* or sin — which then is treated as a dynamic cause. Niebuhr, of all men, should be aware of the depth and creativity of human beings. Yet on the social or ethical level, he clings to concepts of stimulus and response, to forces. Apparently his appreciation of what he calls man's " freedom " is superficial. Has Niebuhr been so myopic as to attribute man's freedom exclusively to his traffic in the transcendental? Has Niebuhr's absolute of sin blinded him to the variety, sensitiveness, creativeness, and infinity within each man as he participates in social life?

The whole causal structure of Niebuhr's world is beset by this force-fallacy. When effects are not caused by meddlings of the eternal, stirring up hosts from what is not, they are sequential occurrences following a " cause," a force, in a necessary manner. Niebuhr's limited understanding of nature and his distorted perspective on scientific methods leave him with the sorry opinion that there is not a grand enough arena for human freedom unless man is permitted to transcend the natural scene. Just as he suspects, sequential cause-and-effect analyses (which for him commit the error of *post hoc, ergo propter hoc*) are not sufficient to the dimensions of modern man. But that does not justify retreat to the transcendental. There are untold promises in the so-far largely untapped concept of cotemporal causation — a concept with which Niebuhr does not appear to be familiar. Prior commitment to his cosmology would in any case obviate his accepting it at its face value.

Just as the transactive approach to the human scene is a more sensitive and inclusive way of handling problems and understanding the human situation than are theories that postulate either interaction or self-action, so the co-temporal approach to causation is more sensitive, more inclusive, and (in the scientific sense) more " simple " than is the older Newtonian sequential cause and effect. Upon close analysis of the minute arena where cause and effect impinge upon one another, they turn out to be interrelational, not relations in time at all but simply non-temporal or cotemporal. The events called " cause " and " effect " become " constituents of a single continuous event." [102] While common sense may continue for some time to function on the macroscopic level of sequential generalization, scientific thought is already beginning to blaze the way toward greater control in the social-physical world on the basis of this broader understanding of causation.

Niebuhr, however, from his partial point of view condemns all science as inadequate because his grasp of it is inadequate. Thus he misunderstands the means-end relationship because he falsely sees the means as a force, a " cause, " and the end as a result temporally separated from the means. In a sense the colors of the original portrait of man as a composite of forces (vitalities) and forms have run, merging with the means-end landscape and distorting the possibility of a scientific treatment of or an actual approach to realistic social ethics.

In brief, through the medium of dialectic Niebuhr finds it possible to agitate for a " scientific " or realistic treatment of problems in the " interim " that is history. Unfortunately for those who hope to find in Niebuhr a wondrous combination of genuine science and Christianity, Niebuhr — despite his dialectic — fails to provide experimentalism with that requisite freedom from dogmatism without which it cannot truly function in the social field. Both his interpretation of history and his so-called " realistic social ethic " are brought by assumptions of *hybris* and human nature to introduce impediments and irrelevancies which block the path of genuine achievement for men on earth.

CHAPTER FOUR

Political Stalemate

[A] point of view has no meaning save as it is used as a vantage point from which to observe and interpret actual phenomena.

JOHN DEWEY [1]

How does Niebuhr's set of concepts, outlined in the preceding chapters, influence his thinking in more strictly political realms? What are the products of his theory — if indeed " theory " is what it is — in the practical field of politics? Is his basic thought productive of useful ideas on the political level? Broadly speaking, two phenomena that are central to the study of political science have been selected for treatment in this chapter in relation to the above questions. The phenomena of the *group* and of *power* are of focal importance to Niebuhr's political thinking; indeed they have pre-empted much of his attention by themselves. As such, a consideration of them will serve the added function of bringing out much of the fuller detail of Niebuhr's political theory — for they cannot be dealt with adequately in isolation.

SACRIFICIAL GROUPS

In respect to the group, two important aspects must be considered. (1) What is the group? What is its character? Are there different kinds of groups? (2) What is its relationship to the individual?

To avoid confusion, Niebuhr's vision of the group will

first be presented as a whole. Then it will be considered
under this twofold division (which is not inherent in
Niebuhr's own analysis) .

The social group as seen by Niebuhr is created in the
first instance by the natural impulses of man. In earliest
human history, the original basis for an organic social
group was a fact of nature — the long period of helplessness in the infancy of the child. The group is held together by the fact that man is a social being. That is, the
sex impulse seeks perpetuation of kind; the impulse of
pity sends man to the aid of his fellow; and besides, such
natural impulses as sympathy, gregariousness, paternal and
filial affection, and a sense of organic cohesion throw men
together.[2] These are the unselfish impulses found in man's
nature along with the selfish.[3]

From the tribal unit, social groups have grown in size
because forced to do so by the necessities of social conflicts,
and because of the application of imagination and intelligence. As the group, in expanding, grew farther and farther away from the intimate, cohesive, organic family, the
basic natural impulses were no longer adequate for the
task of coherence, and they have therefore been altered, re-
fined, and extended.[4] It was the function of reason to
bring about this moral extension of the area within which
man senses an obligation to aid and support man. Man's
social impulses are the deep roots from which the group
springs. Reason does not create; it only extends and stabi-
lizes.[5] " Reason is provisionally an organ of the universal,
as against the particular, interest; and growing rationality
has thus undoubtedly contributed to the extension of human communities." [6]

The most important differences between the individual
and collectives, according to Niebuhr, are (1) that there

are " no discrete or integral collective organisms, corresponding to the life of the individual," [7] and (2) that there
are " no simple distinctions between life and death in collective organisms." [8]　The first difference means that it is
immensely difficult to generalize about communities, cultures, civilizations (which Niebuhr terms " organisms ")
because they vary so much.　Political communities are
fairly discrete as organized through nations, but the rest
are difficult to define or delimit.[9]　The second difference
means that generalizations are dangerous because it is
impossible to tell precisely the fate of collectives — except
in so far as they are organized into nations or empires.

On the other hand, similarities between the individual
and collectives make it possible to draw analogies.　Like
man, the collective feels insecure; it tries to overcome that
insecurity through pride and the will to power — transmuted survival instinct.　In seeking to overcome its
finiteness by its own power, it commits *hybris,* the prime
sin of pretending to be God.[10]　Like man, the collective
organism indulges in impulses of fear, hatred, resentment,
vengeance, forgiveness.　Like man it has a will, a conscience, reason, self-consciousness. . . .

Man seeks to use his collectives as (sometimes) vicarious
means of self-aggrandizement.　He projects his pretensions
of divinity into the larger realm of the group, which, being
larger and stronger, would superficially appear to be more
worthy of divinity.　The frustrated individual — especially
the average man who can never fulfill his aspirations to
power — becomes a willing support and victim of group
pretensions.[11]　Thus the collective's sin is greater.

The self-transcendence of the group is less than that of
the individual.　And, as the group increases in size, self-
transcendence diminishes.　With self-transcendence fol-

lows self-criticism in parallel fashion, likewise diminishing with size. And with less self-criticism there is not only less ethical action, but less check on sin. Thus again the sin of the group outruns the sin of the individual.[12]

The individual is able at times to consider the interests of others and even to choose their advantage over his own, but it is most difficult, if not impossible, to purge societies of egoism. This is due in part to the overpowering egoism of group life, in part to the fact that society's basic cohesion is the product of natural impulses, which cannot be properly constrained by the weak rational force of the group.[13] The reason of the group is weak because individual members cannot see beyond its borders; it cannot see that altruism might benefit in the long run. The group fails to see that, since the impulses of collective behavior belong only to the realm of nature (not spirit), the proportion of reason to impulse increasingly diminishes in the change from the individual to social groups and then to larger groups. In short, all man's failings are present and inflated in the group. And as a result " the achievement of harmony and justice between groups requires a measure of coercion, which is not necessary in the most intimate and the most imaginative individual relations." [14] By comparison only, man is moral and society immoral,[15] and, correspondingly, the individual is capable of purer realizations of " meaning " than is the group.[16]

The death of nations and empires is more obviously self-inflicted than the death of the individual, though they may fall innocent victim of historical caprice just as individuals may die in natural calamity. Groups do not suffer a natural death; [17] they are not physical organisms. " They are created by the ingenuity of human freedom and are destroyed by corruptions of that freedom." [18] " Nations, like individuals, may defeat superior power by special measures of spiritual grace. They may also, within limits, achieve a spiritual victory in the agony of physical defeat," thus gaining new life by dying to self.[19]

Niebuhr attributes all human qualities *except* the spiritual to the state. It is perhaps the very fact that the group does not have a spirit — though it has reason, will, conscience, self-consciousness, and self-transcendence, the last of which is the essence of man's spirit — that is the real distinction between man and his collective and is that which makes the pretenses of the group the more vicious and heinous sin.

When Niebuhr refers to " organic " society or the social " organism," his reference is to the intimate relation he sees between the individual and his group. His notion of ideal group-individual relations is best illustrated by his complaint against the " mechanistic " character of modern life:

> The individual draws the sustenance of his self-conscious individuality from his organic relation to his social group, his family, his craft and his community. While he has always been in the peril of being too completely absorbed in these primary social groups and while his essential liberties have been frequently too rigorously curtailed by them he has also achieved the highest degree of individual self-respect in these intimate relations in which personality is revered, respected, trusted and relied upon. A mechanical civilization weakens these organic relations and thereby destroys robust individuality.[20]

On the other hand:

> Mechanism easily veils the actual realities of life. It makes human life seem to be a series of highly rational social relationships and hides the fact that these relations are actually

the product, not of mind and conscience but of power and impulse.[21]

The individual is related to the community in such a way that his greatest achievements as an individual are dependent upon the group, the social substance, from which he emerged, and are fulfilled and have their end in society.[22]

But, at the same time, the individual transcends the social process and is not just fulfilled in society. He is a " final resource " having a source of moral insight above and beyond the limitations of the group, which can be directed against communal idolatries.[23]

It is fairly obvious that, in Niebuhr's eyes, the character of the phenomenon we call " the group " is greatly influenced by his picture of human nature. Despite the fact that he acknowledges distinctions in kind between the individual and society, Niebuhr constantly personifies the group. If he does so for artistic purposes he has most certainly overshot his mark, for his reader gets an impression of close similarity rather than of analogy. Niebuhr has tended to give the same basic character — that of an evil man — without distinction or qualification to all kinds of groups.

Niebuhr carefully asserts that groups vary greatly from one to the next. But he obscures this astute observation by giving them all a common denominator. The United States, the proletarian class, a county board, and a Ladies' Aid Society are, in his view, basically identical — in so far as each is a community. This means that they are only superficially products of the times and environment. They are characterized by the same sort of eternal composition as is the individual. Their rigidity within Niebuhr's interpretation may be attested to by the fact that their nature, failings, and aspirations are supposedly read out of the

Bible. As they were two thousand years ago, they are now and ever shall be: one true group, sin without end.

Actually groups vary tremendously in fundamental character. Some are even better than the individuals who compose and supposedly transcend them.[24] Group dynamics has discovered that there are creative ways of working together in committees. ". . . Human aggregates are not necessarily and always immoral. It is not even true that the human group always falls below the sum total of the wisdom which its individuals represent. All of us know that there are many cases in which individuals [participating in a group activity] do produce creative results out of all proportion to the wisdom which seems to animate each one of them." [25]

One outstanding feature of Niebuhr's " group " is that it has become a thing in itself apart from the individuals who compose it. It is built up of vitalities, which are inner or psychic forces. And it is propelled by these forces. It is representative of the interest of its members, but it is dominated, directed, and vitalized by the force of its own self-interest (*hybris*). Thus — as in the case of the individual — its actions tend to be interpreted as if explained by simple reference to these inner forces. The group becomes a self-sufficient and self-acting entity largely independent of its surroundings and acting in the world instead of interacting or transacting *within* the world.

When phenomena are " explained " by reference to innate forces, the result is an obstacle to or a cutting short of inquiry. For example, when the factual actions of states are classified under a heading called " selfishness " and are then alleged to be due to a vitality (or a corruption of vitality) — to *hybris* — it is no longer necessary to inquire

into the problem.   The force itself is not to be understood;
it is immutable; it is prior and nothing can be done about
it.   Thus when the actions of states are attributed to it they
are no longer within the reach of human ingenuity.[26]
Niebuhr has not been the only one or the first to comment
on the tendency of individuals and groups, corporations,
labor unions, nations to be concerned exclusively with their
own interests.   But writing off this tendency as a taint in
human nature or in group nature is dismissing it as a factor
to be manipulated by men.   It is a defeatism that recognizes a problem and then abdicates from the effective field
of action.   In Niebuhr's order of things, man cannot set
about changing the eternal " selfishness " of states; as we
shall see,[27] he can only control or balance " selfishness."

Niebuhr does not say that some societies are immoral,
nor simply that societies are immoral.   He puts it in universal terms: society is immoral.   Placing a valuational
stigma upon the interests of all groups does not facilitate
handling of the problems and conflicts that arise between
them.   It leads to the visionary attitude that adjustments
may come about by convincing one side, one group to do
the " moral " thing, to abdicate or sacrifice its interests.
And Niebuhr does think that groups may, through the
agency of grace (though not on their own steam) , " die to
self " and thereby be reborn.[28]

This wholesale condemnation of interests as bad adds an
irrelevancy to perfectly normal phenomena.   Together
with the identification of interests with *hybris* — which
makes of them inevitables and immutables — it conceals
the possibility of mediating between groups, between interests, and of creating new and more satisfactory interests.
It prevents Niebuhr from seeing that there is any possibility of mediation between interests besides the possibility

of compromise based on partial sacrifice of the interests of both parties.

M. C. Otto has very effectively presented these possibilities as the method of " creative bargaining." Briefly, creative bargaining is a method of resolving conflicts of interests in a way satisfactory to both of the opposing parties to the conflict. When two people or two groups of people find themselves in a situation where the interests of each are frustrated by the interests of the other, and there is a complete block, an impasse, the conflict can be resolved (1) by one party riding roughshod over the interests of the other, (2) by one party, in a moment of emotional overflow, sacrificing its interests, (3) by each party sacrificing some of its interests in what is known as compromise, or (4) by creatively intuiting a new set of interests acceptable to both. This latter is creative bargaining. It is a process of interest-changing.

Specific conflicts are very rarely simple affairs; rather, they are complex collisions of patterns of interests, desires, values, or what not. The first step in the creative-bargaining intention is the sharpening of the conflict by pointing up the crucial issues, specifying and identifying as precisely as possible the interests that are in conflict, locating the points at which they conflict, and formulating the disagreement in exact terms. On this foundation the search for a resolution may be instituted — provided a resolution has not already been intuited (as is sometimes the case) during the process of clarification. Out of the greater understanding resultant from candid discussion may come a liberating idea, a hypothetical solution that will reorient the whole situation. A new pattern of interests may be found that is acceptable to both parties and deemed preferable by each to their old interests — *given the fact of conflict*. It is not that a solution has been found which satisfies the old opposing patterns of interest. Rather, a new common pattern has been found which is more satisfactory to both parties than the old interests-*in-conflict*. In any deadlock of opposing interest patterns, the deadlock itself, as part of the total situation, becomes a discordant part of each interest pattern. A creative resolution of the deadlock consists in reorganizing the patterns and changing the interests — the values, if you will — and thus finding a mutually acceptable pattern that is more satisfactory in its situation than the old ones were in theirs. Superficially, this kind of resolution might appear to be a method of sacrifice by all. Actually, in the re-creation of interests, the old is willingly discarded in favor of a more inclusive good; it is simply eclipsed.[29]

A very clear and simple — perhaps over-simple — illustration of creative bargaining is given by Mary Follett:

In the Harvard Library one day, in one of the smaller rooms, someone wanted the window open, I wanted it shut. We opened the window in the next room, where no one was sitting. This was not a compromise because there was no curtailing of desire; we both got what we really wanted. For I did not want a closed room, I simply did not want the north wind to blow directly on me; likewise the other occupant did not want that particular window open, he merely wanted more air in the room.[30]

These two people could easily have spent the afternoon alternately opening and closing the window in the small room, completely disgusted with each other. Instead they reconsidered their patterns of desire (which included the opening or shutting of a particular window) and, on the basis of this sharpening of the conflict, developed an improved pattern for the new situation and intuited a simple solution. Note that neither of them sacrificed his desire in respect to the first window. It simply dropped out of the picture — so much so that in retrospect they felt that they had gotten what they " really " wanted all along.

Creative bargaining is not a utopian pipe dream. It is a method that is in effective use where people are imaginative. Most of us have experienced it within ourselves during the process of education as we mediated between contradicting values and came out with higher syntheses. It is frequently encountered in personal relationships — particularly in sensitive marital relationships. It is also employed, with less frequency and more difficulty, to be sure, but with equal significance, in intergroup relations.

It may be objected that creative bargaining is not a serious alternative to methods of compromise and coercion because in some cases interests may be opposed in a perfect dilemma. Such an objection is no more warranted than its sanguine opposite — that there is a possible creative solution to all conflicts. The mere fact that the resolution in each case is a creation, an intuition of something previously non-existent, precludes any assertion as to its a priori impossibility. The argument for the affirmative, of course, cannot be conclusive either. However, it rests its case on a growing body of usage and on the clear promise creative bargaining shows in spite of the fact that it has not yet been tried in any deliberate and systematic fashion.

Treated in historical context, mythological blinkers removed, as phenomena in which both human nature and particularities of culture participate, selfishness may be alleviated and the problems set by blind and stubborn pursuance of private interests may be solved or partly solved — without recourse to self-sacrifice or grace. (And I refuse to assume that there is any sense in trying to eradicate them

completely.) Indications and achievements of solutions
are already to be found in the mature attitude being taken
by Walter Reuther and the United Automobile Workers;
in imaginative business relationships as described by Mary
Follett; in T.V.A. agricultural and other policies; in the
partial successes of the Montana Study; [31] in the settling of
many labor-management disputes (as, for example, the
mediating work of Nathan Feinsinger in the Hawaiian dock
strike) ; and in such rare international achievements as the
Arab-Palestine mediation by Ralph Bunche. All of these
are characterized by attempts to avoid self-abnegation or
compromise so far as it partakes of self-sacrifice. They embody a radical alteration in emphasis, changing the sphere
of problems from balancing — which, after all, does nothing but frustrate people (as does sacrifice) and evoke sin by
providing challenge to upset the balance — to creation,
representation, and organization. Creation is at a premium to find non-sacrificial resolutions of conflicts; representation, to devise organic bonds whereby the interests of
the people can be tied with the actions of their group
leaders in such a fashion that acceptance of a creative solution by the leaders can result in acceptance by the people;
organization, to assure the tapping and identification of interests and ideas constituent in the total situation.

If the concept of *hybris* in connection with groups is another way of saying that a group by its very nature is for
the good of itself (and/or of its members) and not for the
good of mankind, Niebuhr has most certainly erred. Men
have gathered together for the consolation and advance-
ment of everything under the sun, not excluding mankind.
It would probably be unfair to conclude that Niebuhr has
found no benevolent societies, but if he has found any they
have not profoundly impressed him.

Seeing only too well the bigotries and failings of nations and vested-interest groups, he has neglected the potentialities of democratic grass-roots organization. I have at least not noticed that he has championed them. The smaller, functional group need not necessarily operate on the principles of mob psychology; it *can* be used as a scientific workshop to test and develop the contributions of individuals. It *can* test the preferability of suggested expanded or altered interests; it *can* determine how satisfactory one value is as against another; it *can* mediate between interests by developing new, better interests more satisfactory to all parties and not representing sacrifice by any party.[32]

It is easy to see why Niebuhr may have failed to consider these possibilities. He thinks in terms of sacrifice, not in terms of sharpening interests and developing new ones, not in terms of changing ends along with the means. Reasons for the failure, besides those discussed immediately above, are many: dealing with generalities and general forces it is difficult to descend to concretions; emphasizing the impossible it is difficult to see the possible; being firstly theologian Niebuhr is concerned more for religion than for man-on-earth. But the central reason is traceable to what was said in the last chapter: Niebuhr's social relativism does not envisage a social science. Indeed when it permits Niebuhr to despair of the possibilities of objectivity [33] (because of *hybris,* of course) it displays a misunderstanding of the process of social science as contrasted with physical science. "Objectivity" is neither needed nor desirable. Wants, desires, or interests *are* "subjective" and the determination of a satisfactory resolution of conflicts between them, or the determination of more satisfactory wants, desires, interests must likewise be "subjective." [34]

Niebuhr's pre-emptory condemnation of groups contains

the further disadvantage of obscuring the action of broader, more inclusive groups. In particular, the political party in the United States, while it may pursue interests of its own, is much more remarkable for its mediative action between the interests of sub-groups. And, by the way, let's not forget the vital part egoism or self-interest plays in the democratic running of the American party system — it's called " office-seeking." The function of a group is to arbitrate (or better, to mediate) between the interests of its members (or its member groups) as well as to represent their interest.[35]

The neo-orthodox individual-group relationship partakes, as might be expected, of the dialectical (or paradoxical) quality so prevalent in the rest of neo-orthodoxy. On the one hand, man is a political animal. His greatest achievements are dependent on the group. The development of his capacities is the end of society and cannot be accomplished aside from society. On the other hand, essential man transcends society and is fulfilled beyond history. The one hand, however, is not reduced to nought by the transcendent supernatural importance of the other. They are dialectically clasped.

Society, or the state, is thus partly individualistic and partly corporative. (It is corporate " under the criticism of " individualism, we might say.) Strictly speaking, Niebuhr's individual is not the basic political unit as is the individual of the liberal philosophers. Conversely, the functional group presently epitomized in Communist cells is not an acceptable lowest denominator for Niebuhr's political purposes. The group needs the penetrating insights of disinterested, prophetic individuals.[36]

The group-individual relationship envisaged by Niebuhr is superficially very similar to the instrumentalist picture.

For both it is a two-way affair. For both it is an interdependence. The group is indispensable to the individual, and without the creative individual the group becomes stagnant. Indeed both Niebuhr and Dewey refer to " organic " society. However, the similarity is external; Niebuhr's intimate man-group relation is organic only by the grace of his dialectic. The individual contributes to the group by standing against it. Prophetic criticism is truth independently (and supernaturally) arrived at and then launched at the group from the member's transcendence over it. Such a dialectic approach is a way of avoiding both extremes by accepting both. Its final product is not a genuine organism. The member is not so much identical with as attached to his collective; his contribution to society is impinged upon and not ratified by the collective.

Society is immoral, man moral in comparison. By what standards — those of the individual or of the society? Clearly this strange discordance means that the standards of the two are not in tune. And tuning the individual to an unearthly norm outside the range of societal ears will never foster an organic, transactive individual-group relationship. In final analysis, the transcendental overtones of Niebuhr's philosophy mask his insistence upon " organic " society. The dialectic falters. Perhaps indeed it is as operationally impossible as is the simultaneous utterance by one voice of the advocated opposites. Man is in the end saved as an individual. Though the sins of the father are visited on the children unto the third and fourth generation, even neo-orthodox Protestantism will not retreat from the priesthood of all believers far enough to permit sin to be treated as a problem of organic society. As a prophet himself, Niebuhr is constitutionally individualistic.

INTRACTABLE POWER

As previously suggested, Niebuhr is disturbed by the " mechanical " character of our culture, which prevents the healthy existence of organic groups. He has observed the consequences of industrialism, and he has judged them to be bad. He has noticed the helplessness, the anxiety, the purposelessness of individual men among the mammoth economic forms, the impersonal structures, and the inexorable machinery of present society. His complaint is that through mechanism society has lost the moral forces which hold men serenely together in organic groups.[37]

Niebuhr realizes that a scientific-industrial revolution has taken place since the Middle Ages. But he does not understand that since this was a revolution in culture it was also necessarily a revolution in human nature. He does not see that the new mechanism is an important factor in the changed nature of man. Instead he reads eternal traits of human nature out of the present mechanism-loaded situation — and it spells power.

Attendant upon the breakdown of the medieval organic group, of medieval unity — attendant upon the disintegration, under the impact of the revolution of science, of customs no longer identical with or supporting moral bonds that for a long time held men in social groups — there came about a fundamental change in the nature of man. As a combined result of these changes, power, when applied in old ways, became no longer effective in the new fluid society. Power, which could formerly be fairly easily and effectively wielded because it was applied within and in conformance with an established and living system of customs, became coercive, no longer customarily acceptable, no longer applicable in a way that was felt to be just, no longer effective.[38] Effective (i.e., non-coercive) power tended to be found only in individual and not in social relationships.

Society today has indeed a mechanical in place of the earlier organic character: the growth of economic interdependence has required some sort of organization. Society is still fluid; organic social customs have not crystallized. It is difficult to agree with Niebuhr that the mechanical character of civilization "weakens" organic relations. Mechanism may tend to prevent the regrowth of organic relations; it does not "weaken" something already destroyed. On the other hand, Niebuhr seems very correctly to have observed that the mechanics of contemporary civilization hide the fact that human relations "are actually the product, not of mind and conscience but of power and impulse." [39] But when it is remembered that Niebuhr is addicted to the eternal "are," not to the "are" of the present tense, his opinion is seen to be far from accurate. He really thinks that mechanism is a force destructive of organic society. He actually believes that power (and he understands only coercive power) is an eternal factor in human relationships.

For Niebuhr there are really three moral laws: the law of love or brotherhood, and two natural laws, one universal, arrived at by reason — an individual ethic — equal justice, and one more relative, arrived at in each community as a product of the social mind. This third law is political in that it necessarily represents compromise between reason and the arbitrary impulses within the nation. It is the product of power balanced against power as well as of rational arbitration of conflicting rights.[40] Universal natural law emerges with a logical approximation of the law of love, equally affirming all conflicting claims. Relative natural law, recognizing that love and reason will not resolve conflicts made terrible by man's sin, pits power against power in the interest of tentative solutions.

Within the state men are constantly jockeying for position and power. An impartial community would place fences and boundaries around all men alike. But the community is made up from within, not imposed from without. The justice of the community becomes the interest of the stronger, the interest of whatever group is powerful enough to become the dominant element in society. Rules of justice become rationalizations of the interests of the ruling oligarchy, the group in power.

On the whole, power falls in with the differentiation of social function. Political power is a derivative of ability to manipulate other forms of social power for the purpose of organizing and dominating the community. Soldiers have depended primarily on physical power, priests on " soul-force," industrialists on economic power, and all have relied on the power of reason — so easily corrupted to egoistic ends. All must likewise rely on a certain minimum of physical force and of spiritual force.

The most natural way for man to assert himself and expand his being is through the acquisition of possessions. " Where your treasure is there will your heart be also." Of all kinds of power the most potent is economic — the precise power that organizes democratic states. A tribute to its strength may be extracted from its ability to rule despite its concessions of suffrage and education. Within economic power, however, are the seeds of capitalism's doom. Economic power is not only a derivative of property as Marxists contend; the control and manipulation of economic process is power as well. Though minimal, it gives the proletariat a bludgeon to wield.[41]

Power always corrupts.   A man or group in power in
a nation has an almost invariable tendency to arrogate to
itself still greater dominance and control.   But once an individual, group, or nation has attained power it finds itself
in a vicious circle.   Its attainment places it on a perilous
peak of eminence exposed to even greater dangers than it
feared before.   In attempting to overcome insecurity
through power, it has extended it by power.[42]   Rather
than lose what it has gained, it endeavors to make it secure
by more and more power.[43]   Power is never given up without a struggle or for humanistic motives. Power never
abdicates; it is only forced out.[44]

While power is essential for the sake of creating or
maintaining any social cohesion necessary to preserve peace
within the community, power is inimical to justice — equal
justice.   Any ruling group, whether soldier, priest, in-
dustrialist, or technician, attempts to perpetuate inordinate privileges over and above those requisite for the performance of social function. Correspondingly it limits the
freedom of others.

To obtain obedience with the least outward use of
physical force, the ruling class pretends that its interests
are identical with those of the nation.[45]   It tries to enhance
the religious overtone common to all political loyalties.
It fashions what fictions it can to secure acceptance of what
Niebuhr calls " natural religion " — the pretensions of
human institutions to unconditioned and divine claims.[46]
Without the respect derived from natural religion, government finds itself in a vicious circle of trying to replace
implicit consent by fear and force the more it loses respect
and loyalty.   ". . . mutual respect for each other's rights
in particular communities is older than any code of law;
and . . . machinery for the enforcement of law can be

efficacious only when a community as a whole obeys its laws implicitly, so that coercive enforcement may be limited to a recalcitrant minority." [47]

Accordingly each nation sets up symbols of divinity to aid the imagination of individuals to envisage the national community. The logical symbol for this purpose is a ruler; the most effective is a ruler who has lost all control, all actual power, so that he can be divorced from the ruling oligarchy and represent the pure majesty of the state. The effectiveness of this symbol is attested to by the prolonged cohesion of the British Empire despite rational attacks on the monarchy.

Britain has her queen, Japan has an emperor (only differing from the British monarch in that he is manipulated by a different oligarchy). In America the same is achieved by a religious reverence for the Constitution and the Supreme Court; and in Russia the dictator receives the requisite reverence. " Natural religion . . . finds a God who is majestic, but not majestic enough to threaten human self-esteem." [48]

Besides majesty and force a recent addition to motivation for obedience is the factor of rational consent. Niebuhr dismisses this factor as of only secondary importance: " The giving and withholding of rational consent may make and unmake particular governments within a given state, but it will hardly destroy the state and create a new state structure." [49]

Of course natural religion is not created by the ruling oligarchy, nor is a particular national symbol always consciously created. Furthermore the symbol may carry over, from one historical epoch to another, something of the system wherein it first emerged. Constitutional monarchy carries over, on its monarchical side, taints of feudalism, though its majesty is manipulated for purposes of the capitalistic oligarchy.[50]   Likewise we may presume (though Niebuhr does not mention it) that the American Constitution or the British Parliament, carried over into a socialist state, would bring with it some remnants of capitalism.

Cohesion may also be attained — and the attempt is always made — by claiming general, universal objectives for the nation, such as " civilization," " culture."   And conversely, " no nation defends ' civilization ' or ' truth ' or ' justice ' unless there is some coincidence between those values and its own national self-interest." [51]   Particularly useful in time of war, these claims at any time illustrate to the mere individual the immensity, the worth, the goodness of his country.   Idealism used in this way serves to confuse the real issues, which are mostly group struggles for power or privilege, intra- or inter-nationally.[52]   In short, privileged classes are self-deceptive and hypocritical.   They try to prove that their privileged position serves the general interest, that their privileges are payment for services rendered to the general public.[53]

There are other dangers in cohesion besides the injustices it perpetrates within the nation.   Cohesion is an indication of strength and it tempts to pride.   It is only the highly cohesive nations which form threats to peace among states.[54]   The highly cohesive nation, secure at home with internal harmony, can allow its imagination broader horizons and can imperialistically look across its borders.   It is jealous of its ideals, hypersensitive, and vengeful.   As with mature adults, so with mature nations.   Blessed with a long memory, they alone are prompted to a stubborn vindictiveness.   " Only highly cultured nations like Germany and France allow the accumulated resentments of the centuries to determine their present policies." [55]

Niebuhr thinks it is possible — though very difficult — to approximate politically the ideal of equality. Nearness of approach depends on two principles of communal life: (1) organization of power — power to coerce and organize government; and (2) balance of power. Here again loom Scylla and Charybdis. The first principle may expand to tyranny; the second may degenerate to anarchy. Each may become a contradiction to equal justice; and too great a fear of the one may lead to the perils of the other. Yet there is no strictly middle ground. Man finds himself in the throes of another perfect paradox.[56]

The principle of organization of power is affirmed in the Christian doctrine of divine ordinance of government. It is a principle of justice in so far as it manipulates the various forces and impulses of the community and organizes them into a unity preventing tensions from erupting into overt conflict; preventing capricious disproportions of power from springing up, disjointing things, and instituting tyrannies; and shifting disproportions of power whenever they make for injustice.[57] Government must have conscious control; it must consciously manage its balancing act to prevent disruptions. It should be as impartial as possible and it must have the preponderant power necessary to coerce submission whenever its process of arbitration fails to hold down rising conflict, and tensions overtly erupt.[58]

The principle of organizing power contradicts the law of love and leads to injustice when government becomes over-enthusiastic about establishing order, when it tries to destroy the freedom and vitality of subordinate elements of the community in the name of " order," when it begins to consider itself order incarnate and suppresses all rebellion against its authority as revolt against order per se.[59]

If a proper balance of power is achieved it is possible to approach the ideal of justice. Since it results in tension, which is covert and potential conflict, it can only be an approximation. If driven to extremes, it degenerates into pure individualism, anarchy, in which love and brotherhood are destroyed even more than is equal justice. The principle of balance of power takes cognizance of the fact that struggle between groups in a nation cannot be resolved by dissolving them.

Unfortunately a formula for the balance and organization of power promises little practical value to the politician or statesman unless a scale is provided for the measurement of power and unless power is defined as a measurable quantity. In the absence of a scale or a definition — and Niebuhr does not provide either — how is the statesman to know, except on the basis of intuitive subjective certainty, when the optimum combination of balance and organization has been achieved? Must he rely on genius alone?

Take for example the delicate question of separation of church and state. Religious sects and churches are groups, and as such, in Niebuhr's way of thought, partake of the arch-sinfulness common to all human collectives. If anything their susceptibility to *hybris* could be expected to be greater than that of other groups, for to their greater potentiality for good adheres a greater temptation to evil. They are unquestionably participants in the eternal power struggle, relying perhaps chiefly on soul-force but not eschewing economic or other power resources available to them. In other words they are elements, weighty elements, in the political balance of power. And their proper disposition in the balance is essential to the achievement of a tolerable degree of justice.

How then should the " organizing power " treat them in the interest of justice, freedom, and order? Should it ally itself with one of them or some of them or all? Or should it try to assign them positions in the balance completely apart from governmental favor?

Traditionally the United States, anxious to avoid the blood baths, persecutions, and injustices that have attended the mixture of religious strife with governmental control in Europe, has insisted on a separation of church and state. America's historical decision was that the proper balance was to be obtained (or retained) by governmental alliance with or support of none. The words of the First Amendment are, of course, inadequate — as any words would be — for setting a strict and rigid demarcation between the two realms. It merely says that " Congress shall make no law respecting an establishment of religion, or prohibiting the free exercise thereof." And so it was left to the Supreme Court gradually to define the line of separation by interpreting the Constitution through case by case settlement of specific controversies.

The Supreme Court decision in the 1948 McCollum case,[60] continuing with the attempt to find the proper degree of separation, defined the line too rigidly for the taste of some of the interested parties. By deciding that the use of public classrooms for released-time religious training violated the First Amendment, the Court set the degree of separation so close to the absolute as to evoke a cry of protest from Niebuhr. " We ought not," he warned, " to prejudge [the issue of state support of religion] in the name of a principle of ' separation of church and state ' which in exact constitutional terms goes no further than the prohibition of the establishment of one religion and the suppression of others." [61] " It is not at all clear that [the constitutional fathers] sought to prevent the state's support of religion absolutely, provided such support could be given equitably to all religious groups. Whether that should be done is a question of policy upon which we may have different opinions." [62]

Niebuhr's opinion is that all sects should enjoy state support for selected purposes, or, in the language of Agnes Meyer, " that monogamy between Church and State is illegitimate, while a polygamous marriage between them might be not only legitimate but desirable." [63] His version is typically paradoxical: " Institutions of religion should be politically powerless, if the true principles of our religion are to achieve political influence." But on the other hand, " an absolutely rigorous separation of church and state [means] the secularization of the community." [64]

Surely Niebuhr realizes that " equitable " support to the 256-odd sects in the United States is fantastically impossible and that any state support contributes to the political power of religious institutions — unequally at that. For one thing Catholic power would not permit " equitable " distribution of governmental favor. Yet Niebuhr glibly falsifies history without any attempt at evidence, in order to bolster his position. Contemporary historians have clearly demonstrated that, in the intent of the constitutional fathers, the First Amendment was meant to prevent support to any or all religious sects.[65] The intentions of the constitutional fathers are, of course, not nearly so important as present-day considerations when it comes to present-day problems: our situation may be quite different from theirs. What they said does not indisputably prove the wisdom of a policy for today. On the other hand, such a semi-deliberate historical error on Niebuhr's part shows a revealing lack of concern for facts and for historical accuracy.

Apparently, by so irrationally insisting upon " equitable " support to all American sects and by thus sanctioning the bestowal of political power on religious institutions, Niebuhr has made the fateful decision that " the true principles of our religion " must be sacrificed to the overriding fight against " secularism." He has decided that the second part of his paradoxical statement of the general situation outweighs the first: he is willing to ignore the balance-of-power aspect of this important political problem in order to take arms against a sea of secularism which he believes threatens to swamp our culture with technology.

Even in pointing out that " some very healthy democracies " in Europe do not observe the principle of an " ' absolute wall of separation ' " between church and state,[66] Niebuhr does not rise above the level of expedience. The over-all fact of the situation in European countries may be persuasive in an argument on the propaganda level. If the wisdom of the American decision is to rest upon a careful balance-of-power analysis, however, we must look for more evidence than a barren comparison. What are the elements of power in these various European nations? How are they balanced? Just how do the state-aided religious institutions fit into the balance? And then how do these conditions relate to the particular American balance of power? Can we decide that they are sufficiently similar to American conditions for us to import a European solution to our problem on their authority? We do not adopt the British cabinet system in the United States because we do not feel that it would fit the needs of the American situation. Is their church-aid system in a different category?

Can we even decide, on the basis of our present knowledge, whether Norwegian experience in balancing power, for example, bears more fruitful comparison to the experience of the United States than to the experience of a state within the United States? These are some of the questions we vainly expect Niebuhr to tackle. We expect him to *apply* his theory of power in government to this particular argument of the church-and-state problem. Clearly he feels that he, at least, is able to resolve the problem without a laborious balancing of evidence.

No consideration of the church-and-state question or of religious institutions in power politics can honestly avoid an evaluation of the threat and the power of the Catholic Church. Niebuhr is aware of the pretenses, the authoritarianism, and the political and social evils attributable to the Church, and he has voiced his criticism on many occasions. But he apparently has no fear of augmenting its power through " equitable " state support. Impressed with the democratic spirit of American lay Catholics, he views power-politics Catholicism as different in different countries. " Catholicism," he maintains, " is at its least impressive in feudal-agrarian societies, where it frequently seeks desperately to hold onto special powers and privileges which were essential in the Middle Ages but are so no longer. Catholicism is most creative in highly developed industrial communities." [67] " Catholicism naturally has a greater unity of discipline than other religious communities. But it has the freedom to relate itself to various national situations. It also has many moral and spiritual resources which can act creatively in a free and responsible society." [68] " We fail to appreciate the genuine grace of personal religion within this system of official intolerance." [69]

Of course there is something to be said for Catholicism. But we must ask for evidence — which Niebuhr nowhere provides — before swallowing the story that Catholicism is of two sorts, before accepting the implication that because special powers and privileges are no longer essential to Catholicism (and it is doubtful that they ever truly were) it has seriously repressed its will to power for participation in industrial society. Considering the fact that democracy has not yet grown to flourish in Catholic-dominated countries, we must be forgiven our skepticism, in absence of evidence, of the suggestion that the Church has become creative in democracy once established. To argue from Catholic parties in Europe or from unions in American cities which are predominantly Catholic [70] is a dangerous procedure unless the argument is accompanied by careful analysis. Is it the Catholic influence that has contributed the creativity of these organizations, or is it the ethos of democracy (also informing the members of these organizations), or economic factors, or a combination of many circumstances? To make a valid decision on such matters, more is required than bland assertions. And there is much evidence to be considered. The Italian and French postwar Catholic parties, for example, were catchalls for rightists whose discredited parties had been dissolved. How much of their policy was Catholic? Besides we should take a searching look at the theory of Catholic pluralism [71] currently being pushed — chiefly by the Vatican but also by elements within these parties. Are we sure that its implications are, in the end, democratic rather than feudal? Niebuhr shows no evidence of having made such a careful analysis.

As part of his minimizing of the power position of Catholicism, Niebuhr disparages the idea that Catholicism, being an authoritarian religion, is necessarily hostile to democracy.[72] Evidently in his view authoritarianism in habits or thinking need not transfer from religion to politics — at least in industrial societies. Of course there are innumerable instances where we hold logically and/or practically contradictory habits, tendencies, emotions, desires, beliefs at one and the same time. That fact, however, only slightly mitigates the more general tendency for intolerance in one activity, for example, to spill over into other activities. The naïveté of Niebuhr's view becomes incredible when he inconsistently announces an " affinity between religious individualism and . . . political individualism." [73] Can it be that individualism translates from religion into politics but authoritarianism does not?

We may put our faith in the layman and emphasize the distinction between him and his more militant clergy. Yet his heritage from the Church must remain a worry and we must ponder the warning of another commentator: " When the hierarchy in any authoritarian system finds itself in a position of power, then its ' liberal ' laymen always acquiesce in that authority. Was it not true that the Americans always liked the individual German layman under the Nazi system and the individual layman under the Japanese military system? Yet in a showdown this layman obeyed the authority of his hierarchy — and this is what we may expect in ecclesiastical totalitarianism as well as in political totalitarianism." [74]

Niebuhr's attitude is influenced by two things: (1) his happiness that because " Catholicism has always believed that ' the state has the moral authority to control economic life,' " it in a sense " has never capitulated to pure capitalism " [75] (as if there ever were such a thing as " pure " capitalism) ; and (2) his eagerness for the spiritual rein-

forcements of Catholicism's " genuine grace of personal religion " as a counteragent to the " secularization " of the
state.   Indeed, his whole attitude toward the Catholic
Church sounds strangely like an apology for vested interests in exchange for an anti-secular ally.   Inordinately
frightened by the technical and mechanical aspects of our
culture, Niebuhr has forgotten the tremendous contributions of " secularism " to civic and religious freedom.[76]

Niebuhr's confused stand on the balance-of-power issue
of state aid to religious institutions indicates the weakness
of his formula for power in government as applied to particular issues.   Here it appears that his doctrine of the
balance and organization of power has had little direct influence over his prescription for action.   His solution to
the church-and-state problem derives almost entirely from
other considerations — considerations of therapy for a
" secular " culture.   And where careful weighing of the
power situation would seem to be most appropriate — in
connection with the *hybris* of religious institutions — his
treatment of power is no more adequate, penetrating, coherent, or reliable than the wandering musings of the rest
of us.   This despite the beauty of his abstract general " explanation " of how to mix together a maximum of freedom
and order to attain a tolerable justice.   For lack of any clear
criteria by which to measure instances of power, for lack
of an operative abstract concept of power, he is led to rely
upon his genius alone.

The power of which Niebuhr speaks is clearly non-functional; it does not lead to control and to effectiveness.   It
is, on the contrary, coercive, corruptive, and inimical to
justice.   It is the power of one faction against another.
True, Niebuhr adds majesty (natural religion), consent,
and the claim of universal objectives as elements making up

the cohesion of states. These, however, are for him accomplices of coercive power. Judged by absolute standards, they conspire to conceal the coercive drive of the group in power toward its own selfish interests and contrary to equal justice.

The balance of power advocated by Niebuhr shows that coercive power is a permanent aspect of society, for, if power can be controlled and a relative justice secured only by way of balance, power cannot be changed.

If coercive power were recognized as an evil of the times instead of as an inevitable evil, Niebuhr might accept the opportunity to consider ways of minimizing it by giving it a functional direction; he would be unsatisfied merely to balance it out. The " immorality " of the group and the coercive power of contemporary life are the outcome of specifiable historical circumstances. In large part they are due to a failure of society to adjust itself to the fluid conditions extant since the dissolution of medieval unity.

With no authority to replace the discredited authority of the Church, with no implicitly accepted organic structure of mores within the framework of whose authority it could sink its roots, power became a non-functional use of force. The scientific revolution has so fundamentally transformed conditions in the world that transactive man can no longer hope to find a static authority capable of giving him the much-needed stability and direction he seeks. Change has become so much the order of the day that when men try to wield power in the old way they find they can no longer anticipate the results. Where formerly an exercise of power could fairly effectively achieve its purpose — as much because the permissible uses of power were prescribed as because methods of applying it were well established within the nexus of authority — there is now tremendous uncertainty in the use of power. In other words power has become non-functional; it is felt to be coercive. People do not feel power to be just, and so they maintain with Lord Acton that it corrupts and with Niebuhr that the only thing to do is to balance one corruption against another.

Meanwhile the mighty, also aware that their power is non-functional, seek to make it effective by propaganda. In desperation they try to create an authority of myth and persuasion in the context of which their exercise of power will be accepted by the people and prove functionally effective. And in this way they have a measure of temporary success. Not in the long run, however — for two reasons. (1) Propaganda-authorities are superficial make-shifts, too shallow for the great leagues in depth of man-in-culture. Men have memories. (2) Propaganda-authorities must be, to inspire the blind obedience they seek, unconditional claims to finality; they must be rigid and uncompromising — characteristics which insure their eventual doom within a fluid culture. Yet, in the absence of an adequate understanding of power, these same superficial authorities are reconstructed upon each collapse, in desperate and pathetic hope that this time they will survive the ravages of change.

The " immorality " that Niebuhr sees in society is largely a result of the fact that we have not yet successfully adjusted our institutions to accommodate the revolution in science. Evil (*hybris*), selfishness, irresponsible use of power are more apparent today because morals have been treated in an absolute fashion incommensurate with the changing exigencies of the total situation. The dominant evils of the day are not the product of sin or malice or jealousy but of stupidity, inertia, and circumstance. The

trouble is that we have not yet done enough creative thinking in connection with this central problem. We have not
yet caught up in control of social affairs to the control we
have effected over nature. We have not yet taken seriously
the possibilities of coping with the coercive manifestations
of power and the bankruptcy of authority by way of deliberate development of more adequate and satisfactory
values and a self-improving authoritative method.

Such possibilities are understandably alien to Niebuhr's
trend of thought. The self-interest, the vested interest, the
struggle for power so evident in contemporary society are
embodied in *hybris,* the inevitable sin-force in human nature. In turn sin-force diffuses through man and through
the group image of man to tarnish the coercive power of
today with stains of inevitability.

Niebuhr has succeeded in giving a remarkable account
of the contemporary power scene. His description of the
vicious circle of power brilliantly outlines the bankruptcy
of power when, under conditions of fluid society, it necessarily becomes coercive. Unfortunately, because of his
vision of power in terms of the absolute, he is unable to see
the problem of coercive power as it really is. Indeed, it is
not a true problem for him because he thinks it cannot finally be solved. It permits only of transitory balancing
feats.

He does not understand that the problem is to find a
way of making power functional in a fluid society, to develop a method whereby power can again be effective when
applied in the context of fluid customs. Power is an
amalgam of the desires and values of people. By each of
our desires or values we participate in the creation of
power. Power is not a force but a composite field or structure. It is to be controlled not by weighing and counter-

weighing on the macroscopic level, but by reorganization of desires and value patterns. Power can become effective only as we develop methods for progressively finding more satisfactory values and patterns of values in wide-awake acceptance of the total human situation — including the fundamental and continuously altering dimensions of physical science and technology. Since Niebuhr has postulated *hybris* (as well as power politics) as an uncompromising and eternal fact, he is prevented and prevents others from looking to interconnections. And since he does not investigate the causal interconnections between phenomena, events are, for him, fortuitous for lack of human control.

Until we progress further in the science of human values, Niebuhr is apparently right: we shall have to stumble along protecting ourselves while also frustrating ourselves by balancing power. Creative bargaining presumes that one party to a conflict cannot pursue its goal in defiance of the interests of the other. A balance of power is then necessary until an appropriate authority of method can grow up. But Niebuhr has not essentially advanced thinking about power beyond the outposts of Number 10 of the *Federalist Papers*. His great disservice is that by dogmatically introducing an arbitrary surd he conceals tremendous untapped wells of creative possibility to which he is himself oblivious.

SUMMARY

The questions asked at the beginning of the present chapter have not been fully answered. Only two concepts, or views of phenomena — the *group* and *power* — have so far been considered in their roles as products of Niebuhr's basic theory. Both have been seen to be greatly influenced by the philosopher's fundamental postulates. And both, because of their participation in his a-priori-ism, have been judged to be a hindrance to genuine possibilities of accomplishment in the political field. They have so far proved to be quite the opposite of useful tools for the purpose of guiding either planning or investigation (inquiry) . They have tended rather to stifle productive and progressive actions. The " experimentalist " side of the philosopher has so far failed to bear fruit.

CHAPTER FIVE

Democracy and the World

But this unceasing stress on sacrifice simply indicates
that no satisfactory definition of concrete and democratic aims has yet been made, that no new body of
expectation, capable of fusing hearts and minds into a
fervent whole has been forged.

JAMES H. HART

A set of concepts is more or less operative according to
the degree of precision with which the concepts are drawn
up. It ceases to be operative when the concepts are so
vaguely formulated as to be adaptable to varying exigencies. This is to say that concepts and philosophical sets of
concepts are of social value the day they cease being *mere*
generalities and attain the status of hypothesis and theory.
One of the functions of the theorist in the field of social
science is to clarify ideas, to point up concepts so that they
can be put to use. An idea is a tool; like an ax it must be
sharpened and protected from corrosion. Only when it is
in usable condition can it be effective.

Even a sharpened concept is not automatically a successful conceptual tool. The social theorist must fashion his
tools in such a way that they may be tested. He must forge
his axes so that logical handles can be attached. Only when
logically connected with the actions of men can these rational constructs be shown to have value. If concepts are
precisely formulated and logically bound to hypotheses
concerning the practical world it is possible to test the con-

cepts indirectly. But it is not enough to have a testable hypothesis; the concept itself must also be in such a form that the fate of the practical hypothesis will indicate the usefulness of the concept and, better yet, will indicate needed improvement of the concept.

Among the abstract concepts employed by the political theorist are such things as power, the group, change, freedom, authority, tolerance. In so far as they are made into something more than *mere* generalities — something sufficiently precise so that they can be used as tools instead of as masks — they can be socially constructive or operative. In so far as they are forged into a form permitting logical connection between them and practical affairs, their constructive quality, or usefulness, can be determined; and they can be altered in the direction of greater usefulness.

Any concept or set of concepts may be " useful " in a different sense. The golden rule may function to simplify the making of practical decisions. *Hybris* may help a man decide how to act in a particular situation. As Standards, abstract concepts may facilitate the troublesome process of thinking. If, however, they were fashioned into ideals as functional aims instead of into Standards, they would be more truly useful. They would not suffer from the frequent inapplicability encountered by Standards (as, for example, the golden rule). They would find themselves perfectible in context.

In passing, it is worth noting that general concepts are also used for purposes of deception. Part of the current distrust of reason, of which Niebuhr is an expression, is an inordinate reaction to the use of ideals in propaganda as instruments for manipulating people. Starting after World War I, when it was seen that people could be induced to fight in behalf of false ideologies, the assumption was widely made that *all* ideals were mere rationalizations, either self-deceptions or gloss for the credulous. We find a reflection of this pathological reaction in Niebuhr's statements regarding the secular divinity of nations and methods of inducing acceptance of the state,[1] and in his conviction that *all* ideologies (and all thought) are tinged with *hybris*.

In the preceding chapter Niebuhr's abstract concepts of the group and power were analyzed in somewhat different context. From what has been said, however, they can clearly be seen to fall into the category of *mere* generalities as a result of their participation in and subjection to the overwhelming emphasis in Niebuhr's thought — *hybris*.[2] In their turn, these two general ideas are focal to further concepts that Niebuhr as political theorist employs.

The present chapter will consider what sort of a democracy it is to which Niebuhr finally adheres, what sort of democracy results as end product of his thinking. Democracy will be examined through the medium of some of the abstract concepts (as seen by Niebuhr) which are generally acclaimed as aspects of democracy.

Unfortunately, Niebuhr never really gets down to a specific or detailed treatment of planning or of government — how it should be organized, how it in fact operates. Although it may be dangerous to moralize on the simple basis of a neglect, exclusive consideration of the general on the part of a philosopher may not lightly be passed over as insignificant. It is at least indicative of defect in his relativism, of the influence of *hybris* in drawing attention only to the impossible. It further suggests in advance that his abstract concepts in the political realm are *mere* generalities rather than functional concepts: that is, they are not shaped to sustain the logical connection with practice,

which would submit them to test.[3]   Indeed, this last suggestion is reinforced by his resort to a paradoxico-dialectical
method which is emphatically unfit to serve as medium
through which may be transmitted the shock of test applied
to practical hypotheses.

In the field of international affairs Niebuhr most nearly
approaches a detailed analysis of a political problem. His
view of international relations will, accordingly, be considered, for illustrative purposes, following the examination of democracy.

DIALECTIC DEMOCRACY

Among the concepts relevant to democracy that political theorists have been striving to clarify and perfect are
change, the relation of freedom and authority, tolerance,
faith in human nature, and majority rule.   Together these
concepts may not spell out all relevant aspects of democracy, but from an analysis of Niebuhr's treatment of them
we might expect to obtain a fairly accurate understanding
of his view of democracy and of his contribution to it.
Does he contribute to or hinder the development of more
operative abstract ideas?   Do his particular insights aid or
obstruct the perfection of a functioning democracy?

Change

From the time of his early writings, Niebuhr has shown
a continued interest in change.   The economic injustice
which he has so piercingly felt to be the central problem of
the world is in itself sufficient reason for desiring change.
As a matter of fact, Niebuhr has been so obsessed with the
plight of the proletarian and so anxious for change that for
a long time he failed to see the immense significance of democracy as a method of change.

In the early 1930's he contended:

Political power has been made responsible, but economic power has become irresponsible in society. The net result is that political power has been made more responsible to economic power. . . . At present it must suffice to discount a still widely held conviction that the democratic movement has given society a permanent solution for its vexing problems of power.[4]

The victories of democracy in the eighteenth and nineteenth centuries were triumphs of an alliance of merchants and workers over the aristocrats who defended their position behind the bulwarks of feudalism and monarchy. The contemporary struggle is between the workers on the one hand and an alliance of aristocrats and merchants on the other. . . . This shift of allegiance on the part of the merchants proves to what degree democracy was an instrument of bourgeois class interest for them.[5]

He was skeptical of the potentialities for change within democracy because he had already postulated power as coercion or as coercion thinly veiled behind a curtain of rationalization, propaganda, or " natural religion " — because this power was seen to be of an unyielding character and because the self-interest that led the quest for power was isolated and independent of environment.

He carried the identification of the character of the group with the character of his separated human being to such an extreme that he imagined even groups could be considered in isolation from the broader culture in which they existed. He began to envisage " transcending " groups. And, of course, it was the proletariat that transcended society. Who but the outcasts, the disinherited, he reasoned, can stand without and transcend society enough to evaluate it properly? [6]

This class orientation of the early Niebuhr reflects the

profound influence of Marxism.   Indeed there is a strik-
ing similarity between the Marxian doctrine of class conflict and the Niebuhrian postulate of sin.   The chief difference between the two is that Marxism reads economic,
environmental causes for the phenomenon of vested interest, whereas Niebuhr finds its cause in (a defect of) human
nature.   Thus Niebuhr is particularly critical of the eschatological element in Marxism, which, he says, is " romantic in its interpretation of the possibilities of human nature
and in its mystical glorification of the anticipated automatic
mutuality in the communist society." [7]   Marxism as a
child of liberalism retained faith in human responsibility
for the historic process and for historic progress.[8]

Dominated by a wishful vision of the transcendent disinherited, Niebuhr proceeded to doubt the feasibility of
leveling the disproportion of power (economic) , in which
was rooted the injustice of society, except through unilat-
eral proletarian action.   He did not see any hope in raising
the intelligence of the general community because, as he
said, " unfortunately there is no such general community.
There are many classes, all of them partially deriving their
perspectives from, or suffering them to be limited by, their
economic interest." [9]   There was thus little hope for the
proletariat in Western society.   The chances of their making up a majority party were extremely slim: neither the
middle-class urbanite nor the farmer could be counted as
an adherent to a proletarian party.[10]   Niebuhr did, however, see a faint hope in the fact that the economically
weaker classes had not developed their full potential
strength and that the social intelligence of all classes might
be raised a little.   At any rate, he thought, the proletariat
must hang on to its ideals.   The faith of the proletarian
" is a necessary illusion, without which some truth is ob-

scured." [11] " Once the religious quality of the proletarian creed is abandoned, and the eschatological emphasis in Marxism is disavowed, evolutionary socialism may easily lose the furious energy which alone is capable of moving against the stubborn inertia of society." [12]

Niebuhr disapproved of the tactics of the British Labour Party. " If enterprises are thus taken over piecemeal, it is difficult to develop a systematic and coherent scheme of social ownership and there is a possibility that society will be plunged into a chaos in which the vices of both systems of ownership, private and social, are compounded. Furthermore there is as yet no evidence that a privileged class, which yields advantage after advantage peacefully, will finally yield the very basis of its special position in society without conflict." [13] ". . . social planning is possible only by the rigid circumscription or total abolition of the rights of property." [14]

Niebuhr looked at the Russian experiment and concluded that, under the special circumstances of the case, the violent method of change might be effectual. He began pushing his ideal of equality to the extreme of half-advocating violence. If all force is coercion, he reasoned, how is one morally to choose between the overt and the covert? [15] The industrial magnate who, by his mass hiring and firing, by his business cycles, causes children to die of malnutrition is not morally distinguishable from the outright murderer. Equal justice is a higher law than peace.[16] He argued that violence is disapproved of because it is falsely assumed to be inevitably an expression of ill will and because traditional instrumental values are uncritically identified with intrinsic moral values.[17] " We may argue that the immediate consequences of violence are such that they frustrate the ultimate purpose by which it is justified. If that is true, it is certainly not self-evident; and violence can therefore not be ruled out on a priori grounds." [18]

By 1935 Niebuhr was ready to agree that change forced by non-violent political and moral pressure is to be preferred in terms of results because of the dangers of complete social disintegration once violence is resorted to. [19] He also began to criticize Communist insistence on violent change. " The organic forces of historic tradition, national sentiment, cultural inheritances, and unconscious loyalties, have a more stubborn vitality than mere social mechanisms, and they may complicate the process and retard the tempo of social change. The too mechanistic interpretation of society in the typical philosophy of radicalism throws these forces on the side of fascism and leads to false estimates of the intricate processes of social change." [20] Of course he added that the avoidance of violence also depended on dissuading the privileged from a last ditch stand.

Today Niebuhr is still agitating for greater equality; inequality of power (economic) is still the greatest cause of injustice. But he is not so pessimistic as he used to be. He has found that democracy is a popular as well as a bourgeois achievement; the nation is after all the most cohesive social group in modern life. Instead of insisting that the economic oligarchy makes a sham of democracy by using it as a tool of class interest, he now admits that " democratic principles and traditions are an important check upon the economic oligarchy, even though the money power is usually able to bend democracy to its uses. The proof that this democratic restraint is still vital is given by the effort of the economic power to abrogate democracy when the latter imperils the rule of the financial oligarchs." [21]

Formerly the leveling of economic inequality meant for Niebuhr a rather simple (not complicated) change to public ownership of all property. But he has been watching the Russian experiment and he has remembered that the " right of possession was not regarded in early Christian thought as a natural extension of the power of the person but rather as a right of defense against the inordinate claims of others." [22] Property, he now thinks, is a good defense for individual freedom against societal order — as long as the individual possesses so little of it that he cannot use it for domination over others. Furthermore, it is necessary for the proper performance of function.[23] Not only is Niebuhr now satisfied with halfway measures, but he says that, in submitting economic life " to moral discipline and political restraint, we must be careful to preserve whatever self-regulating forces exist in the economic process. If we do not, the task of control becomes too stupendous and the organs of control achieve proportions which endanger our liberty." [24]

There are other economic powers than property (e.g., managerial power) ; the greatest danger is in throwing all together, and then combining them with political power. It may not be possible to socialize large-scale industrial property without giving economic managers sufficient power to subvert democratic political institutions, which normally constitute a check on political power. The property question must be continually solved by continuous debate and continuous adjustment. ". . . a wise community will walk warily and test the effect of each new adventure before further adventures." [25] In order to arrive at justice, debate must be facilitated by establishment of a common denominator between opposing factions. In America the dominant capitalist dogma must be discredited before such a common denominator can be found, and it must be done before the class struggle rises to such proportions as to threaten the whole democratic process. The problem for America is more difficult than it was for Britain and Scandinavia because America's extravagant bourgeois individualism has not been tempered by property ideas carried over from an agrarian and feudal world.[26]

The progress of Niebuhr's thought shows that he has come to understand that in the present " mechanical " civilization the radical need no longer worry about creating change. Change is rapid enough without an additional shove by radicals. What is needed is to learn to control, to direct the change that is seemingly taking place apart from the efforts of either radical or conservative. Niebuhr has changed from a revolutionist to an evolutionist, from an advocate of socialization to an advocate of caution.

D. R. Davies, describing Niebuhr's thought, has said that " original sin gave Niebuhr the clue to the correct interpretation " of revolutionary frustration, the interpretation being expressed in two ways: " First, that social change never realizes the aims and intentions of its advocates, that, in fact, it frequently results in the opposite. Second, that social change, when the new situation has crystallized and settled, frequently gives rise to other objects which sidetrack and overlay the original aims." [27] While Davies is probably correct in this assertion, something needs to be added to it. Under the aegis of the same *hybris,* Niebuhr earlier tentatively espoused the revolutionary method of violence. A commentator in those days might well have concluded that " original sin gave Niebuhr the clue to a correct understanding of the necessity for revolution."

Hybris is unquestionably a *mere* generality; and Niebuhr's concepts of power and the group appear in the same classification. They have certainly provided no reliable guide to Niebuhr in the question of change. What is more significant, the idea of change has undergone fundamental transformation without causing an alteration of the higher or more comprehensive generalities or even a questioning of them. Thus it is apparent that Niebuhr's concepts of power and the group are indeed vaguely formulated ideas, present in the philosopher's mind in a form not permissive of attachment to and test by the real world. They are not operative concepts.

After a period of skepticism Niebuhr has come to see that ability to change is a perennially valuable aspect of democracy. Here again, however, he fails to present a functional concept. His change is connected by indissoluble bonds to the ephemeral absolutes of his thought; as we saw in an earlier chapter, progress, which is some sort of change, is dependent on grace. Niebuhr finally selects as democratic a system of compromise wherein both sides by grace sacrifice some of their interests.[28] So long as the claims of ruling groups and the challenges of rising groups are arbitrated by God, there is no place for a functional concept of change. The idea is inoperative because celestial interference prevents logical connection and test between idea and action.

Niebuhr fails to discern the closeness of relationship between democracy and change. Democracy is an institutional apparatus whereby human beings produce and control change — whereby they avoid violence in change. In so far as Niebuhr obscures the fact that democracy is a tool of humanity, he has done a disservice and even damage to that tool. Democracy is a way *men* have learned to live together, a way adapted to conditions of fluidity in which custom has ceased to reign and change is the rule of the day.

Freedom and Authority

According to Niebuhr, no matter what the organization of a community it must be resisted in the interests of freedom. Either the oligarchs in their arrogance demand too great submission to their power, or the society in its pride exacts excessive conformance to group ideals and impulses. The sinfulness of man makes it inevitable that the use of coercion should result in injustice. Freedom is essential to social organization because man is " essentially " free. That is, he can transcend the processes and limitations of nature. Freedom is necessary to enable the individual to become his true self. It would seem that since man's true and essential nature is his spirit, freedom would be a transcendent necessity completely eclipsing order in the hierarchy of values. The important points to remember, however, are that man is a unity of spirit and nature, that he is saved as a whole, not by parts, and that his sin can hinder others in attaining realization of their essential selves. Liberty must be preserved, but not at the price of anarchy.

" The limitations upon freedom in a society are justified . . . by the fact that the vitalities may be destructive." [29] The individual may otherwise conflict with or suppress his neighbor. Moreover, human beings are social beings; much more so, indeed, than bourgeois thought has understood.[30] Order must be achieved, but not at the cost of liberty.

For the health of the social organism — to perpetuate its existence, that is — liberty (for its members) is as essential as it is for the health of individuals. The creative capacity of human vitality is indeterminate. Because restraint may suppress these vitalities unknowingly and thus arrest creation (by definition good), society must, for its own good, encourage freedom and hold specific restraints tentatively. Being products of insights contemporary to the time of their inception, legitimate restraints may become unadvisedly and prematurely destructive. " The community must constantly re-examine the presuppositions upon which it orders its life, because no age can fully anticipate or predict the legitimate and creative vitalities which may arise in subsequent ages." [31]

On the other hand, the destructive possibilities of these same vitalities require a coerced order for the welfare of the state.

The two values, freedom and order, are not easily reconciled. An ideal order " seeks unity within the conditions of freedom; and maintains freedom within the framework of order." [32] " Any definition of a proper balance between freedom and order must always be at least slightly colored by the exigencies of the moment . . ." [33]

The value of parliamentary government is that it is a method of " sublimating political struggles in such a way as to avoid violent collisions of interest." [34] Democracy's greatest achievement is a set of institutions which permits the nation to indulge in self-criticism. [35] It is difficult for a group to subject itself to criticism because it is not tempered by spiritual elements as much as is man. Self-criticism permits continual adjustment of the balance between freedom and cohesion.

Niebuhr supports democracy not because it is the best

possible government but because it is better than tyranny. Democracy refutes any purely negative conception of the relation of government and systems of justice to the religious ideal of love. " History reveals adjustments of interest to interest without the interposition of superior coercive force to be possible within wide limits." [36]

" It is the highest achievement of democratic societies that they embody the principle of resistance to government within the principle of government itself." [37] This is the closest man has yet come to appreciating the biblical paradox of grace as applied to justice. The legitimate majesty of government — power, cohesion — is found in the doctrine that government is an ordinance of God. The biblical assertion that " ' rulers ' and ' judges ' of the nations are particularly subject to divine judgment and wrath because they oppress the poor and defy the divine majesty " [38] affirms the balance of power and its democratic expression of resistance to government incorporated within the principle of government.[39]

From this review of Niebuhr's meditations on freedom and order, one fact rises predominantly to the fore. Freedom and order are clearly opposites. The value of democracy is that it is able to unite the two, by means of paradox, to the effect that they support and do not contradict each other. That is, freedom (the principle of resistance to government) is written into order (the principle of government) in such a way that the resisting of order and the ordering of freedom " organically " result in greater possibility of justice.

The paradox of freedom and order entertains close contact with Niebuhr's ideas of the group and power. The opposition between freedom and order can be found in germinal form in the individual's spiritual transcendence

over his collective, whereby he is in a position to criticize
the actions and the divine pretensions of the group. And
the order against which freedom resists can be seen to be a
reflection of coercive power. The selfish interest of the
group as organized into government is conceived by Niebuhr as a coercive order, an order necessarily felt to be
unjust.

Presumably any discussion of freedom and order would
have a rather direct bearing upon the peril of fascism.
It will not be amiss, then, to give a rapid survey of Niebuhr's attitudes toward fascism. In 1934 he described
fascism in Marxist spirit as the delirium which precedes
death: " Fascism represents the class struggle in its final
desperate stages." [40] By 1935 he noticed Communism's
responsibility for the rise of fascism and attributed the
latter at least partially to the " unqualified character of
the radical cynicism toward democratic institutions." [41]
He said that the Communists' recognition of their error at
the International of 1935 came too late.

Along with his defection from Marxist teachings, Niebuhr at this time broadened his view of fascism, attributing it mainly to a substitution of humanism for the-
ism. " A humanism which is sustained only by the obvious
marks of common humanity breaks down when the hysteria of conflict destroys or obscures these obvious human
ties." [42]

The obvious dangers of a natural religion which prompts
undue reverence for both the particular nation and the particular government and state, persuaded eighteenth century
democrats and modern proletarians to attempt a completely
rational political order. . . . In Germany a rationalistic democracy gave way to the demonic fury of a new political movement, explicitly affirming the divinity of nation and ruler. [43]

Niebuhr has since seen that many other factors have
contributed to Nazism: Lutheran defeatism's premature
abandonment of the task of achieving justice, Hegelian
worship of the state as the incarnation of man's universal
will, Nietzschean transvaluation of values, and the romantic movement — especially the emphasis in Herder and
Fichte upon race and vitality.[44]   He has finally admitted
the unique characteristics of Nazism.   But fascism in general he still fits within the comprehensive doctrine of sin:

> Modern tyrannies are not the end product of a long history
> of tyranny in which ancient evils have been consciously re-
> fined to their present consistency of evil.   They are rather
> characteristic corruptions of a mature civilization in which
> technical instruments have become more effective tools of
> tyrannical purpose.[45]

Generally speaking, Niebuhr has always seen fascism as
an over-emphasis on order and an under-emphasis on the
principle of resistance.   He has only vacillated while trying to explain the phenomenon.   If his ideas of freedom
and order had been concise and operative instruments of
thought, it might not have been possible for him to settle
on one explanation for fascism but, as he saw the inadequacy of an explanation derived from these abstract concepts, he would have been able to reformulate the concepts,
thus improving their usefulness and reliability in directing thought.   Since they were *mere* generalities, they were
divorced from the vicissitudes of theories built on them
and from responsibility for these theories.

In 1934 Niebuhr announced:

> If the German fascist venture is not resolved in a revolu-
> tion before the next war it is almost certain to be destroyed
> in the very war which it is helping to generate: for the inter-
> nal unity which it has achieved is too artificial to outlast a

war. A war will merely put weapons into the hands of the suppressed rebellious multitudes who will welcome the opportunity of turning international war into a civil conflict.[46]

If his concept of coercive power and his concept of order, which is closely allied to power, had been formulated as truly operative ideas, they would have undergone alteration as this prediction became falsified by fact. As it was, power and order were conceived in sufficiently vague terms to avoid such a contingency. It was then simply a matter of rejuggling, and of altering the conclusion.

Niebuhr once thought that totalitarianism was external coercion alone; he was obsessed with the idea of will to power on the part of the leaders. What are the chances that his evaluation of democracy as a paradox of freedom and order will weather the ravages of time? From what has been said above, it is possible already to conclude that this Niebuhrian paradox will not be a useful directive of thought. It is, moreover, an ossified concept kept effectively impervious to improvement by the non-logical character which it shares with all paradox and which separates it from the world of practical action.

Niebuhr has avoided the Hegelian, continental, and Catholic [47] meaning of the word " freedom." This usage has been to equate freedom with rationality as an opposite and antidote to vice, passion, or license, a practice which leads to and has become a tool of totalitarianism in so far as rationality is by these philosophies subordinated to law.[48] In contrast, Niebuhr has accepted the British-American usage which identifies freedom with individuality and opposes it to coercion.[49] He does not, however, accept it in the simple form that permitted the economic freedom of individuals to become a source of oppression and coercion in itself. He expects to avoid the evil of economic tyrannies and at the same time the evil of collective tyranny by means of his characteristic device — a paradox.

It is deeply significant that Niebuhr labels the other side of the paradox " order " instead of " authority." Since he is accustomed to think of power as something by its very nature coercive, but more or less hidden, he does not see the possibility or the necessity of setting up a genuine authority. He is blind to the real problem, which is to instate some sort of authority appropriate to our fluid culture in place of the static authority of customs which have become, since the scientific revolution, increasingly inoperative.[50]

Opposition of freedom to authority, or freedom to order, is one of the fallacious attitudes men have fallen into while floundering around trying to adjust to and understand the relatively new situation of social fluidity. It may be that for Niebuhr the acceptance of any authority would entail pretensions to divinity (*hybris*). On the other hand, Niebuhr's alternative may condemn men to an eternity of juggling paradoxes in the dark. If organized inquiry, the method of operative perfectible knowledge, is accepted as authoritative, there is a possibility of organically uniting freedom and authority, freedom and order, in a way attuned to the fluctuating times.

Any sort of transactive approach to the problems of men would deny the actuality of conflict between the individual and society. Individuals are the product of transaction; they are created *with*in the crucible of social arrangements. They may clash with particular social arrangements, but the individual as such and society as such are abstractions between which no clash is possible. Niebuhr, of course, does not understand this because, as a result of his dogmatic definition of human nature, his individual " transcends " the group or society and thus gains a vantage point from which to oppose society.

Similarly, freedom and order are general concepts which cannot actually conflict, although particular acts of freedom may clash with particular efforts at order. So long as these concepts are not handled in terms of the actual referents to which they can be attached, they are useless, or worse than useless — delusive. The simple fact that their proper handling as abstractions is abused and that they are imagined to be things that can oppose one another is an indication of their non-functional character. It is just as well, then, to form them into paradox to emphasize their practical and rational uselessness.

Niebuhr's paradox suffers the probability of being in fact ineffective, of being a mere camouflage to oscillations between coercive authority and uncontrolled freedom. It further conceals the gradual development, in fact, within democracy, and as an essential part of democracy, of an authoritative method, founded on what C. H. Waddington labels the *ethos* of science, " an ethos based on the recognition that one belongs to a community, but a community which requires that one should do one's damnedest to pick holes in its beliefs." [51]

Tolerance

Niebuhr's idea of tolerance develops as follows. Ultimately religious ideas and traditions must be the resource for the highest forms of social realization. It is only through the insights of the individual transcending his society that communal achievement is won. Integrating various subordinate ethnic, religious, and economic groups into community harmony without thereby destroying cultural diversity is the greatest problem of order and freedom. There must be some equilibrium between group forces, and there must be constant shifts of power to conform to development of the social organism. But, in order to approximate most nearly the ideal of brotherhood, a religious tolerance must be added to the social scene.

The Christian interpretation of grace applies to truth as it does to justice; the having and not having of truth is a paradox. " The fulfillments of meaning in history will be the more untainted in fact, if purity is not prematurely claimed for them." [52] The point is " that it is neither possible for man to know the truth fully nor to avoid the error of pretending that he does." [53] All man's thought is invariably beset with " ideological " taint.

The test of how well this paradox of truth is understood and how well it is put into application in the social milieu is to be found in tolerance. " The test is twofold and includes both the ability to hold vital convictions which lead to action; and also the capacity to preserve the spirit of forgiveness towards those who offend us by holding to convictions which seem untrue to us." [54] Modern culture fails on the first part of the test; it is more frequently unable to remain true to and act on its best convictions. It takes the faith of a high religious spirit to be confident in the possibility of attaining the truth with a broken confidence in the finality of our truth. " We will have it the more purely in fact if we know that we have it only in principle." [55] A deep religious humility — not religious indifference — is the foundation for the erection of true tolerance. " For civilization depends upon the vigorous pursuit of the highest values by people who are intelligent enough to know that their values are qualified by their interests and corrupted by their prejudices." [56]

A profound religion requires the only foundation that

will support democracy — a Christian meaningful existence with its test of tolerance. Upon all other dogmas a
Tower of Babel is built.

Niebuhr's " tolerance " emerges in a necessary manner
from his definition of man. It springs from the fact of
man's sin, from the fact that man is incapable of the truth
or incapable of retaining the truth unperverted, from the
insight that the profoundest truth may become the source
of grievous error. It is a method of circumventing sin
and mitigating the effects of sin. It is an attitude which,
if widely held, is expected to prevent the otherwise inevitable development of friction between *hybris*-ridden
men. It is also a resource of transcendent men as individuals, helping them to soften the self-interest of groups.

The question is whether tolerance as a concept is rendered inoperative by reason of its dependence upon sin for
its very existence. The connection with sin in itself would
seem to indicate that it is. A closer inspection indicates
that it is so tightly bound to *hybris* as to partake of its
rigid, non-perfectible character. It is so formulated that
it cannot be altered without altering the outstanding features of human nature. The very fact of its formulation
into a paradox removes it from the jeopardy of practical
test. It can be used as a Standard in appeal to which the
philosopher may object that a man or a culture is failing
on either one or the other half of the " test "; but it is not
truly functional. It is not perfectible in context.

Besides failing as an operative, directing tool for democracy, Niebuhr's tolerance is insufficient to democracy.
Within Niebuhr's definition it is possible to push one half
of the paradox — vigorous pursuit of highest values — to
the extreme of violent revolution while at the same time
stoutly forgiving the offending opposition. Niebuhr him-

self at one time drifted in this direction.[57]   He did not sufficiently realize that forms of democracies, imperfect as they are and secular as they are, encourage freedom of discussion, criticism, and association — the active aspect of the phenomenon of tolerance, without which it would degenerate into prayer.   Tolerance has two aspects; it is a tolerant disposition *and* an act of tolerating.   When it is understood as the first alone, its operation as an important part of democracy is partially obscured.

Tolerance based on the conviction that we imperfectly know the truth is certainly preferable to the intolerance that attends dedication to a fixed goal, the known truth. But it is more difficult to achieve than a democratic tolerance which is part and parcel of a co-operative attempt to find more and more reliable truth*s*.   This latter tolerance prevents judgment of individuals or groups on the authority of an imagined though ungrasped truth.   It permits judgment by the empirically testable direction in which individuals and groups are moving rather than by the distance from the truth; it " makes one severe in judging himself and humane in judging others." [58]   A genuinely tolerant disposition is more than a spirit of forgiveness.   It is a belief in a pluralistic democracy, a belief asserting the importance of individual differences, abetting their existence, and denying the doctrine that the mass of men are constructed from a master pattern.

Faith in Human Nature

Unquestionably Niebuhr does not entertain a faith in human nature.   But on the other hand his opinion of man is not all bad.   During the course of his public career he has made a noticeable shift in emphasis.   Human nature did not undergo a change, but Niebuhr's attention shifted

from pessimistic preoccupation with sin to a more dispassionate, more disinterested consideration, on equal
terms, of sinful corruptions and creative possibilities. His
present stand might be called a paradox of pessimism and
optimism, whereby he tries to avoid the errors he sees in
both:

> A consistent pessimism in regard to man's rational capacity
> for justice invariably leads to absolutistic political theories;
> for they prompt the conviction that only preponderant power
> can coerce the various vitalities of a community into a working
> harmony. But a too consistent optimism in regard to man's
> ability and inclination to grant justice to his fellows obscures
> the perils of chaos which perennially confront every society,
> including a free society.[59]

In place of a faith in man, Niebuhr naturally champions
a faith in God. He thinks that it is a faith in God, not in
man, that sets the tenor for a successful culture.[60] On the
basis of this belief, he develops an interpretation contending that without an adequate foundation in religion all
culture must alternate between moods of complacency and
despair.

The primary root of complacency in modern culture, he
asserts, is found in the belief that through historical development — " progress " — man will achieve perfection
and happiness. Marxism challenges modern liberal culture by discrediting its confidence in reason and its bourgeois confidence in the virtue and stability of democracy.
Marxism saw that reason could be an instrument of interest, but unfortunately it transformed this insight into a
greater complacent confidence in proletarian purity, attributing all ideological taint to other groups. It saw sin,
oppression, and conflict within democratic society, but
unfortunately it substituted new and greater illusions of

progress toward a paradise on earth. It has thus been more fruitful of a demonic idolatry (*hybris*) than the liberal culture; its complacency is even greater; and its challenge has largely wasted away.[61]

The chief bearer of disillusionment about the virtue or wisdom of man and the stability of his institutions in modern culture, according to Niebuhr, has been the romantic movement. With the added impetus of the Communist challenge, the movement from complacency to despair in Europe culminated in the rise of Nazism, which was, " in one of its aspects, the growth of a demonic religion out of the soil of despair. Politically men were willing to entertain the perils of tyranny in order to avoid the dangers of anarchy; and spiritually they were ready to worship race, nation or power as god in order to avoid the abyss of meaninglessness." [62] In France existentialism is a " desperate affirmation of meaning within the framework of despair." [63]

The complacency of liberal culture is still firmest in America because " the opulence of American life and the dominant position of American power in the world create the illusion of a social stability which the total world situation belies." [64] Niebuhr sees a ray of hope for America and all democracy, shining on the virtue of tolerance. Tolerance may mitigate the complacency-despair problem of democracy by its " provisional recognition of the contingent and conditioned character of all forms of historic virtue." [65] But he places final reliance on faith in God:

The hope of Christian faith that the divine power which bears history can complete what even the highest human striving must leave incomplete, and can purify the corruptions which appear in even the purest human aspirations, is an indispensable prerequisite for diligent fulfillment of our historic tasks.[66]

It need hardly be emphasized that this whole business of faith in God and disreliance on man, together with its derivative — the complacency-despair formula — falls into the category of *mere* generality. Where a supernatural realm is invoked there is no place for the practical testing of a concept or for the perfecting of a concept in response to its failure to direct practical control procedures.

The unfortunate thing about the complacency-despair formula is that it requires a prophet-mathematician with a celestial slide rule to insert the unknowns and provide the fine calculations determining which culture fits where in the equation. And when the prophet is done with his necromatic computations he can offer no constructive suggestions as to what men might, themselves, do to alleviate conditions, for despair and complacency are functions of man's inevitable sin.[67] Seeming to explain the ills of the present world by means of a set of terms which in truth only replace a problematic situation with a priori generalities no more genuinely understood than the situation, Niebuhr does the disservice to mankind of letting men think the ills of the world have been simply explained. He conceals possibilities of gradually approaching an understanding of difficulties through the use of tentative, testable, refinable ideas — such as the suggestion above that the sick world may be explained in terms of the ineffectuality of power.[68]

This consideration of Niebuhr's complacency-despair continuum illustrates the irrelevancies arrived at when men rely on transcendence rather than on themselves and their fellows. Democracy has in the past always been allied with a belief in the potentialities of man. It can well be wondered if democracy will not be undermined by a loss of this faith. In so far as democracy rests upon the whole of its citizenry it depends on the reliability and the responsibility of the mass of men and it presupposes the capacity of human nature. In so far as democracy stands opposed to intolerance, in so far as it is built on tolerance, it stands as a memorial to belief in human beings and against the assumption that there are groups of people inherently lacking the good qualities of human nature. To say, in terms of *hybris,* that this view of the capacity of men is idealistic, amounts to a camouflaged distrust of the common man akin to the pessimism of Ortega y Gasset, Mosca, and the neo-Machiavellians.

Despite Niebuhr's insistence on a paradoxical position made up of pessimism with an overcast of hope, it is difficult to see that his position is tenable. The inevitability of *hybris* tends to override all hope. At least the net effect of Niebuhr's doctrines is pessimism for those who are temperamentally unable to embrace impartially both sides of a paradox, or who are unable to understand, in the deepest mystic sense, a paradox.

A faith in human nature need not be subject to the faults of either optimism or pessimism. Niebuhr rightly condemns an optimism that looks to automatic progress or that sees this world as the best of all possible worlds. He also justly condemns pessimism. A melioristic faith in human nature simply believes that no matter how bad things are, or how good they are, they *can* be improved and there is nothing in the nature of man that automatically prevents man's improvement of his lot. In rejecting meliorism because of his assumption of inevitable sin in man, Niebuhr unconsciously throws the weight of his opinion on the side of pessimism by discouraging efforts to discover remediable causes for our evils. ". . . what is antecedently possible is only of human importance when it comes also to be what men believe is possible and are willing to work to bring about." [69] Men do not eagerly exert themselves on behalf of the impossible possible. At least in present society men tend to turn pessimist when they find or become convinced that they personally cannot do something, cannot act to help themselves, but must rely on the supernatural.

Majority Rule

Niebuhr has come to the decision that oligarchical rule is actually inevitable. The ideal of governmental coercive power " established by the whole society and . . . held responsible to it . . . is never completely attained." [70] This conclusion, however, is not as grim as it appears at first glance. An oligarchy may be creative under two headings: (1) when it is creatively interested in the welfare of the community, and (2) when the selfish interest of the ruling group " by grace " coincides with the welfare of the community. An outstanding example of the latter was the temporary coincidence of American capitalism and the development of the country.

Niebuhr does not regard oligarchic rule as the way things should be, but the way things are. Here is a worn strain of the old theme " This Has Been; Therefore It Always Will Be." His conclusion is a distorted image from observations through twisted prisms of *hybris*. When man is laden with sin, and power is perforce coercion, and the potentialities of the mass of men are distorted by a lack of faith in them, inevitable oligarchy seems to follow as night the day. The effective participation and the potentialities of more comprehensive effective participation on the part of the entire electorate pale in the brilliant obviousness of contemporary corruption.

Within democracy Niebuhr envisions the Christian Community as a communion of saints, a priesthood of believers, a small coterie of seeing (and believing) prophets who can function as a ferment toward improvement, as a " saving remnant." Niebuhr has resurrected the prophets of the Old Testament and garbed them in not-so-modern dress to act as a leaven within democracy.[71] His distrust of the common man has culminated in reliance upon saints. His doctrine of sin and depravity has led him to hold a position not dissimilar to that held by the neo-Machiavellians, impressed as they are with the universality of ignorance and the impossibility of imparting wisdom to all.[72]

The great difference, however, between Niebuhr and advocates of government by specialists is that Niebuhr's troop of prophets must act extra-governmentally. Even specialists, according to him, are not free of the selfish interests of the middle class to which they basically belong. The " saving remnant " must disengage itself from the immorality of groups and work at the transcendence which is available to men as individuals.

The implications to democracy of Niebuhr's prophet system are not far to be sought. Democracy may not, as Niebuhr says, have ever worked according to the wishes, or the interest, of the majority; conceivably it may never do so in the future. But to foreclose the possibility before history has run out is a rash and unjustifiable step indeed. To further cull out a self-select group of sensitized individuals and station them as meteorologists to intercept a Word here and there dropped from the heavens, is posi-

tively anti-democratic — especially as there is no democratic way (indeed no way at all) to distinguish between
their true and their false pronouncements. The plodding
progress of democracy in the realm of political affairs has
been made by putting truths found by individuals to the
test of corporate intelligence, not by reproaching mankind with the Truth dropped from on high. Democracy
cannot function if there is a brand of superior knowledge
not open to all but only to the self-chosen.

It is true that experts (not prophets in Niebuhr's sense)
can uncover new facts, and sensitive individuals (again not
Niebuhr's prophets) can proclaim new insights, but only
as these facts and insights become imbedded in collective
intelligence and raise the level of society is progress made.
This is the main problem and Niebuhr with his eagerness
for gratuitous bits of unworldly wisdom ignores it *in toto*.
A prophet may be spectacular, but an organic growth is
effective. Further democratic achievement might be expected by submitting other affairs than the political to
corporate intelligence rather than by withdrawing inquiry
from the democratic method.

Summary

From this analysis of five aspects important to democracy
and important to Niebuhr's understanding of democracy,
a fairly comprehensive picture of Niebuhrian democracy can be drawn together. It is a " democracy " of change
as compromise, of freedom and order (not authority) as
opposites paradoxically united, of " tolerance " based on
man's incapacity for retaining uncorrupted truth, of lack
of faith in man and reliance on a faltering paradox of pessimism and optimism, of oligarchy tempered by a " saving
remnant."

As tools of thought, these concepts of "democracy" have been shown to be inoperative, non-directive generalities, ineffective for the purpose of directing inquiry and aiding in developing more reliable abstract ideas. In this respect they appear of little use to democratic thinking. Furthermore, it has been observed that they contain elements of danger to democracy because of their obstructive effect on genuinely operative possibilities in abstract thought and because of their faulty and inadequate evaluation of the important aspects of democracy to which they refer.

AN AGE BETWEEN THE AGES

Niebuhr is today more involved with international relations than with any other concern of politics. His interest in the subject is obviously greatly encouraged by the excellent opportunities it presents to the moralist in him. International order is a topic "right down his line." It seems just exactly to suit the temper of his thinking. It provides a natural co-ordination in the practical world of most phases of his philosophy, bringing them together in one illustration. It also serves as the best illustration of Niebuhr's thought at its most specific in politics.

Niebuhr's ideas on international affairs have undergone the same change as have many of his other ideas, from deep pessimism to shallow pessimism with an overcast of hope. When he viewed the nation as an assembly of classes without any real over-all community,[73] he very naturally saw little possibility of an international community. Human imagination and human sympathy did not extend any further than the more intimate communities. It was more difficult for communities to be ethical than for individuals, and besides they did not have the direct contact necessary (as it is necessary for individuals) to make a community between them. " There is something to be said for Treitschke's logic, which made the nation the ultimate community of significant loyalty, on the ground that smaller units were too small to deserve, and larger units too vague and ephemeral to be able to exact, man's supreme loyalty." [74] ". . . if powerful classes in national societies corrupt the impartiality of national courts, it may be taken for granted that a community of nations, in which very powerful and very weak nations are bound together, has even less hope of achieving impartiality." [75]

A few years later, when he had become fully aware of the nation as a community, he maintained: " There will never be a community of mankind in the sense that there is a national community. Such a community is too vague, too all-inclusive, and too bereft of the symbols by which common men comprehend the social organization of which they are a part, to arouse the intense loyalties which men are accustomed to pay their national communities." [76]

We are now living in an age between the ages. " The age of absolute national sovereignty is over; but the age of international order under political instruments, powerful enough to regulate the relations of nations and to compose their competing desires, is not yet born." [77] Modern technical skills have created a potential society, but, as usual, political skills must be fashioned to catch up with the technical. Niebuhr foresees a long period in which corrupt attempts at universalism will be made through imperialistic domination, either for the sake of power or for security.[78] The technical situation may be used by particular nations in the interest of particularity.

Niebuhr points out that government cannot create community. It is rather the authority of a community already

achieved. The laws of a government are obeyed because
they correspond on the whole to the community's conception of justice. Police force is an arm of the body of
community and while it may have a limited efficacy in perfecting organization and preserving the integrity of a community, it cannot of itself integrate the community.

". . . the wisest statescraft cannot create social tissue.
It can cut, sew and redesign social fabric to a limited degree. But the social fabric upon which it works must be
' given.' " [79] In the international field " social tissue " is
very thin, Niebuhr maintains. Nations are, in fact, interdependent economically — but there is wide disparity of
economic strength. The fear of mutual annihilation may
be a strong incentive toward creating world organization — but it is not so strong as the fear of a particular
mutual foe. There is a growing feeling of moral obligation to our fellow men — but as yet it is still inchoate.

Nations have achieved community status to a large extent because of their particularity. Such factors as geo-
graphic limitation, ethnic and cultural uniqueness and
unity, common history of struggle and comradeship, common language, have contributed to national cohesion but
are lacking for the world community.[80] " No conceivable
historical growth can . . . make a possible world government of the future as stable and secure as the order of a national community; just as no national community is as
immune to disorder as the family or the tribe." [81]

Since Niebuhr regards all groups or communities as
essentially the same, he considers it " axiomatic that the
less a community is held together by cohesive forces in the
texture of its life the more must it be held together by
power." [82] And this axiom leads him inevitably to " the
dismal conclusion that the international community lack-

ing these inner cohesive forces, must find its first unity through coercive force to a larger degree than is compatible with the necessities of justice." [83] After all, no nation has yet voluntarily made a serious abridgment of its own sovereignty. Niebuhr's greatest insight applies to the world situation: every new freedom represents a peril as well as a promise.

Niebuhr insists that whatever progress is to be made toward world government must be through coalescence of the power of the great nations as the core of the community. In this respect he approves the organization of the United Nations as a realistic approach to the problem. He scorns plans for the elimination of power politics in favor of law. To overcome the anarchy of nations, the balance of power must be brought under the manipulations of the organizing power of government.

Of the three great powers, Russia will have the greatest difficulty in placing moral checks on its will to power, " not because it is communistic or materialistic; but rather because it is informed by a simple religion and culture which makes self-criticism difficult and self-righteousness inevitable." [84] America is not used to its power and consequently alternates between moods of irresponsibility, fearing the corruptions of power, and moods of cynicism, displaying a pride in power and a disregard of responsibilities.[85] A genuine community can be created only with the help of a great degree of humility, tolerance, mutual forbearance and forgiveness,[86] and with knowledge of the limits of the will in creating government and of government in creating community.

At the present time neither Russia nor America is willing to submit to a world authority without reservations so long as there is still a possibility that such authority could annul a nation's system of law and justice. The differences in conceptions of justice are not a product of cultural and religious differences between East and West but of the split in the West between fanatical equalitarian and libertarian creeds.[87] Niebuhr supports democratic justice and institutions, but he prefers a middle ground somewhere near the position of Great Britain.[88] The American oligarchy, he thinks, is jeopardizing our position in Europe by insisting on excessive libertarianism and " free enterprise," [89] when our libertarian conceptions have become irrelevant to the European situation.[90]

Niebuhr entertains the possibility that closer integration of non-Communist nations may, by preponderance of power, save the world from war.[91] The set-up of the United Nations Security Council expresses the ambiguous character of the actual historical situation. We are trying to preserve some unity and to resolve some of the tensions between the halves of the divided world. Yet we are trying to preserve the integrity of our way of life as against the Russian.[92]

The whole question of world community is summed up by Niebuhr in paradox:

. . . World community . . . is a necessity and possibility because history is a process which extends the freedom of man over natural process to the point where universality is reached. It is an impossibility because man is, despite his increasing freedom, a finite creature, wedded to time and place and incapable of building any structure of culture or civilization which does not have its foundations in a particular dated locus.[93]

And atop the paradox he sets a final resource, a Christian hope that the transcendent individual can recognize universal law which idolatrous national communities with their blighted insight into moral obligation have not acknowledged.

Niebuhr's attitude toward world government is of a piece with the rest of his philosophy. His God is a jealous God resenting and preventing accomplishments of men. A Tower of Babel if built by men will be destroyed and prove "impossible." Yet it may be "possible" (through grace) if man submits with abject contrition. Niebuhr seems to be saying that one world is impossible because it would automatically be too great a sin (pride) to be tolerated by God. Thus *hybris* has given him the clue to an over-all interpretation of world-wide order.

On the international level Niebuhr may be making an error comparable to the error he made before World War II in assessing the national cohesion of fascism. His mistaken evaluation of fascism was due to the fact that he was over-impressed with the vitalities of classes and intra-national groups. Today he is perhaps in the same way dazzled by the self-interest of states. A world state is no further beyond a man's imagination and experience than are our colossal nation states — they are both abstract and incomprehensible in terms of direct experiences. As a matter of fact the Marshall Plan alone displays a tremendous advance of the geographical boundaries of ethical concern. Many people would agree with B. E. Meland, that, in America at least, the "will to be sound at heart and of a generous mind in our dealing with neighbors is clearly becoming a national trait." [94]

This is not to say that world government is in the immediate offing. Niebuhr has marshaled an imposing list of difficulties to be overcome. But when he knits a strait jacket for humanity and drags humanity from the working world of meliorism to cast it into a cell of paradox-pessimism, he himself tends to postpone the day of deliverance. The paralyzing implication that because " every community of history has paid a high price in injustice for its wider cohesion " [95] such will always be the course of events, and the supreme freedom will be accompanied by supreme evil, is nothing but a cavernous rehearsal of the tune of the arch-conservative. Just because a pattern or a repetition is found in the past does not mean that men cannot defeat it.

One should note, as Niebuhr does not, that just as the national " organism " does not require the close organic cohesion of the tribe and family, so a world " organism " may not demand the intense loyalties and the unifying factors of particularity required for national cohesion. The national community in Western democracies may not be " as immune to disorder as the family " (a highly questionable assertion of Niebuhr's), but it is less disrupted and very infrequently destroyed by disorder, simply because the cohesion it relies upon is of a different kind. Niebuhr too, in a lucid moment, says that " the transition from a particular to a universal community . . . is a step different not merely in degree. . . . It is different in kind." [96] Perhaps there will be greater difference in kind than Niebuhr anticipates. If so the step may not be so difficult to accomplish.

Niebuhr, with all his talk about cohesion and the organic group, is essentially in tune with the neo-Thomist campaign to return the world to the corporate social structure of the Middle Ages. He is interpreting present problems too much in terms of his theological return to orthodoxy and its derivative — his definition of human nature. In assessing current possibilities it is essential to recognize the profound importance and pervasive influence of the sixteenth century scientific revolution. Malleable human nature has incorporated, and is continuing to incorporate, adjustments to the development of science and technics and, correspondingly, group patterns are reflecting and can be expected in the future to reflect even more the changes in the total transactional situation brought about by science and technics. Thus there can be expected to be different kinds of cohesion in different historical and cultural contexts.

When even the conservative family group is suffering disorganization under the impact and is beginning to reform its bonds of cohesion, it becomes ridiculous to expect cohesion for new dimensional organization to conform to a pattern of the past. It is futile to deplore the fact that technics has " mechanized " society just because medieval organic unity has suffered from technological obsolescence. We should instead direct our efforts to creating a new organic cohesion based on a wide-awake recognition of technics (and science, the father of technics) and its transactional involvement with human nature. We should look for a new type of organization in the international realm which will take form through new kinds of cohesive bonds. We may not require an international organization of a type corresponding at all to the current vision of world government. Real world community in Niebuhr's sense of the terms may be unnecessary.

Again we find Niebuhr thinking exclusively in terms of forces. " Every wide community represents, not some simple triumph of universal over particular interest but an artful equilibration, suppression, extension, and deflection of particular interest for the sake of the wider community." [97] It is power that dictates and it is interest that speaks through power. As long as national groups

are forces, they of course can only be balanced, deflected,
and so forth.   Niebuhr takes particular interests as
"givens."   They are the "social fabric" upon which
statecraft works.[98] He falsely assumes that men will never
be able to create a new fabric. He again fails to see that
the essential problem is not how to balance interests but
how to create new, better, and more comprehensive interests on the international level. Even if Niebuhr is
correct in his opinion that, all communities being essentially the same, the less they are held together by cohesive
forces the more they must be held together by power, the
problem is not only to try to create cohesion but to try to
develop a new, functional kind of power with an appropriate authority of method. Even among nations there is a
possibility that mediation can operate more creatively and
effectively than by sacrifice of interests.

   In the meantime, while world government is an impossible possibility, Niebuhr has some very sensible suggestions
to make for international organization and for American
policy.   He advocates taking advantage of the inchoate
community that exists in the non-Communist world and
permitting the *ad hoc* military and economic arrangements
to grow into quasi-constitutional forms.   He cautions
against proposals for constitutional integration of Western
Europe as a separate unit, because Western Europe is not
a natural economic unit and because any union without
the United States is without significance.   And he realisti-
cally condemns attempts at political co-ordination of Western Germany into Western Europe for fear it may delay
economic co-ordination.[99]

   For the United States he sees two main tasks: (1) to
make the relations of a wealthy nation to an impoverished
world morally tolerable — this in face of Communist ex-

ploitation of world-wide resentment and social upheaval; and (2) to learn to live in a world of continuous insecurity without reacting with hysteria (false estimate of the enemy's position), complacency (false estimate of our own position), or idealistic evasion (utopian, unrealistic schemes for world government). To deal with the first he suggests we avoid giving the impression that our form of democracy is the only valid prototype. " If we declare dogmatically that only our form of economic freedom is compatible with a free society, we persuade our allies, as also the African and Asiatic nations which are as yet neither our allies nor our foes, to regard our form of democracy as a luxury which only a very fortunate nation can afford." [100] Then he suggests vaguely the development of something similar to the *jus gentium* of the Romans to cover international differences. And finally he insists that it is almost impossible to outline the political and economic program which would eliminate the social conditions and resentments exploited by the Communists.[101]

To cope with the second he suggests humility. " Our anxieties are aggravated by the fear that nations, peoples and institutions may not be adequate for this time of testing, that they have not been sufficiently shaken in their pride and self-esteem to do what is necessary for their salvation." [102]

On the great question of the day Niebuhr's realism shines through with reassurance. Recent developments in Korea prove, he feels, " that we have no great reason to fear a final atomic general war with Russia, for the Russians would be at a great disadvantage in such a conflict with us." [103] He suggests as policy that we must establish ourselves " on the narrow edge of morality, consisting in the necessity of manufacturing hydrogen bombs on the one hand, and the awful moral peril of using them on the other." [104]   The core of the conflict is a moral contest between the free world and Communism.   And Niebuhr's final recipe is again humility.   Presumably having interpreted its trials and troubles as judgments on its pride, the nation can be reborn through grace and avoid destruction.

Niebuhr has made a forceful analysis of the power conflict on the international level.   And his policy prescriptions are those of a realist trying to take all pertinent factors into account.   For our day his way of analysis is useful.   But for leading to better ways of solving problems in the future it is inadequate.   Power on the international scene is non-functional today; we do well if we can manage to avoid overt conflict by means of a balance.   But at the same time we should be endeavoring to find ways of making power become functional in the future.

Niebuhr's strictures against the hysteria of American conservatism and the unrealistic idealism of American liberals (who think, for example, that the American type of democracy can be fostered in Asia when actually there is no democratic base upon which to build it) are all very well.   And his championing of a realistic, *ad hoc,* hand-to-mouth method in place of the discredited ideologies is certainly welcome.   But let us not reject ideals per se. They need not necessarily be rationalizations, false claims, or expressions of *hybris*.   They can be held tentatively and improved in context as they are shown to be inadequate — the way of democracy.   Furthermore, they seem to be essential tools without which a people cannot work together in policy as a nation.   Our task is not to learn to do without them, but to learn to make them truly directional and perfectible in light of action taken under their direction.

Again Niebuhr is undoubtedly correct that the present international struggle is a moral contest. But we must question his suggested panacea. Indeed, after all his talk about relativity in morals and scientific treatment of morals we must be surprised, to say the least, at the return to humility. Isn't this a part of the inapplicable ethic of Jesus? Isn't it a part of the perfect law? Perhaps it isn't; it is hard to tell just what is what when you get up among the higher mists. At any rate we can be sure that America will not allay the resentments of the impoverished world or achieve a victory in the moral struggle with Communism simply by the device of having its citizens turn humble. Niebuhr might as well tell everyone to be good. Moral exhortation is a last resort of the tired mind and a resort that has long since ceased to be effective on any level higher than personal relationship.

SUMMARY

All together the democratic and international political aspects of Niebuhr's thought display clearly one thing. He is not a political *theorist*. For him " democracy is a method of finding proximate solutions for *insoluble* problems." [105] A theorist, in the way the term is here used, is a thinker who, when he finds that his problems are " insoluble," questions the problems and tries to reformulate them so that they can be solved. From the insolubility of problems he tries to find clues to the development of more operative ideas. Niebuhr not only isolates his fundamental philosophy in *mere* generality but derives the greater part of his political thought in such a manner that it is reliant upon his basic concepts and immune to the practical world of test.

All the elements in his democracy, as well as his general conclusions concerning world government, are the combined product of deduction from the nature of man and *hybris* via the group and power, and of induction from observations distorted by these powerful dogmas and read under the light of cause as sequence-plus-supernatural-interference. Thus Niebuhr loiters on the " upper " level of generalization even in politics, instead of coming down to a working, grass roots level of operative generalization.

Niebuhr remains essentially a moralist, a preacher in the old-time sense of the word. His radicalism is ephemeral because it consists in a vision of the inadequacies of the creeds of others (a vision distorted, to be sure, by overmuch faith in *hybris*) but in no clear, comprehensive, progressive program — besides " what seems to us right " — for directing deliberate action. It merely dramatizes the perils in the thoughts of others without indicating a road for surer travel. We cannot help wondering if such paralysis is not the inevitable effect of a faith in sin.

CHAPTER SIX

The Course of a Faith in Sin

> . . . We have a curious way of regarding our fellows as especially honest and straightforward when they behave in the way in which our theories expect them to behave. . . . A theory which asserts that all men are necessarily selfish will give moral credit to the men who are openly selfish rather than to those who seem to be unselfish.
>
> A. D. LINDSAY

In an address in 1952 at the University of Wisconsin, entitled "The Two Dimensions of the World Crisis," Niebuhr added a new turn to his evaluation of the world situation.

Polishing up an old distinction between civilization and culture, he gave an excellent statement of what seems to be a common-sense distinction in usage. In his analysis, civilization was defined to include all the relations among men that have been more or less formalized into institutions — economic, political, social, legal, religious. Culture was said to comprise all expressions by individuals of their ultimate beliefs and aspirations, including the realms of art, philosophy, religion. This distinction, Niebuhr cautioned, could be only generally delineated because the two factors are interdependent and causally interrelated. Yet he made the distinction the basis for a new interpretation of historical crisis.

It seems that in the past minor crises have occurred when contradictions or oppositions have arisen on one of these levels, major crises when they have occurred on both. Thus the Roman Empire collapsed under the major crisis of administrative and spiritual disorder, and medieval Christianity fell victim to the major disruptions of capitalism on the one level and of the Renaissance and Reformation on the other.

Today is major-crisis time again. On the level of civilization, crisis is caused by the impact of technics on the community, resulting in the loosening of the communal bonds of cohesion and in turn accentuating the differentials in the power structure. On the level of culture, crisis is caused by deepening doubt of the basic belief grounding our culture — the belief that all the difficulties that man faces, the inadequacies that he feels, can be removed and resolved by him through the empirical use of reason.

To cope with the crisis in *civilization* Niebuhr recommended accepting the terms set by modern technics and recreating the human community in accordance with their demands. While modern technological advances had *actually* loosened communal bonds, they had *potentially* provided a base for greater and stronger communities. However, he emphasized, technological refinements would not automatically create broader communities. On the contrary, their first effects had been to accentuate the power differentials among men, magnifying the problem of securing justice in the world, the problem of managing society so as to obtain maximum relative justice while preventing management from becoming over-powerful and thus tyrannical. To handle this problem of securing justice Niebuhr thought it essential to avoid commitment to the ideology of either *laissez-faire* or dialectical materialism and to follow, instead, an *ad hoc* procedure using parts of either or both of them as common sense and the necessities of the moment seemed to dictate. This he alleged to have been what the healthy countries of Europe (Britain, Norway, Sweden, Denmark, the Netherlands) had done.

To cope with the crisis in *culture* Niebuhr recommended that man recognize his limitations and attain humility. By this means man might avoid the futile and catastrophic errors (for example, preventive war) that he would inevitably commit if he worked logically from the assumption that man could completely shape his own destiny. This dominant belief had been subject to growing doubts during the last three decades. The supreme danger lay in our reaching, in the face of unmanageable events, a point of despair from which we should reaffirm this false faith with brute force.

In this one lecture Niebuhr brought together, in clearly organized form, the familiar basic elements of his thought. The division of man into natural and transcendental parts is apparent in the two dimensions, civilization and culture. So are also the two ways of knowing (the cultural being the level where knowing relies on grace), and the two moral laws (*eros* and *agape*). The inevitability of sin is evident in the problem of coercive power, which is still controllable only through careful balance, and in the espousal of an *ad hoc* procedure distrustful of the directional use of all ideals. And, finally, the arbitrary limitation on social science is visible in the relegation of technics to civilization and out of culture.

But the frightening aspect of this lecture is the blind insistence that the prime danger in the world today is a false belief that man can overcome all difficulties by use of reason. In this connection Niebuhr's difference in attitude toward the two crises is noteworthy. On the plane of civilization, where the conflict is between technics and

the community, he champions the new — technics. This
is his radicalism. On the plane of culture, where the conflict is between belief in the omnipotence of reason and
doubts of this belief, he champions the old — doubts.
(The doubts are perhaps new in that they are rising to
challenge the modern belief, but very, very old in that they
have been with us from creation in the form of superstition.) This is his neo-orthodoxy. In so far as his doubts
in the guise of humility impinge on the lower plane (civilization), the edge of his radicalism is turned to dull reaction.

At this point objections must be raised to this cultural
crisis that Niebuhr fancies. A belief that man can resolve all of his problems by use of empirical reason simply
does not exist in any proportion sufficient to deserve granting it first rank as the grounding of our culture. The
romantic movement alone provided enough impact to
shake any foundations laid by the Age of Reason. But just
come down to the present day and look at the man in
the street. Surely if there is such a basic belief it will be
found in him too; the culture of an age is not to be isolated
in the minds of a handful of philosophers. Any person
half-heartedly alive will realize that the average citizen has
little if any over-confidence in reason and, even if he is confident at all, shows little inclination to rely on it. Where,
for instance, is the rational attitude toward social problems
and conflicts that we could expect if our culture basically
believed they could be removed by reason? In America
there is a prevalent attitude — found more extensively
than in other countries — that if something is unsatisfac-
tory we should try to do something about it. But it is a
practical attitude, not based on conviction that everything
is possible nor insisting on reason over feeling.

If on the other hand this grounding belief in the capacity of reason to resolve human difficulties is supposedly implicit, subconscious, hidden below the surface, we still have trouble explaining fascism within this theory. America is by all odds the land that has most thoroughly accepted the utopian belief in reason — if any land has. Yet we find the first outbreak of despair in fascist Germany. This discrepancy cannot be explained away by assertion that fascism is a minor crisis, for fascism unquestionably has cultural as well as civilizational dimensions — even by Niebuhr's own testimony.[1] It must be a part, at least, of the major crisis. If we follow Niebuhr's outline for crisis, the areas with least basic reliance on reason would be expected to have the least violent reaction to the loss of human control over human affairs — unmanageable events in Niebuhr's terms. The facts of the case, as it turns out, are just the reverse.

To be sure, the despair of which fascism is an expression is partly, perhaps largely, due to the failure of customary methods to solve important problems. It is a desperate emotional attempt to force a desired resolution of difficulties. But it is the *failure* to control human affairs that leads to despair, not the *belief* that they can be controlled. The unsolved problems (e.g., depression, unemployment, hunger, abuse of power, war) are in themselves serious enough, tragic enough for men to react with despair and fanaticism, completely irrespective of their hopes or " basic " beliefs. Human problems and conflicts are not merely intellectual puzzles; they are deep-seated, imperative calls for change. They can even be so unbearable that any change, no matter how fraught with peril, will be clutched at in desperation. In face of an unbearable situation human beings can be expected to *do* something no matter how persuasively they are told it is paradox and exhorted to humility.[2]

As for unmanageable events: if a particular event is unmanageable, Niebuhr, with his faith in sin, is the only one who *knows* it. There are of course many events that have not been managed, but the only way we have of knowing an event to be unmanageable is to try to manage it and fail. And then we can never be sure that another method of attack might not have been successful. As has already been emphasized, today's " uncontrollable " events are largely attributable to the possibly remediable non-functional character of power and to the lack of appropriate authority. When power is coercive, events are unmanageable; they refuse to be coerced. If we believe we can handle events by use of reason and then find we have not succeeded, would not a belief in reason require us to try again in an equally reasonable fashion, leaving to the distrust of reason the advocacy of coercion, the council of despair? To this we can say " no " only if, through some such stratagem as *hybris,* we define reasoning to be essentially in some respect unreasonable.

If the belief in the power of reason is so fundamental as to ground our culture, it is incredible that it could lead to reliance on desperate irrational measures. Fundamental beliefs supply a basic habitual bias that tends to spring forth invigorated from the pressure of difficult circumstances. As an atheist's childhood faith in God wells forth into prayer from the depths of a foxhole, so would a belief in reason break forth under stress into paeans of thought. This, of course, sounds ridiculous simply because a belief in reason is not and never has been basic to any culture. How could it be any deeper in culture than it is in men whose basic attitudes have been formed under the influence of childhood fears, gropings, superstitions, tyrannies, and prejudices?

No, it is the other way around; thinking is a fragile faculty, and reliance on it or " basic belief " in it has never been much more than sporadic. It is when we weaken in our determination to use our rational faculties (together with whatever non-rational elements of our being we can bring to bear) to deal with human problems that despair, superstition, prejudice, and fanaticism take over. And this is the crucial moment when Niebuhr does his bit to muddy the waters of thought and fertilize the weed of doubt. Doubts of the ultimacy of reason may be healthy in themselves. But when they grow, under such fertilizers as paradox and *hybris,* into doubts of the usefulness of reason, they become rankly pernicious. They put a premium on loose thinking.

Niebuhr, however, does more than undermine the human enterprise with doubts. His campaign against the critical use of reason is grounded in a pretense to inside information about the ultimate nature of reality. He reinforces it by an interpretation of God's incomprehensibility to man that in effect enshrines the irrational as a mark of the divine. In effect he throws the whole weight of his authority on the side of unreason, playing into the hands of reaction and clearing the way for unsupported assertion, denunciation, and cruelty.

Niebuhr himself is saved from carrying his own predilections to their most violent extremes partly because of his earlier training in ethical philosophies. But we are justified in fearing the results of his formulations in the minds of less sophisticated people, especially those who may confront it in their formative years. The chances are that the popular mind, unable to accept his bewildering assortment of paradox with all the nicety, balance, and humility demanded, will rather pick and choose, and will in the end, if not completely revolted, accept his dogmatisms. The human mind has become too accustomed to thinking rationally (albeit defectively) to find easy accommodation to systematic obscurity. Reports from Germany, the homeland of neo-orthodoxy, have it that neo-orthodoxy has already proven almost unintelligible to the laity.[3] The great danger is that people will be persuaded to stop thinking and accept isolated dogmas of the prophet.

Sidney Hook and John Herman Randall, Jr., have suggested that Niebuhr's thought is divisible — that his theology and his political policy can be accepted or rejected separately, that there is no organic connection between his theology and the practical action he advocates.[4] They are correct in that Niebuhr's theological concepts do not necessarily require particular social actions or policies. However, Niebuhr does use such concepts as *hybris* and grace in interpreting current affairs. The catch is that there are no criteria for telling what are instances of them in the practical world. For example, in locating the greatest manifestation of sin Niebuhr is no better off than other political thinkers and so can shift the locus in a very few years from capitalism to Communism. We have seen throughout the last several chapters the close relation between Niebuhr's political concepts (power, the group, democracy) and his theological dogmas; but we are still left with a hiatus between his political concepts and his practical prescriptions because his concepts are formulated as generalities, not as directional theories or hypotheses. Niebuhr really has no functional theory. At most, the direction we can get from him is a process of empirical patching carefully gauged to fit within the hems of generalities.

On the other hand, there is a negative organic connection between his theology and his practical suggestions, if such a thing can be. This consists in the great realm of possibilities for practical action ruled out by his theological dogmas. In this connection Niebuhr disfigures social science by reducing it to materialism and then declaiming the errors and limitations of materialism as if it were social science. He subverts the directional use of ideals. He desecrates reason, nature, and man, thus putting a discount on resources potentially available for human betterment. He hamstrings effort by declaring soluble problems insoluble (e.g., power).

We cannot avoid wondering whether, in spite of the fact that his own concern with politics is progressive and moral, his net influence may not be quite otherwise — especially if his views are not accepted in all their dialectic subtlety. There is the element of distrust of the state that tends to induce withdrawal from participation. There is the aggravation of individualism by giving the individual transcendent resources above the group, which may tend to break down sense of community and of social responsibility. There is the asceticism implied in a dual set of values wherein the lower set becomes ultimately not *really* important. There is the problem of moral commitment, when the doctrine of grace is allowed to come close to interfering with the exercise of moral effort. There is the lack of any constructive leadership, of any positive direction to help Christianity attain a progressive role in a society that has lost confidence in the ideas and principles that once served to interpret and justify conduct. Instead men are left drifting in distrust of their own resources and quaking under *hybris*.

And finally there is the purely destructive impact upon democracy of many aspects of Niebuhr's thought. Under his influence, democratic citizens will stray to a world of make-believe where they will be enjoined to act scientifically but will find themselves under a withering scrutiny forbidding scientific method. There they will encounter new difficulties, but they will be unable to form new concepts to deal with them. Indeed, they will gladly retain the old ones and diligently defend their comprehensive vagueness. They will have lost the spirit of investigation, for they will know This is impossible (though possible) and That is inevitable (though unnecessary). They will interpret international affairs by means of generalities and forces, and await the coming of a larger community through grace.

In this new land, Niebuhrians will establish a democracy actually run by an oligarchy. They will be forever frustrated because morally bound to sacrifice their interests upon the altar of compromise. They will find that powers and forces have been " given " in their land, and they will eternally maneuver to balance them. Their freedom will be rootless, paradoxically united with coercive order into a discordant harmony. And they will tolerate each other only because they are not sure whether they have or have not the truth, meanwhile awaiting Word from the hovering saints who have escaped the shackles of immoral society.

CHAPTER SEVEN

Epilogue: *The Irony of Sin*

This time, like all times, is a very good one, if we
but know what to do with it.

EMERSON

With *The Irony of American History* [1] Niebuhr returned to one of his favorite themes to revel in fantasy
and fugue on the failings of American liberalism and
American materialism. It is a performance in which he
has now had much practice and his fingers run over the
noisy keys with greater precision, conviction, and force
than ever before. And there is no doubt that the tune
will linger long in the ears of his audience. It is well
turned, rings true, and is supported by a harmony of
profound analysis excellent but for the *faux-bourdon* that
rumbles subdued but relentless in the bass.

The book, however, pretends to a significance over and
above the mere pointing out to Americans of the errors
of their ways. It presents with welcome humility a framework for finding in the ironic a category to apply to historical events. In history Niebuhr finds pathos, tragedy, and
irony. Pathos is the suffering that arises from purely
fortuitous cross-purposes and confusions for which no
reason can be given or guilt ascribed, as for example the
buffetings of nature. [2] Tragedy is a product " of conscious choices of evil for the sake of good "; [3] it " combines
nobility with guilt." [4] Irony is found where an apparently
fortuitous incongruity of life (which elicits laughter) dis-

closes upon closer examination a hidden relation within the incongruity. " Comic incongruity is transmuted into irony, when one element in the contrast is found to be the source of the other." [5]   Comparing three types of situations, Niebuhr decides that an " ironic situation is distinguished from a pathetic one by the fact that a person involved in it bears some responsibility for it. It is distinguished from a tragic one by the fact that the responsibility is not due to a conscious choice but to an unconscious weakness." [6]   The great significance of the category of the ironic for contemporary history is that an " ironic situation must dissolve, if men or nations are made aware of their complicity in it." [7]   When men or nations become aware of the hidden vanity or pretensions that make the comic ironic, they either abate their pretensions (which means contrition) or accentuate them (turning irony into pure evil) .

In general terms, a situation is ironic if " virtue becomes vice through some hidden defect in the virtue; if strength becomes weakness because of the vanity to which strength may prompt the mighty man or nation; if security is transmuted into insecurity because too much reliance is placed upon it; if wisdom becomes folly because it does not know its own limits . . ." [8]   In each instance the hidden defect is a human pretension or vanity: pretensions of virtue, strength, wisdom, and so on and on. In each case the limits of human capacities of power, wisdom, virtue, volition are forgotten. In other words, the old familiar taint in human nature, corruption of human freedom and whatnot — original sin — is the discordance that, for Niebuhr, turns comic incongruity into irony.

Niebuhr maintains that " the Christian faith " (meaning presumably his own Christian faith) " tends to make the ironic view of human evil in history the normative one." [9] Undoubtedly he is right. Behind the ironic interpretation are marshaled all the familiar aspects of his dogmatism. In Niebuhr's scheme, by definition of human nature, man " is an ironic creature because he forgets that he is not simply a creator but also a creature." [10] What is more to be expected than that from a transcendent point of view the vain dreams, misjudgments, and paltry pretensions of men should appear to emanate from their creatureliness and sinfulness into systematic irony? So it is the " observers " — those who transcend the situation — who are " not so hostile to the victim of irony as to deny the element of virtue which must constitute a part of the ironic situation; nor yet so sympathetic as to discount the weakness, the vanity and pretension which constitute another element," [11] who must detect and proclaim the ironies of history to the world. Other observers can of course find irony in history, but those who see in the category of the ironic a systematic interpretation for history will have a superior understanding through the transcendence of faith of the incomprehensible mystery and meaning of the universe.[12]

On the other hand, the " participants " in an ironic context have too limited a perspective, are too immediately concerned — that is, too corrupted by sin — to divine the ironic. If, however, the irony of their ways is pointed out to them, they can grasp the situation and mend their ways. This almost sounds as if Niebuhr had found a simple technique for combatting inevitable sin through the miracle of ironic awakening. It is certainly true that in this book he shows an extension of this trend toward greater emphasis on the optimistic side of the paradox of impossible possibilities. The whole book sustains the commendable purpose of awakening us to the dangers of our ways in order that we may avoid injustice and international conflict. But Niebuhr has not abjured his dialectical position. For example, " powerful nations and individuals [still] inevitably tend to use the weak as instruments of their purposes," [13] and " there are [still] irresolvable contradictions both between prosperity and virtue, and between happiness and the ' good life.' " [14] The tenor of the book as a whole is deceptive: Niebuhr still insists on the paradoxical relation of the possible and the impossible in history.

Perhaps the cue to this deceptiveness may be found in the following passage:

> Nothing that is worth doing can be achieved in our lifetime; therefore we must be saved by *hope*. Nothing which is true or beautiful or good makes complete sense in any immediate context of history; therefore we must be saved by *faith*. Nothing we do, however virtuous, can be accomplished alone; therefore we are saved by *love*. No virtuous act is quite as virtuous from the standpoint of our friend or foe as it is from our standpoint. Therefore we must be saved by the final form of love which is *forgiveness*.[15]

The therapeutic effect upon the " participants " that Niebuhr expects from dissertation on irony by the " observers " is in line with faith, hope, love, forgiveness. If, in the process of dissolving ironic incongruities, we would avoid accentuating our pretensions and thus crystallizing out pure evil, we must, through awareness of our pretensions, come to terms " with the limits of all human striving, the fragmentariness of all human wisdom, the precariousness of all historic configurations of power, and the mixture of good and evil in all human virtue." [16] But this requires religious humility, faith in a paradoxical universe, repentance, contrition, and, in the end, charity and sacrifice. All of which is to say that the *final* reliance for ironic awakening is not on enlightenment of the masses by the " observers " but on the grace of God. Here, then, is the characteristic Niebuhrian paradox: Americans can and cannot resolve the ironies of their history. They can do it themselves but, in the end, only when it is done for them by grace through the miracle of ironic awakening.

As a principle for the interpretation of current history, the category of the ironic proves to be decidedly less of a touchstone than it might seem at first. The particular ironies that Niebuhr uncovers are easily agreed upon even by those who lack his specific religious background. And, although literary theories may disagree in definition of irony, as they do also in explanation of tragedy and pathos, the pretension-emphasis that Niebuhr employs seems to provide a legitimate and sensitive account of the mechanics of irony. In order to understand current history, however, we need something more than poetic interpretation. We need general concepts sufficiently precise both to have meaning in specific contexts and to be perfectible as a result of their relationships with particular happenings.

This is where irony as a category breaks down. As treated by Niebuhr, the category makes a certain amount of fuzzy sense when the elements of ironic contrast are such vague catch-alls as virtue and evil, strength and weakness, wisdom and foolishness, innocence and guilt — whatever they all mean in their eloquent generality. The sense quickly disappears when a particular occurrence of irony is examined as a test of the category.

The chief stumbling block of the category in this respect is the insistence that one element of an ironic contrast is the source of the other: innocency with its pretension is the source of evil; strength with its pretension is the source of weakness; and so forth. How, for example, can we, in accordance with the formula, establish American dreams of virtue and innocence as a source of America's guilt-edged security? For it is undoubtedly ironic that " our dreams of a pure virtue are dissolved in a situation in which it is possible to exercise the virtue of responsibility toward a community of nations only by courting the prospective guilt of the atomic bomb." [17] How can dreams or illusions, or pretenses of virtue or innocence, on the part of the American nation (including all the easy beliefs that America has avoided the wars, tyrannies, oppressions of Europe and the facile pretense that America has been providentially set aside as a land of prosperity, justice, freedom) have been the source of America's present world position in which she has become the prospectively guilty leader of the West in its clash with Communism?

Pretenses, beliefs, ideologies are certainly factors in historical development. But there are many others, including the economic and the scientific, and pretensions are not the most important — even " in final analysis." It is this sort of fault in applying the theory of irony that gives large sections of the book a tone of unreality; this in turn makes the reader perversely wonder if this whole business of categorical irony is not just an excuse for a renewed criticism, in somewhat more systematic fashion than before, of American liberalism, and for vindicating [18] Niebuhr's own pet dogmas on the strength of its weaknesses. A dream or pretense in this particular context is not the source of the ironic evil alleged, in any sense that we can know, but only in the dogmatic sense that a jealous God smites sinful pretenses to divinity.

A similar difficulty hedges the irony Niebuhr has found

in "an age of reason culminating in a life-and-death struggle between two forms of 'scientific' politics." [19] Wisdom plus pretense yields folly. Yet Niebuhr recognizes and commends the American pragmatic approach to politics and economics [20] and glories in the " ironic triumph " [21] of " common sense " in American politics over the theories of the foolish wise men.[22] How can an age of reason, no matter how over-confident and pretentious, be the source of a struggle between two forms of " scientific " politics if it has itself been triumphed over by common sense — especially since at least one of the two forms of " scientific " politics does not then exist? This incessant harping on the evils of the utopian dreams of America strikes a false note when it is seen that in practice the dreams are largely ignored and a pragmatic method espoused. Our dreams do, of course, have their impact; but again they are not the all-significant source of our woes — except in the negative sense that so long as we persist in occupying our minds with disembodied theories, utopias, and dreams we shall not effectively make use of thought that can be productive in practice.

There is indeed irony in the failure of utopian dreams to materialize and in the refutation of them by history. But it is an irony that does not fit into the Niebuhrian pattern. Failure of dreams is not so much the result of pretense as the fate to be expected for thought separated from action, theory divorced from practice. Such a fate involves much of what Niebuhr means by pretenses: false estimation of the unlimited dimensions of men, over-confidence in one man's or one group's point of view, misunderstanding of the degree to which men can be managed by others. But it excludes original sin. The irony of Niebuhr's position is that, in denouncing the ideals of others and their superficial reasoning, he himself pretends to an absolute dogma (that all reasoning is corrupt) which would subvert any genuine collective attempt to develop ideals as theories organically and self-correctively connected with the actions of men.[23]

Irrespective of systematic ironies compounded from hidden human defects, unrealistic beliefs and ideologies — as Niebuhr rightly insists — *are* dangerous in the present situation. Too great confidence in our national strength, in the purity of our motives, in the absolute rightness of our cause, in the wisdom of our policy or the virtue of our particular social institutions — all of these can have ill effects upon the nation's foreign policy. In this respect, Chapter 6 of *The Irony of American History* is particularly excellent. There Niebuhr analyzes the development of Communism into a creed for the agrarian world and explains the ineffectiveness of American power, virtue, and influence in combating Communism in the agrarian East. He concludes that we must maintain strength enough to prevent aggression, at the same time teaching ourselves sufficient restraint and patience to endure a long wait — perhaps hundreds of years — until Communism crumbles (as did Islam) from the internal errors of its creed.

At this point Niebuhr discards all the implications of what he has said about the " common sense " or " pragmatic " method of American democracy. He vaults clear over it to the conclusion that a religious faith which grounds tolerance, humility, charity, hope, and sacrifice in a recognition of original sin is the only " final " or " ultimate " way we have of maintaining our position and our patience today. Niebuhr shows continued progress in his gradual understanding and appreciation of de-

mocracy. He falls short, however, of an adequate realization of its value and importance. Its " common sense "
attribute is much more significant than he realizes. Incidentally, it is to the enduring credit of the much-maligned
liberals that, despite their illusions, they have consistently
supported, both in practice and in ideal, the democratic apparatus for arriving at decisions.

Democracy is more than a constitutional mechanism for
balancing faction against faction, power against power,
interest against interest, in the manner of James Madison.
It is more than a cautious, step-by-step pragmatism tempered by worship and tradition in the spirit of Edmund
Burke. (Madison and Burke are the heroes of Niebuhr's
mature thought.) There is an ethos, a tolerance and humility habitually embedded in democracy's method of self-
adjustment and self-correction. This is the element Niebuhr disregards when he relegates the " common sense "
method to the strictly internal affairs of America. It can
and does spill over into our relations with the rest of the
world. And it can be extrapolated even further. It is a
more promising and reliable resource than Niebuhr's final
resort: it is backed by the ways of the people rather than by
pious exhortation. Yet Niebuhr not only underrates its
potential but undermines it with a moral washout. For
what else is the indiscriminate dogma that any decision —
including the decision not to decide — involves us in
guilt, and the corollary that power cannot be wielded or
disavowed without guilt? [24] Niebuhr's agonized conscience
tends to deprive guilt of meaning in the more-and-less
framework of morality, for when our practical actions are
indiscriminately guilty the term loses its comparative
function. He seemingly continually forgets his own

scheme of "relative ethics" in order to reproach us with the impact of the eternal. And democracy, a primarily moral endeavor, is thereby imperiled.

The fact that American democratic method, or the ethos of American democracy, has begun to bubble over into our foreign relations is duly noted by Niebuhr: he is acutely perceptive despite his ideological blinkers. His example is the "creative synthesis" that was achieved, *notwithstanding America's disproportionate power,* between the too precipitate American policy of rearming Germany and European fears which might have prevented the inclusion of Western Germany in the Western community.[25] Such an achievement is one step beyond the Madisonian or Niebuhrian balance of power. Niebuhr's recognition of it is a promising development; and we can only hope that some time he will, in line with its implications, revise his conception of power (and original sin, unless he finds some new ingenious way for self-contradiction) into something more sensitive, realistic, and useful. As it is, he slips lightly by, shifting quickly into overdrive, so eager is he to expound his religious biases — humility, charity, mystery, and sacrifice — as the final strategy for bringing power under discipline.

Still thinking of power as necessarily coercive force, Niebuhr has apparently not yet grasped the main problem. In international affairs he discards the strategy of balance of power because there is no international force (or government) capable of organizing such a balance. He briefly mentions the capacity of the United Nations to present a limited amount of check in the form of social and moral review.[26] And then he hastens on to champion the "inapplicable ethic" of inner religious and moral checks. Actually our problem is to eliminate coercive power, to make power functional in terms of an authority appropriate to the present day, to remake power so that it is no longer a force to be balanced by force or checked by restraint, but a legitimate and essential part of the social structure, working *with*in a nexus of authority.

Power as force can only be frustrated or sacrificed. Power that is functional knows neither of these; there is simply no sense in speaking of frustrating or sacrificing it; there is no occasion, no need. The fact is that power can be one-sided and still not overweening if it is functionally integrated with a growing and self-correcting authority.

America seems to be developing such an authority in its " pragmatic," " common sense " (to use Niebuhr's terms) method for political democracy. It is also to be found in many instances of business administration where power is exercised in co-ordination with the authority of the total situation. (This is an instance of ironic success; Niebuhr, dealing always with the macroscopic, has persuasively argued, and not without some basis in truth, that " it is the nature of a business community that it deals with the covert forms of power in economic life and to be insensible to significance and the complexity of more overt forms of power." [27]) And a self-correcting authority is in evidence in some collective-bargaining situations where creative solutions have been evolved. Our task is to try to extend these promises, to functionalize power under an authoritative method, particularly in realms other than the political (i.e., the economic, the moral, even the ideal). In the political arena the " common sense " method as self-improving authority is already partially supplementing balance of power.

When, despite America's preponderant power, a creative

synthesis (meaning no sacrifice, no frustration) is wrought out of a conflict of interests on the international level, there is indication that the " common sense " authority in our democratic ethos is beginning to brim over national boundaries to functionalize even external power potentials. A creative bargaining context does not require power parity between participants where the power involved is non-coercive. The American democratic method, to be sure, is peripheral to our power relations with other countries. But the ethos of that method is conditioning our actions beyond our borders.

To many people, as to Niebuhr, such imaginative operations in external relations must seem the result of commendable self-restraint or moral check. When carefully observed, however, they appear quite otherwise: they exhibit a creative opening-out rather than a frustrating penting-in, and they show a promise of *progressive* practical achievement in the resolution of problems. Beneath the sublime current of disembodied pretentious ideologies, beneath the vague prescriptions of " inapplicable " religious ethics, beneath the shifty interpretations of historical ironies, exists a potential of the " common sense," workaday world.

If we would develop our potentialities we must look into the microscopic as well as the macroscopic; we must delve into the details beneath irony. Our problems deserve attack on all levels. Thus, while it is easy to sympathize with Niebuhr's disparagement of the pseudo social scientists in their pretentious attempts to develop a body of wisdom that will make possible the management of men and history, Niebuhr's across-the-board condemnation of all social science is fantastic. He does it by brilliantly analyzing abortive attempts at science and by then implying that the results of his analysis apply to all social science, particularly to Dewey and to contemporary sociology and psychology. His analysis and judgment are as follows:

> Sometimes the historical process is conceived as a purely natural one, in which case all men are regarded as merely the instruments and fruits of the process. But generally it is assumed that some group of men has the intelligence to manipulate and manage the process. The excessive voluntarism which underlies this theory of an élite, explicit in communism and implicit in some democratic theory, is encouraged by the excessive determinism, which assumes that most men are creatures with simple determinate ends of life, and that their "anti-social" tendencies are quasi-biological impulses and inheritances which an astute social and psychological science can overcome or "redirect" to what are known as "socially approved" goals. . . . This belief which has found classic expression in the philosophy of John Dewey, pervades the academic disciplines of sociology and psychology.[28]

But why this monstrously incorrect interpretation of John Dewey's philosophy? Why this flagrantly indiscriminate lumping of all social science under the banners of the would-be managers of history? It is a cry of fear, a primary reaction to danger. A genuine social science is a direct threat to all of Niebuhr's cherished dualistic illusions of transcendence and to his claim to have divined the nature of man's depravity. In defending himself, Niebuhr has, in effect, become an accomplice to Catholic efforts, fair and foul, for the defense of institutional interests against this same cardinal threat.

Niebuhr's impatience with the specific assumes its full dimensions when he breaks into a tirade against the attempt of a group of anthropologists to ascertain the roots of aggressiveness by means of extensive research into the toilet training of children of various national groups.[29]

" Significantly," Niebuhr decides, " it has not been determined whether collective aggressiveness is merely the cu-
mulation of individual forms of aggressiveness or whether
it is the fruit of an undue docility among the individuals
of a nation which provides fodder for the aggressiveness of
its leaders." [30]   By the word "significantly" he implies
that inquiry into the specific is by definition (of human
nature) futile and we might as well desist.   " When political science is severed from its ancient rootage in the hu-
manities and 'enriched' by the wisdom of sociologists,
psychologists and anthropologists, the result is frequently
a preoccupation with minutiae which obscures the grand
and tragic outlines of contemporary history, and offers
vapid solutions for profound problems." [31]   Since Niebuhr
has given us the grand and tragic outlines, since he has
already found the roots of aggressiveness to be planted
firmly in human nature, we can forget the minutiae, we
can cut inquiry short.   This is obviously not what Niebuhr
says in so many words, but it is present in the air.   And
it tends to smother progress in the solving of problems.

As his tirades against excessive attention to detail tend
to overreach themselves, so do his strictures against would-
be managers of history.   They verge, in their negativism,
on the brink of a paralyzing do-nothingness — think not,
strive not, but only believe!   The purposes of history, the
destiny of man, the will of God, are indifferent to the
conscious intents of men.   This is a position not fundamentally different from that of Tolstoy (whom Niebuhr
chides for his pessimism) ,[32] which makes people the pawns
of history and their purposes totally irrelevent.

The irony of irony is that Niebuhr's wisdom, with its
claim to a final insight into human nature, should culminate in the foolishness — avoided by " common sense " —

of discouraging rational and moral effort at improving the estate of man. The hidden fault, in this final case, is unveiled when the pretense is seen to have become, as pretenses will, a dogma — not a simple doubt of human ability but a dogma of arbitrary limitation upon human existence. The ultimate outcome of this kind of wisdom, this kind of thinking, is self-frustration — unnecessary self-frustration, dissipation of specifically human resources. What wisdom dare direct men to hypnotize themselves with paradox while there still remains the living option of directing rational and moral effort toward the development of whatever promise humanity shows? The end is not yet.

Postscript: Notes on Conservative Tendencies

The last few years have seen a determined effort on the part of would-be organizers of American conservatism, notably Russell Kirk,[1] to establish Niebuhr as one of the proud displays of American conservatism. Such a classification of Niebuhr in face of his earlier radicalism and his present advocacy of radical, though gradual changes, derives in no small part from the opinion of the organizers of the new conservatism that " the religious man, whatever his party allegiance or outward politics, in some considerable degree is at heart a conservative, for he appeals to an authority beyond the vanity of Demos or Expediency and he trusts in the wisdom of our ancestors and in enduring values." [2] And it finds its plausibility in recent writings of Niebuhr which have expressed appreciation for some aspects of the conservative creed,[3] found fault in some aspects of democratic socialism,[4] and carried on a continuous offensive against " extreme voluntarism " with its abstract schemes for social reform.

It is very easy to oversimplify Niebuhr's views. Indeed, it has come to the point where almost any statement about his views is challenged from some quarter as not having " done justice to the complexities of " his thought. A particular stumbling block in this respect is Niebuhr's way of emphasizing different portions of his analysis of the human situation at different times according to what he believes to be currently needed for social correction.

Niebuhr clearly does not fall into the camp of conservatism in the field of American daily politics. His inclination is, if anything, more obviously in the direction of the welfare state. He is not satisfied with the current internal balance of power or the inequality and conformity it demands. As he says, " Any conservatism which is merely interested in the preservation of some *status quo* would be anathema for any one who had drawn inspiration from the Old Testament prophets." [5]

Niebuhr particularly distrusts American conservatism, which he considers "nothing more than a decadent liberalism." [6] "American conservatism," he contends, " is not conservative at all in the traditional sense; it is a part of the traditional liberal movement and it exhibits the defects of its creed; but it has not retained many of its virtues." [7] The liberal creed, he feels, was a weapon developed by the bourgeois class in its fight against the old feudal aristocracy. The freedom from aristocratic society gained as a result of the American Revolution left America without a truly conservative creed, leaving the right wing of this liberal view to develop into a " conservatism " of the business community dedicated to resisting innovation and to defending laissez faire. [8]

The occupation of sorting people into neat categories of conservatives and liberals and radicals and reactionaries, with perhaps refinements of hyphenated sub-categories plus prefixes of " neo," tends to be a fruitless trade in vanity goods. It is a vocation well left to those who have direct stake in the organizing of group processes. Most of us in any case defy logic or history (whichever is the basis for setting bounds to the categories) by stubbornly maintaining ourselves in two or many groups at once. And Niebuhr is among us.

Niebuhr's latest book, *The Self and the Dramas of History,* is the writing of a man who, having settled upon his doctrine, has now settled in to preach it with as grand a manner as he can muster. However, at the same time it reveals glimpses of a slow movement in his thought, a movement made up of conservative tendencies which are not merely timely emphases for sermonizing's sake. As noted above[9] there is a fundamental conservatism attached to his basic assumptions and central concepts. The same attitude deeply infects his philosophy of history and then comes to the surface in prescriptions for social health and in defenses for the *status quo.*

Complete with brave overabstract oversimplification,[10] *The Self and the Dramas of History* surveys modern Western history as a dramatic encounter between Biblical-Hebraic and Hellenic components of our culture,[11] incidentally complicated by the development of technics. The Biblical-Hebraic component views history as drama, respects the organic aspects or forms of life and society, accepts divine providence, piously bases historical revelation in the mystery of creation and has an essentially traditional outlook. The Hellenic component looks for structure in history, glorifies the artifacts of man's reason and will, considers man the master of historical destiny, rationalistically approaches history ontologically from the idea of being and has an essentially voluntaristic outlook. Niebuhr retains his regular dialectical position by seeing virtue in both parts of our cultural heritage.

From the rational (Hellenistic) side he tries to uphold the dialectic by insisting that we must think rigorously.[12] For example, he contends that, " for the fulfillment of our task [of integrating the world community] it is obvious that we require all the instruments of rational discrimination which our various social and historical sciences are able to develop." [13]   But on the other hand one of the prime intents of the book is to expose the tendency of the Hellenistic side of our culture to be overconfident in the efficacy of artifact.   It goes so far as to insist that " the chief problem [of the world] arises from our inclination to accentuate all the errors and illusions of Western civilization in regard to man's mastery of historical destiny." [14]   It clearly discards the Hellenic view of man and bestows supreme favor on the "historical" (Biblical-Hebraic) view of the "self" — which turns out to be the creature described in *The Nature and Destiny of Man*.   And it champions a corresponding view of history which finds history to be the bearer of deep meanings not to be arrived at by reason — as if there were such a thing as pure reason.

There is a vast difference between learning from history, from experience, benefiting from what others have learned, and accepting history as the bearer of meanings that surpass our understanding.   History may not fit into neat logical categories, but there is great danger in uncritically accepting its supposed frame of meaning as final wisdom.   Niebuhr of course does not eschew the process of thought for the analysis of history, but he has often enough and in enough different contexts, repeated the bit about foolish wise men failing to understand the wisdom of history that it is safe to say that he contributes to the tendency to venerate rather than analyze history.   [And this is said in full awareness of Niebuhr's own cautions against undue reverence.]

Niebuhr has returned home from his jaunty travels through history with a deepened appreciation of the wisdom carried by tradition.   He is impressed with " the positive contribution of traditional societies in restraining

self-interest by historically established norms and by setting limits to the inordinate ambitions of men." [15]   He
makes an oversimple opposition between "traditional"
and "voluntaristic" societies, the one aware of the "organic" factors in the human situation, the other given to
dreaming up "artifacts" without base in human nature.
The opposition seems to become an either-or proposition
and he makes his choice without considering that there
may be middle grounds.   Of course he dialectically bal-
ances this with the "duty to challenge the inherited traditions" and the "obligation to exercise discriminate
judgement in rearranging or reconstructing any scheme of
togetherness which has been faulty in providing justice." [16]
   Nevertheless, in sympathy with this appreciation of tradition and as marks of conservative tendency, we now find
signs of renewed respect for property, privilege, status.
"The two instruments of property and social stratifica-
tion . . . are necessary instruments of justice and order,
and yet both are fruitful of injustice," he says.[17]   Conservatism shows in this statement — not through the emphasis on property and status as historical tools for retention of justice, after all this is balanced by cautions of the
injustice also implicit in them, but through the conviction
that the more things change the more they are the same.
The attitude of fundamental conservatism expressed in the
assumption of unchangeable factors — *hybris,* power —
reappears on the lowly level.   The real possibilities of
converting status from a rigid aspect of personality to a
more flexible adjunct of function, from hierarchy constructed around persons to organization arranged and re-
arranged in respect to jobs to be done and problems to be
solved, is thereby obscured.
   Niebuhr is now explicit in his respect for European

traditional conservatism, especially of the British variety. His position might be described, with qualification of the final term, as Burke plus universal suffrage minus *status quo*.[18]   What he appreciates in traditional conservatism is its realistic understanding of power, its appreciation of contingency in history, its full acceptance of the whole organic self, its restriction of policy to limited and forseeable ends.   As Kenneth Thompson says, Niebuhr has taken over Burke's " prudence " as " first in the rank of political virtues." [19]

The final indication of conservatism in Niebuhr's thought is not a tendency but a long standing, confirmed defense of the *status quo*.   This is his persistent opposition to the extension of the scientific method into the realms of moral concern, about which much has already been said in this volume.   His attitude here is clearly due to a failure to understand.   He continues to restrict science to " civilization " and to exclude it from " culture," that is, to consider it merely a "context," a technical context for the cultural conflicts of modern times,[20] and thus betrays himself into a distorted and oversimplified recounting of Western history.   He falsely persists in believing the scientific method to be a necessarily ontological endeavor engaged in the search for causes, indissoluably connected with prediction, dealing exclusively with sense data for facts and requiring an objective detachment of scientist from subject-matter.[21]   It is of course true that many scientists themselves fall into these common errors.   By perpetuation of this *status quo* which declares false " limits " for science, however, Sin postpones the day when Science, meaning a social scientific method, will be equipped to supplant our present crude, *ad hoc* methods of attack on social problems.

Notes

Full titles and publication data of books and articles here referred to by the author's surname will be found in the Bibliography (pp. 221–34).

Chapter One
Introduction: Retreat from Reason

1 Sperry, p. 200.

2 As early as 1927 Niebuhr was bothered by this separation: "It seems to me rather unfortunate that we must depend upon the 'publicans' for our social conscience to so great a degree while the 'saints' develop their private virtues and let the city as such fry in its iniquities." *Cynic*, p. 144.

3 D. R. Davies puts it this way: "The inevitable tendency of Niebuhr's work . . . is toward the sharpening of the issue of Church versus World." Davies, p. 100. If this is true, Niebuhr's work is having effects somewhat tangential to his express aims. He has probably spilled as much ink damning churches as institutions as he has castigating any other single comparable phenomenon.

4 *Ibid.*

5 Niebuhr, *Cynic*, p. 152.

6 Niebuhr, *Faith and History*, p. 173.

7 Niebuhr, *Cynic*, pp. 56–57.

8 Niebuhr, however, develops a distinctive natural law of his own. See pp. 71–72 below.

9 Cf. Niebuhr, *Faith and History*, Chap. 11.

10 Reason's rebuttal to the irrationalists' contentions has been well handled by L. Harold DeWolf, *The Religious Revolt Against Reason*, and by Arthur E. Murphy, *The Uses of Reason*.

Chapter Two
The Chains of Dogma

1 "To say that He is the Creator of the World means that the processes of nature and history are not self-derived and self-explanatory." Niebuhr, *Europe's Catastrophe*, pp. 26–27.

2 *Ibid.*, p. 30.

3 Niebuhr, *Human Nature*, p. 3.

4 *Ibid.*, pp. 26–27.

5 "Any careful reading of the works of Thomas Aquinas must impress the thoughtful student with the element of pretension which informs the flowering of the Catholic faith in the 'golden' thirteenth century. . . .

The mysteries of the human soul and spirit are mastered and rationally defined in the most meticulous terms. . . . The new age of science attempted an even more rigorous denial of mystery." Niebuhr, *Signs of the Times*, p. 158.

[6] Niebuhr, *Europe's Catastrophe*, p. 30.

[7] *Ibid.*, p. 22.

[8] Niebuhr, *Human Nature*, p. 252.

[9] In his books before *Human Nature*, Niebuhr does not consider the sin prior to sin; it seems to be a later refinement of thought.

[10] Niebuhr, *Human Nature*, p. 242.

[11] Niebuhr, *Christian Ethics*, p. 76.

[12] Niebuhr, *Europe's Catastrophe*, p. 28.

[13] Niebuhr is not sure whether the " positive " and " negative " are two types of sin or whether one is derived from the other. Cf. *Beyond Tragedy*, p. 296. In *Human Nature*, the sin of sensuality is developed into a three-faceted affair: an extension of self-love, an effort to escape the self, and an effort to escape the confusion of sin and guilt. Cf. Niebuhr, *Human Nature*, pp. 228–40.

[14] Augustine, *Confessions*, Book III, Par. VIII.

[15] *Ibid.*, Book VII, Par. XIII.

[16] *Ibid.*, Book VII, Par. XVII.

[17] Niebuhr, *Human Nature*, p. 258.

[18] *Ibid.*, p. 260.

[19] " To an external observer no conscious choice of evil is ever discernible. There is always a previous condition or the force of an antecedent impulse which seems to offer a complete explanation of the inevitability of the act. . . . The full dimension of depth in which all human actions transpire is disclosed only in introspection." Niebuhr, *Christian Ethics*, p. 80.

[20] Niebuhr, *Human Nature*, p. 4.

[21] *Ibid.*, p. 27.

[22] Niebuhr, *Europe's Catastrophe*, pp. 18–19.

[23] Niebuhr, *Social Work*, p. 69.

[24] " The fatal error of rationalistic humanism is its failure to recognize that reason is universal only in purely formal terms. Logic and mathematics may be universal; but no judgment which fills logical forms with material content is universal." Niebuhr, *Beyond Tragedy*, p. 236.

[25] Niebuhr has not been consistent in his use of the term " reason." In some of his earlier works it is indistinguishable from what he now calls " spirit " (see e.g., *Christian Ethics*, p. 76). I have here relied primarily on his use of the term in *Human Nature*, which is his present view. Where this difficulty of inconsistency has been encountered in later chapters I have accordingly " translated," where necessary, the old usage to fit the present description of man.

[26] Dewey and Bentley clarify the concept very nicely by reduction to the simplest case. " Suppose a man engaged in but one transaction and that with but one other man, and this all his life long. Would he be

viewed in distinction from that transaction or from that other man? Hardly." Dewey and Bentley, *Knowing and the Known*, p. 138.

27 For illustration of the transactional approach as it can fruitfully be used in business and industry, see Mary Follett, *Dynamic Administration*. Her terminology is different, but her approach is mainly transactional.

28 See page 32 below for a discussion of meaning as seen by Niebuhr.

29 " *Potentially*, perhaps, man has remained more or less constant in certain gross features of his emotional make-up. . . . But *actually*, instead of being aloof, man has been the very creature of his surroundings, and his supposedly impregnable human nature has undergone fantastic acrobatics, not merely from one millennium to another, but from war to war, treaty to treaty, and even from one ruler (or election) to the next." Geiger, " Dewey's Social and Political Philosophy," p. 350.

30 Niebuhr, *Faith and History*, p. 160.

31 Dewey, *Freedom and Culture*, p. 108. Cf. also *Human Nature and Conduct*, Chap. 5. Dewey uses for historical example Hobbes with fear, and Plato, the archetype, with his threefold human nature explicitly drawn from the three-faceted society of the city-state wherein man was seen writ large.

32 Sperry, p. 180. Similar appraisals of Niebuhr are made by Lewis, *Morals and the New Theology*, p. 120; and Murphy, p. 206. Following Murphy, Niebuhr's preoccupation can be classed as part of the post World War I reaction against propaganda, a reaction that swung to the opposite extreme of doubting all ideologies as " rationalizations " — Niebuhr's " ideological taint."

33 For example, love of power is an important part of our present democratic process as it operates in the job competition of candidates for office. A certain amount of pride is essential to achievement. And pride is important to the cohesion of the small group. Anyone who has observed the operation of local government will have noticed the importance of pride in locality for any sort of local accomplishment. Other observers of man have found in this same urge of divine unrest, of man's striving to surpass his accomplishments, a source of creative behavior.

34 Niebuhr, *Faith and History*, page viii.

35 Niebuhr, *Europe's Catastrophe*, p. 8.

36 Niebuhr, *Why the Christian Church Is Not Pacifist*, p. 13.

37 Jacobson, p. 241.

38 " . . . a limited rational validation of the truth of the Gospel is possible. . . . Negatively the Gospel must and can be validated by exploring the limits of historic forms of wisdom and virtue. Positively it is validated when the truth of faith is correlated with all truths which may be known by scientific and philosophical disciplines and proves itself a resource for coordinating them into a deeper and wider system of coherence." Niebuhr, *Faith and History*, p. 152.

39 " Unfortunately, for all their talk of appeal to experience, direct or indirect, religious experimentalists dare not appeal to any experience of sufficiently determinate character to permit of definite tests. There is

a certain wisdom in this reluctance. For if experience can confirm a belief, it can also disprove it. But to most supernaturalists the latter is an
inadmissible possibility. We therefore find that the kind of experience
to which reference is made is not only unique but uniquely self-authen-
ticating." Hook, " The New Failure of Nerve," p. 7.

40 " . . . all relevant problems had been mooted. Then came the
unanswerable puzzles, the paradoxes that always mark the limit of what
a generative idea, an intellectual vision, will do. The exhausted Christian mind rested its case, and philosophy became a reiteration and ever-
weakening justification of faith." Langer, p. 8.

41 Niebuhr, *Human Destiny*, p. 97.

42 It seems inevitable to me that, if all man's thoughts and actions are
tainted by sin, so are his experiences (except for brief moments of
grace). I don't see how the truth could conform to, much less organize,
even the experience of the converted.

43 Davies, page ix.

44 Niebuhr, *Human Nature*, p 3.

45 *Ibid.*, p. 38.

46 *Ibid.*, p. 120.

47 Niebuhr, *Faith and History*, p. 178.

48 Niebuhr, *Human Destiny*, p. 213.

49 An excellent example of Niebuhr's use of paradox may be seen in
an excerpt he takes from Kierkegaard: " Truth [in the human situation]
is exactly the identity of choosing and determining and of being chosen
and determined. What I choose I do not determine, for if it were not
determined I could not choose it; and yet if I did not determine it
through my choice I would not really choose it. It is: if it were not I
could not choose it. It is not: but becomes reality through my choice, or
else my choice were an illusion. . . . I choose the Absolute? What is
the Absolute? I am that myself the eternal personality. . . . But what
is this myself? . . . It is the most abstract and yet at the same time the
most concrete of all realities. It is freedom " (from *Entweder Oder Band*,
II, p. 182). Niebuhr, *Human Nature*, p. 163. This is allegedly a suc-
cinct statement of the paradox of human freedom.

50 Niebuhr, *Human Destiny*, p. 50.

51 *Ibid.*, p. 123.

52 *Ibid.*, pp. 218, 246.

53 Niebuhr, *Human Nature*, p. 263.

54 Cf. Thelen, pp. 82–83, 114–15. Thelen interprets Niebuhr's dialectic as centering around the concept of sin, with sin (the antithesis of
freedom) destroyed by God in the synthesis. I have not been able to agree
with this interpretation of Niebuhr's dialectic. It is unlikely that he
would handle the dialectic so that sometimes the antithesis is incorporated
in the synthesis and sometimes it is destroyed.

55 " The relation between the truth, apprehended in God's self-disclosure, and the truth about life which men deduce through a rational
organization of their experience, might best be clarified through the anal-

ogy of our knowledge about other persons. We know what we know about other persons, partly through an observation of their behavior. But human personality, unlike animal life, has a depth and uniqueness which cannot be understood purely in terms of external behavior. The depth is partly comprehended by assuming that the depths of self-consciousness within ourselves correspond to that in the other person. The uniqueness of the other person is partly falsified, however, by our effort to understand him in terms which we have drawn from the knowledge of ourselves." Niebuhr, *Human Destiny*, p. 64.

56 Niebuhr, *Beyond Tragedy*, p. 5.

57 *Ibid.*, p. 10.

58 *Ibid.*, pp. 12–13.

59 " Not that there are no ineffable experiences, but to ground the judgment of all human conduct on that which is clearly unspeakable suggests an obscurity and fuzziness in which flourishes sentimentalism, if nothing worse." Geiger, " Philosophic Humanism Today," p. 461.

60 Niebuhr, *Faith and History*, p. 48.

61 Niebuhr, *Cynic*, p. 141.

62 If human nature were completely predetermined and constant, Niebuhr could (possibly) have derived all truth and meaning from Scripture. As man's nature is not completely set but may change " within limits," Niebuhr has been able to discover revealed truths in history since Christ.

63 McCown, p. 157. McCown also deplores Niebuhr's use of " meaning " and suggests that meaning implies that a question has been answered or a confusion or obscurity removed.

64 Loomer, p. 91. Cf. also Macintosh's opinion in respect to Karl Barth, in *The Problem of Religious Knowledge*, pp. 343–44.

65 Banning, p. 1322.

66 *Ibid.*, p. 1322.

67 Barth, p. 203.

68 Niebuhr, " An Answer to Karl Barth," p. 235.

69 Sperry, pp. 167–68.

70 *Ibid.*, pp. 31–32.

71 *Ibid.*, p. 194.

72 *Ibid.*, pp. 204–05.

73 Tillich, p. 733. In contrast, C. C. Morrison celebrates neo-orthodoxy as an extension of the spirit of liberalism beyond the point at which " static liberalism " has stagnated. By reviving revelation, " by distinguishing the Bible from the revelation, and finding the primary locus of the revelation in the living historical experience of which the Bible is the product ['the reflecting mirror'], it set man free to exercise his intelligence in reading the Bible." Morrison, p. 731.

74 Niebuhr, " Coherence, Incoherence, and Christian Faith," p. 165.

75 *Ibid.*, p. 165.

76 *Ibid.*, p. 163.

77 In Chapter 4.

[78] Niebuhr, " Coherence, Incoherence, and Christian Faith," pp. 155–56.

[79] Jacobson, p. 260.

[80] Banning, p. 1322.

[81] Banning, p. 1322.

[82] Klausner, pp. 229–30. See DeWolf, pp. 203–11, for an able refutation of this belief.

[83] Klausner, p. 230.

[84] Cf. DeWolf, p. 114.

[85] Cf. Murphy, pp. 10–12. For a detailed point-by-point refutation of the irrationalists' case against reason see DeWolf's *The Religious Revolt Against Reason.* It is a thorough rebuttal, unfortunately limited by the circumscribed understanding of social science which the author shares with Niebuhr.

[86] Niebuhr, " Coherence, Incoherence, and Christian Faith," p. 164.

[87] Murphy, p. 12.

[88] Sperry, p. 183. As Sperry points out, " anti-intellectualism manifests itself most often in times of intellectual perplexity and among persons who are intellectually sophisticated rather than naively simple." Sperry, p. 182.

[89] " A free decision need not be uncaused or self-caused, as has mistakenly been supposed, but it must be caused by the self and therefore not fully determined apart from the specific contribution which the man *as a self* or person makes to its determination." Murphy, p. 122. See also Murphy, p. 278; and Dewey, *Logic: The Theory of Inquiry,* especially Chap. 22.

[90] Niebuhr, *Faith and History,* p. 165.

[91] " Formally there can be of course no conflict between logic and truth. The laws of logic are reason's guard against chaos in the realm of truth. They eliminate contradictory assertions. But there is no resource in logical rules to help us understand complex phenomena, exhibiting characteristics which seem to require that they be placed into contradictory categories of reason. Loyalty to all the facts may require a provisional defiance of logic, lest complexity in the facts of experience be denied for the sake of a premature logical consistency. Hegel's ' dialectic ' is a logic invented for the purpose of doing justice to the fact of ' becoming ' as a phenomenon which belongs into the category of neither ' being ' nor ' non-being.' " Niebuhr, *Human Nature,* pp. 262–63.

[92] Murphy comments, rather superficially: " Mr. Niebuhr appears to know a good deal about this incomprehensible reality, which proves, in fact, to be of a recognizably Calvinistic complexion and to require of men something much more specific than the unqualified affirmation of its incomprehensible transcendence. Perhaps he is right in this but how are we to know? And how is he to know? For while the transcendent reality may indeed pronounce judgment from a standpoint beyond all human standards, it is hard to see how Mr. Niebuhr can pretend to do so without exhibiting the sin of pride in its most sinful form." Murphy, p. 332.

[93] In view of the Marxist influence on Niebuhr's thought, it is of inter-

est to point out the similarity of this dialectic to the Marxian belief in the inevitability of Communism *and* the moral duty to further it. Niebuhr's sin and responsibility have a reverse twist but the same emotional overtones.

94 ". . . when it comes to convincing men of the truth of doctrines which are no longer to be accepted upon the say-so of custom and social authority, but which also are not capable of empirical verification, there is no recourse save to magnify the signs of rigorous thought and rigid demonstration." Dewey, *Reconstruction in Philosophy*, p. 20.

95 Communist moral pressure to work towards an inevitable goal has led to uncritical planning and striving, to a divorce of means and ends, and has resulted in missing the X marked " classless society," hitting instead on dictatorship. Will not Niebuhr's moral exhortations to work against an inevitable force result in equally uncritical and undirected strivings?

96 Recent anthropological studies have lifted this interpretation of human nature well out of the abyss of unbased assumption to the status of respectable scientific hypothesis. Cf., e.g., Benedict, *Patterns of Culture* Chap. 8; and " Human Nature Is Not a Trap," pp. 159–64.

Chapter Three
EXPERIMENTALISM BETWEEN TWO CHRISTS

1 Niebuhr, *Human Destiny*, p. 3.

2 *Ibid.*, p. 36.

3 *Ibid.*, p. 16.

4 " It is possible for a character, event or fact of history to point symbolically beyond history and to become a source of disclosure of an eternal meaning, purpose and power which bears history." Niebuhr, *Human Destiny*, p. 61.

5 *Ibid.*, p. 56.

6 *Ibid.*, pp. 76–78.

7 *Ibid.*, p. 110.

8 *Ibid.*, p. 300. " Christianity . . . knows by faith of some events in history, in which the transcendent source and end of the whole panorama of history is disclosed." Niebuhr, *Faith and History*, p. 22.

9 Niebuhr, *Human Destiny*, p. 118.

10 *Loc. cit.*

11 *Ibid.*, p. 137.

12 *Ibid.*, p. 142. " The medieval-Catholic synthesis is inadequate because it rested upon a compromise between the twofold aspects of grace. It arrested the fullest development of each aspect. Its conception of the fulfillment of life was marred by its confinement of the power of grace to a human-historical institution." *Ibid.*, pp. 207–08.

13 *Ibid.*, p. 159.

14 *Ibid.*, p. 169.

15 *Ibid.*, p. 200.

16 *Ibid.*, p. 207.

17 *Ibid.*, p. 156.

18 *Ibid.*, p. 211.

19 *Ibid.*, pp. 291–93.

20 *Ibid.*, p. 295.

21 Jacobson, p. 241.

22 " Paradoxes . . . are useful so long as we look for the truth, not in them, but in a new rational synthesis beyond them." DeWolf, p. 142.

23 Klausner, p. 228.

24 Macintosh, *The Problem of Religious Knowledge,* pp. 342, 343.

25 Williams, p. 822.

26 Jacobson, p. 262.

27 " Traditionally, the relation or the bridge between God in Jesus Christ and God as contemporaneously encountered is God in his character as the Holy Spirit. The neo-orthodox presupposition seems to be some form of transcendental philosophy in which God or the Holy Spirit is interpreted as being a nonmaterial spirit. But unless ' Holy Spirit ' means some process of dynamic events, the term smacks of sheer magic." Loomer, p. 91. Interestingly enough, Karl Barth, from this very perspective of " sheer magic," also criticizes Niebuhr for neglecting the Holy Spirit. Cf. Barth, pp. 201–04.

28 Williams, p. 822.

29 McCown, p. 155.

30 Morrison, in contrast, argues that neo-orthodoxy's diverted attention to the *Weltanschauung* or world view is an extension of thought in accord with the best liberal tradition. Morrison, " The Liberalism of Neo-Orthodoxy," pp. 760–63.

31 Morrison, p. 699.

32 Cf., e.g., McIntyre, p. 16.

33 ". . . the liberal cannot be blamed for his disquiet at the disproportion, in the newer orthodoxy, between the space given on its pages to the recorded life and words of Jesus and to speculation as to the part played by the eternal Word in the cosmic drama of salvation. He would have supposed that the latter requires initial warrant in the former." Sperry, p. 203.

34 Jacobson, p. 255.

35 McIntyre, p. 30.

36 Sperry, p. 194.

37 See p. 49 above.

38 ". . . in order to sustain the doctrine of the guilt in which all men are steeped through the fall, it is thought necessary to postulate such an alienation of man from God as to veil the nature of God altogether from the eyes of man. For the sinner there can be no natural knowledge of God, there is no normal channel by which the Divine can communicate with us. Hence the mysterious act of grace." Lewis, *Morals and the New*

Theology, p. 108. If man's reason is arbitrarily limited by *hybris*, the dualistic barrier between man and God is complete. Only an act of grace can break through it.

[39] Niebuhr, *Faith and History*, pp. 187–88.

[40] Dewey, " Anti-Naturalism in Extremis," p. 526.

[41] *Ibid.*, p. 528.

[42] Dewey, " Progress," pp. 311–22. Niebuhr has run across a clear statement of Dewey's to this effect. He quotes Dewey as saying " ' All I know about the future of progress, . . . is that it depends upon man to say whether he wants it or not ' " — and blandly uses this as proof that there is a persistent flaw (*hybris*) attached to human nature. " Thus the responsible self (and the guilty self insofar as it always falls short of its highest responsibilities) peeps through even the most intricate and elaborate facades of modern thought," Niebuhr concludes. *Faith and History*, p. 95.

[43] In an entry in his diary during 1920, Niebuhr muses: " I think since I have stopped worrying so much about intellectual problems of religion and have begun to explore some of its ethical problems there is more of a thrill in preaching." Niebuhr, *Cynic,* p. 27.

[44] Niebuhr, *Christian Ethics*, p. 150.

[45] Niebuhr, *Reflections*, p. 221.

[46] ". . . Christian orthodoxy in one moment pessimistically consigns the world of politics to the world of nature unredeemed and unredeemable. In the next moment it sanctifies the institutions which have brought relative order into its chaos, and the relative justice which they have achieved, into ordinances of God. The moral possibilities in political life are gravely imperilled in each instance." *Ibid.*, pp. 217–18.

[47] Niebuhr, *Christian Ethics*, pp. 170–71.

[48] *Ibid.*, p. 182.

[49] *Ibid.*, p. 171. ". . . the plutocracy of America has found the faith of the liberal Church in purely moral suasion a conveniently harmless doctrine just as it appropriated Jeffersonian and *laissez-faire* economic theory for its own purposes, though the theory was first elaborated by agrarian and frontier enemies of big business." *Ibid.*, pp. 171–72.

[50] Niebuhr, *Reflections*, p. 220. Considering this unique definition of the divine ordinance of government, it is possible to say that in a sense Niebuhr is concerned with government — indeed, that he is a political scientist — because of his preoccupation with *hybris*.

[51] Niebuhr, *Moral Man*, p. 175. " Every society needs working principles of justice, as criteria for its positive law and system of restraints. The profoundest of these actually transcend reason and lie rooted in religious conceptions of the meaning of existence. But every historical statement of them is subject to amendment." Niebuhr, *Children of Light*, p. 71.

[52] Niebuhr, *Christian Ethics*, p. 164. Obviously Niebuhr doesn't think he is hostile to a critical use of reason.

[53] *Ibid.*, pp. 204–05.

54 Niebuhr, *Moral Man,* p. 27.
55 *Ibid.,* p. 31.
56 *Ibid.,* p. 28.
57 Niebuhr, *Christian Ethics,* p. 206.
58 *Ibid.,* p. 208.
59 Niebuhr, *Children of Light,* p. 72.
60 Niebuhr, *Christian Ethics,* p. 12.
61 R. M. MacIver has made a notable attempt to eliminate the conflict of free will vs. determinism by insisting that the problem does not exist, since constraint is the opposite of free will and indeterminism the opposite of determinism. MacIver, *Social Causation,* pp. 234–42. Niebuhr considers the two to be opposites; a will that is not free — that is constrained — is determined. "To the degree that men are not free, their actions . . . may be predicted with something of the assurance with which a natural scientist charts the recurrences of nature." Niebuhr, *Faith and History,* p. 55.
62 Niebuhr, *Reflections,* p. 290.
63 Niebuhr, *Christian Ethics,* p. 99.
64 Niebuhr, *Moral Man,* p. 80.
65 Niebuhr, *Christian Ethics,* pp. 82–83.
66 *Ibid.,* p. 166.
67 *Ibid.,* p. 147.
68 Niebuhr, *Moral Man,* p. 59.
69 Niebuhr, *Human Destiny,* p. 254.
70 Niebuhr, *Faith and History,* pp. 189–90.
71 Maritain, *The Rights of Man and Natural Law,* p. 69.
72 "My quarrel with the moral philosophers is that most of them misconceive their task to be the determination of what men *ought* to value instead of the discovery of the conditions under which actually experienced values occur, their compatibility with the conditions for realizing other values, and so on." Ramsberger, p. 156.
73 Niebuhr, *Reflections,* p. 94.
74 Niebuhr, *Faith and History,* pp. 183–84.
75 Niebuhr's "radicalism" has also been softened with passage of time. See also pp. 128–36 below.
76 Randall, p. 149.
77 Meland, p. 46.
78 Williams, p. 822.
79 See pp. 98–100 below.
80 Murphy, p. 112.
81 Lewis, *Morals and the New Theology,* pp. 68–69.
82 *Ibid.,* p. 64.
83 *Ibid.,* p. 67.
84 *Ibid.,* p. 68.
85 *Ibid.,* p. 70.
86 *Ibid.,* p. 72.
87 Sperry, p. 180. "My own misgivings in the matter have been con-

firmed by the reflections of thoughtful friends returning from one or another of the great ecclesiastical gatherings of recent years, who had come away feeling that the transactions had been in occasional danger of a touch of moral unreality in their uncritical appeal to the dogmas of man's worthlessness and helplessness." *Ibid.*, p. 181.

88 Lewis, *Morals and the New Theology*, p. 63.

89 Lewis, *Morals and Revelation*, p. 103.

90 Lewis, *Morals and the New Theology*, p. 25.

91 *Ibid.*, p. 156.

92 Lewis seems to assume that a relative ethic must judge an individual's worth " strictly proportionate to the course of events which his action initiates." *Ibid.*, p. 63. This is an unfortunate mistake. Men may still be judged by ethical standards. It is the standards that are subject to instrumental check — to judgment, if you will — according to results or effects.

93 Geiger, " Dewey's Social and Political Philosophy." p. 351.

94 James Breasted's *The Dawn of Conscience*, a landmark in historical studies, admirably demonstrates the historical development of morals as a form of social control.

95 See pp. 28–30 above.

96 Dewey, *Freedom and Culture*, p. 58. See also his *Reconstruction in Philosophy*, Chap. 4, for a fuller treatment of experience.

97 Niebuhrian science is not dissimilar to Communist science, which exists " under the criticism of " the class struggle.

98 Needless to say, there is as yet little that is truly scientific (as the term is here used) in present-day social action. And if people continue to be persuaded to accept such blighted views of science as Niebuhr perpetuates there is little likelihood of it in the future. The best illustrations of science in social action that I can think of are to be found in Fries, " Scientific Mediation: Tool of Democracy "; and in Follett, *Dynamic Administration*.

99 " The rational use of ideals in the organization and evaluation of conduct is . . . justified in its fruit, which is moral wisdom. If those who deny the authority of reason have meant to say that in this usage it cannot perform what it promises, or that there is some other or better way of judging the worth of conduct than that which it provides, we can show that they are mistaken, because they have failed to understand the good of which human nature is capable, and to which, when it achieves self-knowledge and self-mastery, it is addressed." Murphy, p. 18.

100 When ends are fixed and men find themselves, in their desperate search for means, deviating further and further from the stated goal, they frequently turn to intellectual subterfuge and justification. The outstanding case in point today is Communist Russia.

101 Niebuhr, *Christian Ethics*, p. 192.

102 Cf. Dewey, *Logic: The Theory of Inquiry*, p. 458; see also the whole of Chap. 22.

Chapter Four

POLITICAL STALEMATE

1 Ratner, ed., p. 819.

2 Niebuhr, *Christian Ethics*, pp. 202–03.

3 " Man is the kind of animal who cannot merely live. . . . to his true nature belongs his fulfillment in the lives of others. The will to live is thus transmuted into the will to self-realization; and self-realization involves self-giving in relations to others. . . . Thus the will to live is finally transmuted into its opposite in the sense that only in self-giving can the self be fulfilled." Niebuhr, *Children of Light*, p. 19.

4 Niebuhr, *Moral Man*, p. 2.

5 *Ibid.*, p. 26.

6 Niebuhr, *Children of Light*, p. 66.

7 Niebuhr, *Faith and History*, p. 216.

8 *Ibid.*, p. 217.

9 Niebuhr makes a distinction between nation and state. The state is that through which the nation is organized and its will is articulated. The nation is a territorial society. Frequently a state incorporates several nationalities; this " indicates that the authority of government [the state] is the ultimate force of national cohesion. The fact that state and nation are roughly synonymous proves that, without the sentiment of nationality with its common language and traditions, the authority of government is usually unable to maintain national unity." Niebuhr, *Moral Man*, pp. 83–84. Except for occasional note of this difference, Niebuhr uses the terms interchangeably. Cf. also Niebuhr, *Nation Belong to God or the Devil?*, p. 7.

10 Niebuhr, *Faith and History*, p. 218. See pp. 14–15 above.

11 Niebuhr, *Moral Man*, p. 18.

12 *Ibid.*, pp. 88, 48. " The ' vain imaginations ' of collective man are so plausible from the standpoint of the individual, the mortality of nations is so shrouded in the seeming immortality of their long life, and the pomp and power of the community is so impressive in comparison with the individual's impotence, that the final words of judgment and mercy scarcely penetrate to the heart of nations. They are furthermore involved in a despair which the individual does not know. They have no other life than their life in history, since they lack those organs of self-transcendence which place them within reach of a meaning of existence beyond their physical life. Collective man clings more desperately to this life than the individual because he is not certain of a deeper dimension of meaning." Niebuhr, *Faith and History*, pp. 229–30.

13 Niebuhr, *Moral Man*, page xi.

14 *Ibid.*, p. 172.

15 " Men are clearly not very lovely in the mass. One can maintain confidence in them only by viewing them at close range. . . . The same middle classes which seem so blind to the larger moral problems of soci-

ety have, after all, the most wholesome family life of any group in society." Niebuhr, *Cynic*, p. 95.

16 Over-simple belief that the individual is able to attain purer realizations of meaning than the collective is alleged to have led to the following errors: (1) the optimism of liberalism and the pessimism of Lutheranism, (2) the Catholic and Calvinist attempts to bring the community under an unambiguously righteous will, and (3) the assumption of some sectarian Christians (Levellers, Diggers) that sin could be wholly eliminated from political and economic institutions. Furthermore, the germ of the civil war in Western civilization between Fascism and Communism is found in the conflict between the half-truth of orthodox Christianity (Protestant and Catholic) and the half-truth of sectarianism. Cf. Niebuhr, *Faith and History*, pp. 198–209.

17 On this point Niebuhr's idea has changed. In *Reflections*, he spoke of senility causing death of social organisms (p. 31).

18 Niebuhr, *Faith and History*, pp. 218–19. "If we sought to do full justice to all the various possibilities of decline and causes of decay we would find ourselves merely recapitulating the various types of human sin." Niebuhr, *Human Destiny*, p. 304.

19 Niebuhr, *Faith and History*, p. 219. "It must be admitted, of course, that there are genuinely tragic elements in the human enterprise, simply because nobility and strength, dignity and creative ambition are mixed with this sin [i.e. pride], and frequently make it more destructive. Thus Japan lives in greater ultimate insecurity than China because Japanese patriotism has created a nation of greater unity and force than China, a nation playing for higher stakes, at greater risks and with the certainty of ultimate disaster. In the same way the British Empire could not have been built without the solid achievements of British statecraft, a statecraft which made moral qualities serve political purposes. But the British aristocrats who built the Empire are also sealing its doom by policies which are prompted by some of the same class characteristics which were responsible for their original success." Niebuhr, *Beyond Tragedy*, p. 167.

20 Niebuhr, *Reflections*, pp. 99–100.

21 *Ibid.*, p. 4.

22 Niebuhr, *Children of Light*, p. 48. "Perhaps the real reason that we live such chaotic lives in urban communities is because a city is not a society at all, and moral standards are formed only in societies and through the sense of mutual obligation which neighbors feel for one another ... its people are spiritually isolated even though they are mechanically dependent upon one another." Niebuhr, *Cynic*, p. 116.

23 Niebuhr, *Children of Light*, pp. 82–83.

24 Cf., e.g., remarks about the early workings of the Atomic Energy Commission under Lilienthal in *Educator's Washington Dispatch*.

25 Raven, p. 353.

26 "By forming our view of the morality of human conduct, not on the basis of such loyalty to the agent's own ideal as our experience war-

rants us to attribute to men, but in terms of their conformity collectively, in substance as well as intention, to the pattern of an ideal society or of the Kingdom of God, we exaggerate the extent of sinful action. Thereby we set in the path of progress obstacles of our own making, we obtrude into a situation already sufficiently complicated and fraught with dangers, complications that have no foundation outside our own misconceptions and heated imagination. The most immediate result is a substantial reduction of our estimate of the progress and reform which is possible for society." Lewis, *Morals and the New Theology*, p. 133.

27 See pp. 111–12 below.

28 For an example of dying to self he cites the replacement of absolute monarchy by constitutional monarchy. "But," as *Time* points out, "he significantly fails to mention any example of 'dying to self' on the part of a great nation." *Time*, "Niebuhr on History," p. 69.

29 For a much more adequate statement of creative bargaining see Otto, "Creative Bargaining," pp. 263–69, and "Professional Philosophy and the Public," pp. 159–67. See also Otto, *The Human Enterprise*, Chap. 5, and *Things and Ideals*, Chap. 5, although the phrase "creative bargaining" does not occur in those chapters.

30 Follett, *Dynamic Administration*, p. 32. See also Follett, *Creative Experience*, especially Chap. 9, for other illustrations. Follett uses the term "integration" to mean very nearly the same thing as creative bargaining.

31 See Brownell, *The Human Community*, and Poston, *Small Town Renaissance*.

32 There is no a priori reason why eventually collective testing and developing of new hypotheses cannot be carried on at the national and even the international levels.

33 Niebuhr, *Faith and History*, p. 84.

34 The plea for "objectivity" furthermore is a cry from the heavens. It assumes, firstly, that there is some absolute standard by which judgments can be judged for "objectivity." Secondly it assumes that there is a separate individual who can sit aside to look at his society.

35 "The contrast between self-interest (non-moral) and self-sacrifice (moral) is radically misleading. For . . . a moral community is also a natural community, and the *content* of its purpose will be precisely the satisfaction of identifiable human interests, at the level at which such interests are capable of joint satisfaction on terms of mutual understanding and good will. A morality of self-sacrifice that cannot be justified by reference to such a harmony of interests is not something nobler than the ideals of liberal democracy. It is either a superstitious and anti-human reverence for needless and wasteful suffering, or a fraudulent false front for special groups which seek to advance their own interests at the expense of those who are gullible enough to be imposed on by their claims." Murphy, pp. 131–32.

36 Unfortunately, this attempt to explain Niebuhr's organic society is predestined to fail. "The organic character of the individual's relation

to society can be comprehended and illumined by an adequate mythology but hardly by rationalism; for reason mechanizes human relations." Niebuhr, *Reflections*, p. 93.

37 " Modern industry, particularly American industry, is not Christian. The economic forces which move it are hardly qualified at a single point by really ethical considerations." Niebuhr, *Cynic*, p. 197.

38 " When men find that they do not know how to *control* events so as to achieve their aims, they try to *compel* events to comply with their demands." Fries, " Scientific Mediation: Tool of Democracy," p. 390.

39 Niebuhr, *Reflections*, p. 4.

40 Niebuhr, *Moral Man*, p. 31.

41 Niebuhr, *Human Destiny*, p. 262.

42 " The insecurity of the French after the world war, and their desperate effort to gain security by emasculating Germany, had as its consequence the creation of a new Germany, not strong in resources but strong for a moment in the desperation of its resentments and the hysteria of its vindictive passions." Niebuhr, *Europe's Catastrophe*, pp. 20–21.

43 Niebuhr, *Moral Man*, p. 42.

44 An excellent example of this phenomenon today might be the desperate struggle of the AMA. Niebuhr might analyze it thus: If the AMA can be altruistic enough to avoid a last-ditch stand (with the aid of grace) it may gain new life; if not it will, by its fanatic resistance, dig for itself a grave of socialized medicine, instead of assuming the halfway burden of medical insurance.

45 Niebuhr, *Nation Belong to God or the Devil?*, p. 14.

46 *Ibid.*, p. 9.

47 Niebuhr, " The Illusion of World Government," p. 380.

48 Niebuhr, *Nation Belong to God or the Devil?*, p. 32.

49 *Ibid.*, p. 8.

50 *Ibid.*, p. 35.

51 Niebuhr, *Europe's Catastrophe*, pp. 24–25.

52 This is, incidentally, one of Niebuhr's criticisms of American liberalism. According to him, it is batting ideals around profusely and uncritically, and thus proves very useful to the privileged class.

53 Niebuhr, *Moral Man*, pp. 117–18.

54 Niebuhr, *Christian Ethics*, p. 73. This statement is clearly excessive, as Niebuhr undoubtedly recognizes on second thought: wars have been started for the purpose of uniting the home front.

55 *Ibid.*, p. 94.

56 Niebuhr, *Human Destiny*, p. 258.

57 ". . . political morality must be morally ambiguous because it cannot merely reject, but must also deflect, beguile, harness and use self-interest for the sake of a tolerable harmony of the whole." Niebuhr, *Children of Light*, p. 73.

58 Niebuhr, *Human Destiny*, p. 266.

59 *Ibid.*, p. 267.

60 Illinois *ex rel.* McCollum *v.* Board of Education.

[61] Niebuhr, " Our Relations to Catholicism," pp. 6–7.

[62] *Ibid.*, p. 6.

[63] Speech given by Agnes E. Meyer in 1947.

[64] Niebuhr, " Our Relations to Catholicism," p. 6. See also the 1948 " Statement on Church and State," signed by 27 Protestant leaders including Reinhold Niebuhr. Niebuhr suggests resolving the school-aid question by granting federal scholarships to individuals, not to schools. Would this apportion support " equitably " to all religious groups? See Niebuhr, " The Rising Catholic-Protestant Tension," p. 108.

[65] Cf., e.g., Butts, *The American Tradition in Religion and Education.* A part of the difficulty encountered in trying to understand the original meaning of the First Amendment revolves around the changed (restricted) meaning of the word " establishment."

[66] Niebuhr, " A Protestant Looks at Catholics," pp. 119–20.

[67] Niebuhr, " Catholics and Politics: Some Misconceptions," p. 10.

[68] *Ibid.*, p. 11.

[69] Niebuhr, " Our Relations to Catholicism," p. 6.

[70] Cf. Niebuhr, " Catholics and Politics."

[71] For one statement of Catholic pluralism, see Maritain, *The Rights of Man and Natural Law.*

[72] Niebuhr, " Catholics and Politics," p. 9.

[73] *Ibid.*, p. 11.

[74] Fitch, " The Catholic Church as a Power Polity," pp. 6–7.

[75] Niebuhr, " Catholicism and Politics," p. 10.

[76] Cf. Meyer, " The School, the State, and the Church."

Chapter Five
DEMOCRACY AND THE WORLD

[1] See pp. 108–10 above.

[2] " When ' individual ' or ' society ' is looked upon as something in itself and factitiously separate; when the two are urged to cooperate or to remain opposed; when it is graciously admitted that ' in reality ' their interests are mutual — then we are in truth in the land of dialectic. We are using general ideas to solve particular problems. And that, for Dewey, is the mortal sin." Geiger, " Dewey's Social and Political Philosophy," p. 346.

[3] " Mere general ideas can be argued for and against without the necessity of recourse to observation. The arguments are saved from being a mere matter of words only because there are certain emotional attitudes involved. When general ideas are not capable of being continuously checked and revised by observation of what actually takes place, they are, as a mere truism, in the field of opinion." Dewey, *Freedom and Culture*, p. 116.

[4] Niebuhr, *Moral Man*, p. 15.

[5] Niebuhr, *Christian Ethics*, pp. 131–32.

[6] Niebuhr, *Moral Man*, p. 226.

7 Niebuhr, *Moral Man*, p. 194.

8 Marxist theory of history with its belief in determinism *and* indeterminism is not unlike Niebuhr's Christian idea. " Lenin's insistence that the objective forces of history must be consciously directed toward a revolutionary goal by a revolutionary class seeks to preserve a proper ' dialectic ' balance between ' religious ' determinism and the voluntarism of an adequate moral theory." Niebuhr, *Reflections*, p. 131. Niebuhr's later Christian position between the Renaissance and the Reformation, between Christian orthodoxy and Christian liberalism — his new synthesis for the paradox of grace — very likely developed from his appreciation of the Marxian " dialectic " position. " Neither [Christian orthodoxy nor liberal Christianity] is in any sense morally preferable to a possible compromise between the Marxian and the pure Christian mythology." *Ibid.*, pp. 134–35.

9 Niebuhr, *Moral Man*, p. 213.

10 It is interesting to note here that Niebuhr made the reservation that " another war might completely change the picture." *Ibid.*, p. 219.

11 *Ibid.*, p. 221.

12 *Ibid.*, p. 222.

13 *Ibid.*, pp. 209–10.

14 *Ibid.*, p. 213.

15 " The powerful man . . . is under the temptation of using his power for selfish rather than social ends. There is therefore no reason to suppose that the substitution of non-physical for physical, and nonviolent for violent, forms of coercion will make a permanent contribution to the problem of power, though any intelligent society will seek to increase non-violent forms of social pressure and discourage violence." Niebuhr, *Nation Belong to God or the Devil?*, pp. 39–40.

16 Niebuhr, *Moral Man*, p. 235.

17 *Ibid.*, p. 173.

18 *Ibid.*, p. 172.

19 Niebuhr, *Christian Ethics*, p. 189.

20 *Ibid.*, p. 192.

21 *Ibid.*, p. 190.

22 Niebuhr, *Children of Light*, p. 91.

23 Niebuhr, *Faith and History*, p. 191.

24 Niebuhr, *Children of Light*, p. 76.

25 *Ibid.*, p. 117.

26 *Ibid.*, p. 89.

27 Davies, p. 43.

28 Niebuhr, *Faith and History*, p. 226.

29 Niebuhr, *Children of Light*, p. 64.

30 " If you want love and cooperation in any kind of society, and most of all in the family, it is necessary to sacrifice some freedom for its sake. What strange fanatics these moderns are! Imagining themselves dispassionate in their evaluation of all values, they are really bigoted protag-

onists of the one value of freedom. Every other value must be subordinated to it." Niebuhr, *Cynic*, p. 151.

[31] Niebuhr, *Children of Light*, p. 64.

[32] *Ibid.*, p. 3.

[33] *Ibid.*, p. 78.

[34] Niebuhr, *Power Politics*, p. 11.

[35] Niebuhr, *Children of Light*, p. 183.

[36] Niebuhr, *Human Destiny*, p. 249.

[37] *Ibid.*, p. 268.

[38] *Ibid.*, p. 269.

[39] *Ibid.*, pp. 267–69.

[40] Niebuhr, *Reflections*, p. 79.

[41] Niebuhr, *Christian Ethics*, p. 190.

[42] *Ibid.*, p. 231. This is substantially identical with the Catholic explanation of anthropocentric humanism as expressed by Maritain. See " Christian Humanism," pp. 106–07. See also Maritain, *Principes d'une Politique Humaniste*, Chap. 1, especially pp. 27–33.

[43] Niebuhr, *Nation Belong to God or the Devil?*, pp. 35, 36.

[44] Niebuhr, *Power Politics*, p. 57.

[45] Niebuhr, *Human Destiny*, p. 318.

[46] Niebuhr, *Reflections*, pp. 59–60.

[47] Cf. Maritain, *Education at the Crossroads*, pp. 10–12.

[48] Dewey, *Freedom and Culture*, pp. 24–25.

[49] Incidentally, Niebuhr's choice of freedom of individuality over freedom of rationality derives from as far back as his construction of human nature.

[50] Cf. John Dewey's article, " Authority and the Individual," in Ratner (ed.), *Intelligence in the Modern World*, pp. 343–63.

[51] Waddington, p. 112.

[52] Niebuhr, *Human Destiny*, p. 213.

[53] *Ibid.*, p. 217.

[54] *Ibid.*, p. 219.

[55] *Ibid.*, p. 243.

[56] Niebuhr, *Cynic*, p. 127.

[57] " [Niebuhr] realizes the pitfalls of claiming finality for one's view; he depreciates any attempt to bolster one's views in a final manner even upon Scriptural authority. One wonders what to think of a man who seems to realize the mistakes of all manner of absolutisms and then leaps in the precise direction in which he has seen great danger." Jacobson, pp. 257–58.

[58] Dewey, *Reconstruction in Philosophy*, p. 176. Cf. also Otto, " Intolerance," pp. 242–45.

[59] Niebuhr, *Children of Light*, pages x–xi.

[60] " The man who cannot find the freedom and happiness of his fellow citizens, as well as his own, worth defending without a supernatural validation of their claim to respect must take a very low view of human nature.

And if he cannot love his neighbor whom he has seen, without such extrinsic sanction for it, how shall he love a cosmic spiritual power which he has not seen?" Murphy, p. 176.

61 Niebuhr, *Faith and History,* p. 160. "The social harmony of which Marxism dreams would eliminate the destructive power of human freedom; but it would also destroy the creative possibilities of human life." Niebuhr, *Children of Light,* p. 60.

62 Niebuhr, *Faith and History,* p. 162.

63 *Loc. cit.*

64 *Ibid.,* p. 161.

65 *Ibid.,* p. 160.

66 Niebuhr, *Children of Light,* p. 189.

67 "The common destiny of mankind need not be always as insecure as our present state. War will not last forever. But we will be the more able to bear the present insecurities if we recognize that there is always an element of moral ambiguity in historic responsibilities, a hazard in all historic ventures, and no certain promise of success for any of our hopes. Our survival as a civilization depends on our ability to do what seems to us right from day to day without the distractions of alternate moments of illusion and despair." Niebuhr, "The Conditions of Our Survival," p. 491.

68 See pp. 122–23 above.

69 Murphy, p. 238. "We must not ask the impossible, but if we cease to ask the possible which is not yet actual, when it is also the humanly excellent, we shall have run counter to at least one inherent, and very valuable, tendency in human nature, the tendency to use ideals as guides for action." *Ibid.,* pp. 237–38.

70 Niebuhr, *Faith and History,* p. 220.

71 *Ibid.,* p. 230.

72 ". . . what is the faith of democracy in the rôle of consultation, of conference, of persuasion, of discussion, in formation of public opinion, which in the long run is self-corrective, except faith in the capacity of the intelligence of the common man to respond with common sense to the free play of facts and ideas which are secured by effective guarantees of free inquiry, free assembly, and free communication? I am willing to leave to upholders of totalitarian states of the right and the left the view that faith in the capacities of intelligence is utopian. For the faith is so deeply imbedded in the methods which are intrinsic to democracy that when a professed democrat denies the faith he convicts himself of treachery to his profession." Dewey, "Creative Democracy — The Task Before Us," p. 224.

73 See p. 130 above.

74 Niebuhr, *Moral Man,* p. 48.

75 *Ibid.,* p. 110.

76 Niebuhr, *Reflections,* p. 181.

77 Niebuhr, *Signs of the Times,* p. 40.

78 Niebuhr, *Children of Light,* p. 160.

[79] Niebuhr, "The Illusion of World Government," p. 386.

[80] Niebuhr, *Children of Light*, p. 166.

[81] Niebuhr, *Destiny of Man*, p. 316.

[82] Niebuhr, *Children of Light*, p. 168.

[83] *Loc. cit.*

[84] *Ibid.*, p. 183.

[85] *Ibid.*, p. 185.

[86] Niebuhr, "The Illusion of World Government," p. 388.

[87] In 1928 Niebuhr perceived a possibility of co-ordinating the values of the East (religion) and the West (science). "The western man must bring his energy under moral control. The eastern man must learn the moral value of energy." Niebuhr, "The Confession of a Tired Radical," p. 1047. "Let the East learn to live in time and the West to view its temporalities with indifference." Niebuhr, *Does Civilization Need Religion?* (New York: Macmillan, 1927), p. 186. "The greatest hope lies in the missionary enterprise, which through its very effort toward the universalization of the Christian faith has a tendency to strip it of its Occidental accretions, so that it may become intrinsically worthy of its world expansion." *Ibid.*, p. 187.

[88] Niebuhr, "American Liberals and British Labor," p. 682.

[89] Niebuhr, "The Fight for Germany," pp. 65–68.

[90] Niebuhr, "Hazards and Resources," pp. 194–204.

[91] Niebuhr, "The Illusion of World Government," p. 382.

[92] *Ibid.*, p. 383.

[93] Niebuhr, *Children of Light*, p. 187.

[94] Meland, p. 1.

[95] Niebuhr, *Faith and History*, p. 223.

[96] Niebuhr, *Children of Light*, p. 168.

[97] Niebuhr, *Faith and History*, p. 98.

[98] See p. 156 above.

[99] Niebuhr, "The Conditions of Our Survival," p. 490.

[100] *Ibid.*, p. 483.

[101] Niebuhr, "American Conservatism and the World Crisis," pp. 385–99.

[102] Niebuhr, "The Pope's Domesticated God," p. 75.

[103] Niebuhr, "The Conditions of Our Survival," p. 488.

[104] *Ibid.*, p. 491.

[105] Niebuhr, *Children of Light*, p. 118. Italics added.

Chapter Six
THE COURSE OF A FAITH IN SIN

[1] See pp. 139–140 above.

[2] "Niebuhr would frighten men out of their mistaken belief in omnipotence by a fairy tale about a creature that is absolutely omnipotent. The humility it induces is one of fear, not the humility which is fostered by knowledge of human limitations and ignorance. His wisdom does not

carry further than the caution that no claim is completely justified, but he is helpless before the problem of determining the degree and extent of its justification, so necessary in order to get on with the problems in hand." Hook, "The New Failure of Nerve," pp. 15–16.

3 Sperry, pp. 12–13.

4 Hook, "The New Failure of Nerve," p. 13; and Randall, pp. 149, 164.

Chapter Seven
Epilogue: The Irony of Sin

1 Niebuhr, *The Irony of American History*. The body of the book is taken from lectures given in May, 1949, and January, 1951.

2 *Ibid.*, page vii.

3 *Ibid.*, page vii.

4 *Ibid.*, pages vii–viii.

5 *Ibid.*, p. 155.

6 *Ibid.*, pp. 166–67.

7 *Ibid.*, page viii.

8 *Ibid.*, page viii.

9 *Ibid.*, p. 155.

10 *Ibid.*, p. 156.

11 *Ibid.*, p. 153.

12 *Ibid.*, p. 88.

13 *Ibid.*, p. 113.

14 *Ibid.*, p. 45.

15 *Ibid.*, p. 63.   Italics added.

16 *Ibid.*, p. 133.

17 *Ibid.*, p. 2.

18 Here is an illustration of Niebuhr's deceptive and premature idea of proof: "The inadequacy of both [the idealistic and realistic] types of escape from our moral dilemma proves that there is no purely moral solution for the ultimate moral issues of life." *Ibid.*, p. 40.

19 *Ibid.*, p. 45.

20 *Ibid.*, p. 89.

21 We can assume, I suppose, that ironic triumph and ironic success are the obverse of some ironic failure, though they seem to add more confusion than clarity to the historical category.

22 *Ibid.*, p. 106.

23 The category of the ironic fits closer to the facts in the U.S.S.R., where what action there is on the common-sense level is constantly interfered with and redirected by deliberate and violent insistence on conformity to ideology.

24 *Ibid.*, p. 37.

25 *Ibid.*, p. 137.

26 *Ibid.*, pp. 136–37.

27 *Ibid.*, p. 76.

28 *Ibid.*, p. 80.

[29] *Ibid.,* p. 85. Incidentally, " the irony of the contrast between the careful study of human ' aggressiveness ' in our socio-psychological sciences, and our encounter with a form of aggressiveness in actual life which is informed by such manias, illusions, historic aberrations and confusions, as could not possibly come under the microscope of the scientific procedures used in some of these studies " (*ibid.,* p. 60), if interpreted according to Niebuhr's category, would make the first part of the contrast or its pretensions the source of the second. Thus analysis of Niebuhr's own ironies by means of his own category would lead us to conclude that pseudo-scientific studies (meaning, for Niebuhr, Dewey) were the source of fascism. The absurdity of such a conclusion only points to the unreliability of the category of the ironic for purposes of historical interpretation.

[30] *Ibid.,* p. 86.

[31] *Ibid.,* p. 60.

[32] *Ibid.,* p. 171.

POSTSCRIPT
NOTES ON CONSERVATIVE TENDENCIES

[1] See Kirk, p. 100. Cf. also Freund, pp. 2–3 and Herberg, p. 29. Other prominent figures in the new conservatism are Peter Viereck, Francis Wilson, Clinton Rossiter.

[2] Kirk, p. 99.

[3] See Niebuhr, *Christian Realism,* Chap. 5, " The Foreign Policy of American Conservatism and Liberalism."

[4] Niebuhr, " The Anomaly of European Socialism," (Reprinted as Chap. 4 in Niebuhr, *Christian Realism.*) Also Niebuhr, " The Fate of European Socialism."

[5] Niebuhr, " Reply to Interpretation and Criticism," in Kegley and Bretall, p. 434.

[6] *Loc. cit.*

[7] Niebuhr, *Christian Realism,* p. 55.

[8] *Ibid.,* p. 56.

[9] See above pp. 9, 160.

[10] For example, Niebuhr says that " the panacea of the socialization of property [in post war Britain] proved inadequate in overcoming the collective poverty of a war-impoverished nation and . . . proved to be unnecessary in view of the measures of justice which had been accomplished without socialization." Niebuhr, *Self,* p. 179. This sounds like a political candidate grandly disposing of the opposition. Does Niebuhr realize the degree to which the reversal of the program of nationalization, especially the nationalization of land under the Town and Country Planning Act of 1947, was due, irrespective of necessity, to the lack of democratic techniques for making tolerable the administration of such expanded govern-

mental activity? Cf. Orlans, pp. 192–95. The problem in this area may be to find more democratic administrative techniques so that governmental activity can, when necessary, be extended without becoming coercive.

For other illustrations of the frailty of Niebuhr's political judgments see Arthur Schlesinger, Jr., " Reinhold Niebuhr's Role in American Thought and Life," in Kegley and Bretall, eds., pp. 126–50 and Kenneth Thompson, "The Political Philosophy of Reinhold Niebuhr," in Kegley & Bretall, eds., pp. 152–75.

11 Niebuhr, *Self,* p. 159.

12 Curiously, some of Niebuhr's disciples deny his irrationalism on the ground that he makes use of reason, i.e., that he thinks. Cf. e.g., Miller, p. 14.

13 Niebuhr, *Self,* p. 203.

14 *Ibid.,* p. 212.

15 *Ibid.,* p. 182.

16 *Loc. cit.*

17 *Ibid.,* p. 184.

18 Niebuhr, *Christian Realism,* Chap. 5; Niebuhr, *Self,* pp. 179–82; Niebuhr, " Winston Churchill and Great Britain."

19 Kegley and Bretall, eds., p. 174. Cf. Niebuhr, " The Sources of American Prestige," p. 8.

20 Niebuhr, *Self,* pp. 162, 182. As corrective to this misreading of the implications of science see George Simpson, *Science as Morality.*

21 See above pp. 81–84, 102.

Selected Bibliography

A. BOOKS BY REINHOLD NIEBUHR

Most of the short titles used in the Notes may be easily identified from the alphabetical list given here. The following short titles are out of alphabetical order:

Power Politics	*Christianity and Power Politics*
Social Work	*The Contribution of Religion to Social Work*
Signs of the Times	*Discerning the Signs of the Times*
Nation Belong to God or to the Devil?	*Do the State and Nation Belong to God or the Devil?*
Christian Ethics	*An Interpretation of Christian Ethics*
Cynic	*Leaves from the Notebook of a Tamed Cynic*

Beyond Tragedy: Essays on the Christian Interpretation of History. New York: Charles Scribner's Sons, 1937.

The Children of Light and the Children of Darkness: A Vindication of Democracy and a Critique of its Traditional Defense. New York: Charles Scribner's Sons, 1944.

Christian Realism and Political Problems. New York: Charles Scribner's Sons, 1953.

Christianity and Power Politics. New York: Charles Scribner's Sons, 1940.

The Contribution of Religion to Social Work. (Forbes Lectures, 1930.) New York: Columbia University Press, 1932.

Discerning the Signs of the Times: Sermons for Today and Tomorrow. New York: Charles Scribner's Sons, 1946.

Does Civilization Need Religion? A Study in the Social Resources and Limitations of Religion in Modern Life. New York: The Macmillan Company, 1927.

Do the State and Nation Belong to God or the Devil? (Burge Memorial Lecture.) London: Student Christian Movement Press, 1937.

Europe's Catastrophe and the Christian Faith. London: Nisbet, 1940.

Faith and History: A Comparison of Christian and Modern Views of History. New York: Charles Scribner's Sons, 1949.

Human Destiny. (Volume II of *The Nature and Destiny of Man: A Christian Interpretation.*) New York: Charles Scribner's Sons, 1943.

Human Nature. (Volume I of *The Nature and Destiny of Man.*) New York: Charles Scribner's Sons, 1941.

An Interpretation of Christian Ethics. New York: Harper & Brothers, 1935.

The Irony of American History. New York: Charles Scribner's Sons, 1952.

Jews After the War. (Reprinted from *The Nation,* etc.) United Jewish
  Federation of Great Britain, 1943.
Leaves from the Notebook of a Tamed Cynic. Chicago: Willett, Clark &
  Colby, 1929.
Moral Man and Immoral Society: A Study in Ethics and Politics. New
  York: Charles Scribner's Sons, 1932.
The Protestant Opposition Movement in Germany, 1934–37. London:
  Friends of Europe, 1937.
Reflections on the End of an Era. New York: Charles Scribner's Sons,
  1934.
The Self and the Dramas of History. New York: Charles Scribner's Sons,
  1955.
Why the Christian Church Is Not Pacifist. London: Student Christian
  Movement Press, 1940.

B. Articles by Reinhold Niebuhr

" After Capitalism — What? " *The World Tomorrow,* XVI (1933) , 203–05.
" Alternatives to the H-Bomb," *The New Leader,* XXXVII (August 2,
  1954) , 12–14.
" America and the War in China," *Christian Century,* LIV (1937) , 1195–96.
" American Attitudes On World Organization; Comment," *Public Opinion
  Quarterly,* XVII (1953) , 435–38.
" American Conservatism and the World Crisis: A Study in Vacillation,"
  Yale Review, XL (1951) , 385–99.
" American Liberals and British Labor," *The Nation,* CLXII (1946) ,
  682–84.
" American Pride and Power," *American Scholar,* XVII (1948) , 393–94.
" The American Scene," *Spectator,* CLXXVIII (1947) , 198.
" American Trends," *Spectator,* CLXXI (1943) , 573.
" America's Precarious Eminence," *Virginia Quarterly Review,* XXII
  (1947) , 481–90.
" Anatomy of Power," *The Nation,* CXLVII (1938) , 326–27.
" Anglo-Saxon Tensions," *Spectator,* CLXXIV (1945) , 142–43.
" The Anomaly of European Socialism," *Yale Review,* XLII (1952) , 161–67.
" An Answer to Karl Barth," *Christian Century,* LXVI (1949) , 234–36.
" The Atomic Issue," *Christianity and Crisis,* V (October 15, 1945) , 5–7.
" Awkward Imperialists," *The Atlantic Monthly,* CXLV (1930) , 670–75.
" Barth — Apostle of the Absolute," *Christian Century,* XLV (1928) , 1523–
  24.
" The Basis of World Order," *The Nation,* CLIX (1944) , 489.
" Beauty as a Substitute for Righteousness," *Christian Century,* XLIV
  (1927) , 1133–34.
" Britain Bewildered," *Christian Century,* LIII (1936) , 1081–82.
" The British Conscience," *The Nation,* CXLIX (1939) , 219–21.

" Can Schweitzer Save Us from Russell? " *Christian Century,* XLII (1925), 1093–95.

" Capitalism — A Protestant Offspring," *Christian Century,* XLII (1925), 600–01.

" The Case for Coexistence," *The New Leader,* XXXVII (October 4, 1954), 5–6.

" Catastrophe or Social Control? " *Harper's Magazine,* CLXV (1932), 114–18.

" The Catholic Heresy," *Christian Century,* LIV (1937), 1524–25.

" The Catholic Hierarchy's Analysis of the Ills of Our Day," *Christianity and Crisis,* XIV (1954), 171–73.

" Catholics and Politics: Some Misconceptions," *The Reporter,* VI (January 22, 1952), 9–11.

" Christian Faith and Social Action," in *Christian Faith and Social Action,* ed. John Hutchinson (New York: Charles Scribner's Sons, 1953).

" The Christian Faith and the World Crisis," *Christianity and Crisis,* I (February 10, 1941), 4–6.

" A Christian Philosophy of Compromise," *Christian Century,* L (1933), 746–48, 950–51, 1006–08.

" Christianity and Communism: Social Justice," *Spectator,* CLVII (1936), 802–03.

" Christianity and Contemporary Politics," *Christian Century,* XLI (1924), 498–501.

" Christianity and the Moral Law," *Christian Century,* LXX (1953), 1386–88.

" Christian Witness in a Secular Age," *Christian Century,* LXX (1953), 840–43, 1051–52.

" Christ vs. Socrates," *The Saturday Review,* XXXVII (December 18, 1954), 7–8, 37–39.

" The Church and Political Action," *Christian Century,* LI (1934), 992–94.

" The Church and the Industrial Crisis," *Biblical World,* LIV (1920), 588–92.

" The Churches and Society," *New Statesman and Nation,* XXXVI (1948), 232–33.

" The Churches in Germany," *American Scholar,* III (1934), 344–51.

" Clericalism in Europe," *The New Leader,* XXXIX (January 2, 1956), 17–18.

" Coherence, Incoherence, and Christian Faith," *Journal of Religion,* XXXI (1951), 155–68.

" Communism and the Clergy," *Christian Century,* LXX (1953), 936–37.

" The Conditions of Our Survival," *Virginia Quarterly Review,* XXVI (1950), 481–91.

" The Confession of a Tired Radical," *Christian Century,* XLV (1928), 1046–47.

" Coronation Afterthoughts," *Christian Century,* LXX (1953), 771–72.

" Democracy and the Party Spirit," *The New Leader*, XXXVII (March 15, 1954), 3–5.

" Democracy as a Religion," *Christianity and Crisis*, VII (August 4, 1947), 1–2. (Initialed editorial.)

" Democracy, Secularism, and Christianity," *Christianity and Crisis*, XIII (1953), 19–20 *et seq.*

" Does Religion Quiet or Disquiet?" *The World Tomorrow*, IX (1926), 220–21.

" Dr. William Temple and His Britain," *The Nation*, CLIX (1944), 584–86.

" Economic Perils to World Peace," *The World Tomorrow*, XIV (1931), 154–56.

" An End to Illusions," *The Nation*, CL (1940), 778–79.

" England Teaches Its Soldiers," *The Nation*, CLVII (1943), 208–10.

" English Church: An American View," *Spectator*, CLVII (1936), 373–74.

" European Impressions," *Christianity and Crisis*, VII (May 12, 1947), 2–4.

" European Reform and American Reform — How They Differ," *Christian Century*, XLI (1924), 1108–10.

" Europe, Russia and America," *The Nation*, CLXIII (1946), 288–89.

" Factors of Cohesion," *Spectator*, CLXX (1943), 562–63.

" Failure of German-Americanism," *The Atlantic Monthly*, CXVIII (1916), 13–18.

" A Faith to Live By," *The Nation*, CLXIV (1947), 205–09.

" The Fate of European Socialism," *The New Leader*, XXXVIII (June 20, 1955), 6–8.

" The Federation of Western Europe," *Christianity and Crisis*, VIII (1948), 17–18. (Initialed editorial.)

" The Fight for Germany," *Life*, XXI (October 21, 1946), 65–68, 70, 72.

" Fighting Chance for a Sick Society," *The Nation*, CLII (1941), 357–60.

" The Forms of Liberalism," *The Nation*, CLXI (1945), 553–56. (Review of *The Liberal Tradition* by William A. Orton.)

" A Fourth Term for Roosevelt," *New Statesman and Nation*, XXV (1943), 315–16.

" German Church Girds for Battle," *Christian Century*, LIII (1936), 1129–30.

" The German Klan," *Christian Century*, XLI (1924), 1330–31.

" The German Problem," *Christianity and Crisis*, III (January 10, 1944), 2–4.

" Germans and Nazis," *Spectator*, CLXIII (1939), 401–02.

" Germans: Unhappy Philosophers in Politics," *American Scholar*, II (1933), 409–19.

" Germany and Modern Civilization," *The Atlantic Monthly*, CXXXV (1925), 843–48.

" God Wills Both Justice and Peace," *Christianity and Crisis*, XV (1955), 75–78. (Angus Dun co-author.)

" The Godly and the Godless," *Christianity and Crisis*, VIII (1948), 161–62. (Initialed editorial.)

" Great Britain's Post-War Role," *The Nation*, CLVII (1943), 39–40.

" Greek Tragedy and Modern Politics," *The Nation*, CXLVI (1938), 12–16.

" Halfway to What? " *The Nation*, CLXX (1950), 26–28.

" Hazards and Resources," *Virginia Quarterly Review*, XXV (1949), 194–204.

" The Heresy Trials," *Christianity and Crisis*, XV (1955), 171–72.

" Heroes and Hero Worship," *The Nation*, CXII (1921), 293–94.

" Hitler and Buchman," *Christian Century*, LIII (1936), 1315–16.

" Hope Needs Faith and Love," *Ecumenical Review*, V (1953), 358–63.

" How Philanthropic Is Henry Ford? " *Christian Century*, XLIII (1926), 1516–17.

" Human Nature and Social Change," *Christian Century*, L (1933), 363–64.

" Idealists as Cynics," *The Nation*, CL (1940), 72–74.

" Ideology and Pretense," *The Nation*, CXLIX (1939), 645–46.

" If America Enters the War," *Christian Century*, LVII (1940), 1578–80.

" The Illusion of World Government," *Foreign Affairs*, XXVII (1949), 379–88.

" The Impact of Protestantism Today," *The Atlantic Monthly*, CLXXXI (February, 1948), 57–62.

" Is History Predictable? " *The Atlantic Monthly*, CXCIV (July 1954), 69–72.

" Is Protestantism Self-Deceived? " *Christian Century*, XLI (1924), 1661–62.

" Is Social Conflict Inevitable? " *Scribner's Magazine*, XCVIII (1935), 166–69.

" Is There a Revival of Religion? " *New York Times Magazine*, November 19, 1950, pp. 13, 60–63.

" Is This ' Peace in Our Time '? " *The Nation*, CLX (1945), 382–84.

" Japan and the Christian Conscience," *Christian Century*, LIV (1937), 1390–91.

" Jerome Frank's Way Out," *The Nation*, CXLVII (1938), 45–46.

" Job's Problem and St. Paul's," *Christian Century*, LX (1943), 1298–1300.

" Labor Coalition in Holland," *The Nation*, CLXIV (1947), 447–48.

" Leaves from the Notebook of a War-Bound American," *Christian Century*, LVI (1939), 1298–99, 1405–06, 1502–03, 1607–08.

" A Lecture to Liberals," *The Nation*, CLXI (1945), 491–93.

" Liberalism: Illusions and Realities," *The New Republic*, CXXXIII (July 4, 1955), 11–13.

" Limitations of the Scientific Method: An Answer to Pierre Auger." *Bulletin of the Atomic Scientists*, XI (1955), 87.

" The Limits of Military Power," *The New Leader*, XXXVIII (May 30, 1955), 16–17.

" The Long Cold War," *The Nation*, CLXXI (1950), 268–69. (Review of *Truman, Stalin and Peace* by Albert Z. Carr.)

" Making Peace with Russia," *The World Tomorrow*, XIV (1931), 354–55.

" Making Radicalism Effective," *The World Tomorrow*, XVI (1933), 682–84.

" Man's Disorder and God's Design," in *The Report of the Second World*

Conference of Christian Youth, ed. Paul G. Macy (Oslo, 1947), pp. 176–87.

" Marxism in Eclipse," *Spectator*, CLXX (1943), 518–19.

" Mechanical Men in a Mechanical Age," *The World Tomorrow*, XIII (1930), 492–95.

" Missions and World Peace," *The World Tomorrow*, X (1927), 170–71.

" Modern Utopians," *Scribner's Magazine*, C (September, 1936), 142–45.

" Moralistic Preaching," *Christian Century*, LIII (1936), 985–87.

" More on Kinsey," *Christianity and Crisis*, XIII (1954), 182–83.

" The Myth of World Government," *The Nation*, CLXII (1946), 312–14.

" The Nation's Crime Against the Individual," *The Atlantic Monthly*, CXVIII (1916), 609–14.

" A New Strategy for Socialists," *The World Tomorrow*, XVI (1933), 490–92.

" A New View of Palestine," *Spectator*, CLXXVII (1946), 162–63.

" Nobody Predicted Today," *The New Leader*, XXXVIII (January 3, 1955), 9–10.

" The North Atlantic Pact," *Christianity and Crisis*, IX (1949), 65–66. (Initialed editorial.)

" One World or None," *Christianity and Crisis*, VIII (1948), 9–10. (Initialed editorial.)

" The Opposition in Germany," *The New Republic*, LXXV (1933), 169–71.

" Oriental v. Occidental Strategy of Life," *The World Tomorrow*, XI (1928), 21–23.

" Our Country and Our Culture," *Partisan Review*, XIX (1952), 301–03. (A symposium.)

" Our Dependence is on God," *Christian Century*, LXXI (1954), 1034–37.

" Our Fifteenth Birthday," *Christianity and Crisis*, XV (1955), 1–3. (Initialed editorial.)

" Our Relations to Catholicism," *Christianity and Crisis*, VII (September 15, 1947), 5–7.

" Our Relations to Japan," *Christianity and Crisis*, V (September 17, 1945), 5–7.

" Our Secularized Civilization," *Christian Century*, XLIII (1926), 508–10.

" Pacifism Against the Wall," *American Scholar*, V (1936), 133–41.

" Pacifism and America First," *Christianity and Crisis*, I (June 16, 1941), 2–6.

" Pacifism and the Use of Force," *The World Tomorrow*, XI (1928), 218–20.

" Palestine: British-American Dilemma," *The Nation*, CLXIII (1946), 238–39.

" Pawns of Fascism — Our Lower Middle Class," *American Scholar*, VI (1937), 145–52.

" Peace and the Liberal Illusion," *The Nation*, CXLVIII (1939), 117–19.

" Peace Through Cultural Cooperation," *Christianity and Crisis*, IX (1949), 131–33.

"The Pillars of Peace," *Spectator*, CLXXI (1943), 378–79.

"Pius XI and His Successor," *The Nation*, CXLIV (1937), 120–22.

"Plans for World Reorganization," *Christianity and Crisis*, II (October 19, 1942), 3–6.

"Political Action and Social Change," *The World Tomorrow*, XII, (1929), 491–93.

"Politics and Religion in Britain," *Christianity and Crisis*, III (July 26, 1943), 2–3.

"Politics and the Children of Light," *Christianity and Crisis*, III (November 29, 1943), 2. (Initialed editorial.)

"The Pope's Domesticated God," *Christian Century*, LXVII (1950), 74–75.

"Positive Defense," *Christianity and Crisis*, VI (April 29, 1946), 1–2. (Initialed editorial.)

"The Presidential Campaign," *Christianity and Crisis*, VIII (1948), 137–38. (Initialed editorial.)

"The Protestant Clergy and U. S. Politics," *The Reporter*, VI (February 19, 1952), 24–27.

"A Protestant Looks at Catholics," *The Commonweal*, LVIII (1953), 117–20.

"Protestantism in a Disordered World," *The Nation*, CLXVII (1948), 311–13.

"Protestantism in Germany," *Christian Century*, XL (1923), 1258–60.

"Puritanism and Prosperity," *The Atlantic Monthly*, CXXXVII (1926), 721–25.

"The Reach for One World," *The New Republic*, CXXIX (November 23, 1953), 16–17. (Review of *Foundations of the World Republic* by Guiseppe Antonio Borgese.)

"Reason and Religious Ultimates," *The New Republic*, *CXXXIII* (September 12, 1955), 17–18. (Review of *Reason and Existenz* by Karl Jaspers.)

"Religious Imagination and the Scientific Method," in *Proceedings of the National Conference of Social Work* (Chicago: University of Chicago Press, 1928), pp. 51–57.

"The Religious Level of the World Crisis," *Christianity and Crisis*, V (January 21, 1946), 4–7.

"Reply to Professor Macintosh," *Review of Religion*, IV (1940), 304–08.

"The Republican Victory," *Christianity and Crisis*, XII (1952), 153–54. (Initialed editorial.)

"The Reverend Doctor Silke," *Christian Century*, XLIII (1926), 316–18.

"The Revised Communist Faith," *The Nation*, CXLVI (1938), 247–49. (Review of *The People's Front* by Earl Browder.)

"The Revival of Feudalism," *Harper's Magazine*, CLXX (1935), 483–88.

"The Rising Catholic-Protestant Tension," *Christianity and Crisis*, IX (1949), 106–08.

"The Role of Prophetic Religion in the World Crisis," in *Men of To-*

morrow, ed. Thomas H. Johnson (New York: Putnam, 1942) , pp. 105–24.

"Roosevelt's Chances," *Spectator,* CLXXIII (1944) , 166–67.

"Russia and Karl Marx," *The Nation,* CXLVI (1938) , 530–31.

"Russia and the Peace," *Christianity and Crisis,* IV (November 13, 1944) , 2–4.

"The Secular and the Religious," *Christian Century,* LIII (1936) , 1452–54.

"Sex and Religion in the Kinsey Report," *Christianity and Crisis,* XIII (1953) , 138–41.

"Shall We Proclaim the Truth or Search for It?" *Christian Century,* XLII (1925) , 344–46.

"Should We Be Consistent?" *Christianity and Crisis,* X (1950) , 1–2.   (Initialed editorial.)

"The Sickness of American Culture," *The Nation,* CLXVI (1948) , 267–70.

"The Significance of the Growth of 'Christian Action'," *Christianity and Crisis,* XIV (1954) , 30–32.

"Social Justice," in *Christianity and Communism,* ed. H. Wilson Harris (Oxford: Blackwell's, 1937) , pp. 62–69.

"The Sources of American Prestige," *The New Leader,* XXXVIII (January 31, 1955) , 6–8.

"The Spirit and the Mechanism of Partnership," *Christianity and Crisis,* IX (1949) , 121–22.   (Initialed editorial.)

"Streaks of Dawn in the Night," *Christianity and Crisis,* IX (1949) , 162–64.

"The Supreme Court on Segregation in the Schools," *Christianity and Crisis,* XIV (1954) , 75–77.

"Survival and Religion," *Contemporary Jewish Record,* VII (1944) , 239–46.

"Synthetic Barbarism," *New Statesman and Nation,* XVIII (1939) , 368–69.

"Tensions in British Politics," *The Nation,* CLVI (1943) , 889–90.

"Ten Fateful Years," *Christianity and Crisis,* XI (1951) , 1–4.

"Ten Years that Shook My World," *Christian Century,* LVI (1939) , 542–46.

"The Terrible Beauty of the Cross," *Christian Century,* XLVI (1929) , 386–88.

"The Theory and Practice of UNESCO," *International Organization,* IV (1950) , 3–11.

"They All Fear America," *Christian Century,* LXIV (1947) , 993–94.

"The Truth in Myths," in *The Nature of Religious Experience,* ed. J. S. Bixler (New York: Harper & Brothers, 1937) , pp. 117–35.

"The Two Dimensions of the Struggle," *Christianity and Crisis,* XI (1951) , 65–66.   (Initialed editorial.)

"Two Forms of Tyranny," *Christianity and Crisis,* VIII (1948) , 3–5.

"The Tyranny of Science," *Theology Today,* X (1954) , 464–73.

"Understanding England," *The Nation,* CLVII (1943) , 175–77.

"The United Nations and World Organization," *Christianity and Crisis,* II (January 25, 1943), 1–2. (Initialed editorial.)

"Unity and Depth in Our Culture," *Sewanee Review,* LII (1944), 193–98.

"Utilitarian Christianity and the World Crisis," *Christianity and Crisis,* X (1950), 66–69.

"Wanted: Christian Morality," *Christian Century,* XL (1923), 201–03.

"We Are Being Driven!" *Christian Century,* XLVI (1929), 578–79.

"We Are Men and Not God," *Christian Century,* LXV (1948), 1138–40.

"What Are the Churches Advertising?" *Christian Century,* XLI (1924), 1532–33.

"What the War Did to My Mind," *Christian Century,* XLV (1928), 1161–63.

"Which Way, Great Britain?" *Current History,* XLV (November, 1936), 35–39.

"Why I Am Not a Christian," *Christian Century,* XLIV (1927), 1482–83.

"Why We Need a New Economic Order," *The World Tomorrow,* XI (1928), 395–98.

"Will America Back Out?" *The Nation,* CLX (1945), 42–43.

"Will Civilization Survive Technics?" *Commentary,* I (December, 1945), 2–8.

"Will Germany Go Communist?" *The Nation,* CLXIII (1946), 371–73.

"Will of God and the Van Zeeland Report," *Christian Century,* LV (1938), 1549–50.

"Winston Churchill and Great Britain," *Christianity and Crisis,* XV (1955), 51–52.

"World Community and World Government," *Christianity and Crisis,* VI (March 4, 1946), 5–6.

"World War III Ahead?" *The Nation,* CLVIII (1944), 356–58.

"Would Jesus Be a Churchman Today?" *World Tomorrow,* XI (1928), 492–94.

"The Youth Movement in Germany," *Christian Century,* XL (1923), 1316–17.

C. OTHER BOOKS AND ARTICLES

Allen, E. L., *Christianity and Society: A Guide to the Thought of Reinhold Niebuhr.* London: Hodder and Stoughton, 1950.

Auger, Pierre. "Who? Why? How?" *Bulletin of the Atomic Scientists,* XI (1955), 74–76.

Augustine. *Confessions.*

Banning, Andrew. "What Kind of Theology?" *Christian Century,* LXVI (1949), 1322–24.

Barth, Karl. "Continental vs. Anglo-Saxon Theology," *Christian Century,* LXVI (1949), 201–04.

Benedict, Ruth. "Human Nature Is Not a Trap," *Partisan Review,* X (1943), 159–64.

Benedict, Ruth. *Patterns of Culture*. New York: Penguin Books, Inc., 1934.

Bennett, John C. "Implication of the New Conception of 'Separation,'" *Christianity and Crisis*, VIII (1948), 89–90. (Initialed editorial.)

Blackmur, R. P. "The Scandals and Embarrassments of Modern Man," *Yale Review*, XLV (1956) 276–86.

Bouma, Clarence. "Calvinism in American Theology Today," *Journal of Religion*, XXVII, 1947, 34–45.

Breasted, James Henry. *The Dawn of Conscience*. New York: Charles Scribner's Sons, 1934.

Brightman, Edgar Sheffield. Review of *Faith and History* by Reinhold Niebuhr, in *Crozer Quarterly*, XXVI (1949), 249–252.

Brownell, Baker. *The Human Community*. New York: Harper & Brothers, 1950.

Brunner, Emil. "Toward a Missionary Theology," *Christian Century*, LXVI (1949), 816–18.

Butts, R. Freeman. *The American Tradition in Religion and Education*. Boston: The Beacon Press, 1950.

Canham, Edwin D. "The World at Mid-Century: Crisis Thinking Pulls Theology Both Forward and Backward," *Christian Science Monitor Magazine Section*, January 6, 1951, pp. 3, 12.

Davies, D. R. *Reinhold Niebuhr: Prophet from America*. New York: The Macmillan Company, 1945.

Davis, H. R. "The Political Philosophy of Reinhold Niebuhr." Unpublished Ph.D. dissertation, University of Chicago, 1951.

Dewey, John. "Anti-Naturalism in Extremis," in *Partisan Reader* (1943), pp. 514–28.

———. "Creative Democracy — The Task Before Us," in *The Philosopher of the Common Man*, ed. Sidney Ratner (New York: G. P. Putnam's Sons, 1940), pp. 220–28.

———. *Freedom and Culture*. New York: G. P. Putnam's Sons, 1939.

———. *Human Nature and Conduct*. New York: Henry Holt & Company, 1922.

———. "Liberating the Social Scientist," *Commentary*, IV (1947), 378–85.

———. *Logic: The Theory of Inquiry*. New York: Henry Holt & Company, 1938.

———. "Progress," *International Journal of Ethics*, XXVI (1916), 311–22.

———. *Reconstruction in Philosophy*. Enlarged ed. Boston: The Beacon Press, 1948.

Dewey, John, and Bentley, Arthur F. *Knowing and the Known*. Boston: The Beacon Press, 1949.

DeWolf, L. Harold. *The Religious Revolt Against Reason*. New York: Harper & Brothers, 1949.

Educator's Washington Dispatch. Supplement, January, 1948, "So You Appointed a Committee. . . ."

Ferré, Nels F. S. "Beyond Liberalism and Neo-Orthodoxy," *Christian Century*, LXVI (1949), 362–64.

Fitch, Robert E. "The Catholic Church as a Power Polity," *Christianity and Crisis,* VII (November 10, 1947), 5–7.

———. "Reinhold Niebuhr as Prophet and as Philosopher of History," *Journal of Religion,* XXXII (1952), 31–46.

———. "Reinhold Niebuhr, Excubitor!" *Pacific Spectator,* IV (1950), 308–18.

Follett, Mary Parker. *Creative Experience.* New York: Longmans, Green & Company, 1924.

———. *Dynamic Administration.* Edited by Henry C. Metcalf and L. Urwick. London: Bath Management Publications Trust, 1941.

Freund, Ludwig. "The New American Conservatism and European Conservatism," Mimeo. Paper presented at the Annual Convention of Midwest Political Scientists at the University of Iowa, April 30, 1954.

Fries, Horace S. "On the Origin of Communication," *American Journal of Economics and Sociology,* V (1946), 411–14.

———. "Scientific Mediation: Tool of Democracy," *Antioch Review,* V (1945), 388–401.

———. "Social Planning," in *The Cleavage of Our Culture,* ed. Frederick Burkhardt (Boston: The Beacon Press, 1952), pp. 81–104.

———. "Some Democratic Implications of Science in Scientific Management," *Advanced Management,* V (1940), 147–52.

———. "World Revolution Number Five," *Antioch Review,* III (1943), 425–37.

Geiger, G. R. "Philosophic Humanism Today," *Antioch Review,* VIII (1948), 447–62.

———. "Dewey's Social and Political Philosophy," in *The Philosophy of John Dewey,* ed. P. A. Schilpp (Chicago: Northwestern University, 1939), pp. 337–68.

Gilmore, R. E. Review of *The Religious Revolt Against Reason* by L. Harold DeWolf, in *Christian Century,* LXVI (1949), 1294–95.

Hammar, George. *Christian Realism in Contemporary American Theology: A Study of Reinhold Niebuhr, W. M. Horton, H. P. Van Dusen.* D.D. dissertation, University of Uppsala. Uppsala: Lundequistska Bokhandeln, 1940.

Hauge, Hendrik. "Barth as Church Politician," *Christian Century,* LXVII (1950), 47–49.

Herberg, Will. "The Three Dialogues of Man," review of *The Self and the Dramas of History* by Reinhold Niebuhr, in *The New Republic,* CXXXII (May 16, 1955), 28–31.

Hiltner, Seward. "Niebuhr on Kinsey," *Christianity and Crisis,* XIII (1954), 179–82.

Hook, Sidney. "Intelligence and Evil in Human History," *Commentary,* III (1947), 210–21.

———. "The New Failure of Nerve," *Partisan Review,* X (1943), 2–23.

———. "The Philosophical Presuppositions of Democracy," *Ethics,* LII (1942), 275–96.

Hook, Sidney. "Prophet of Man's Glory and Tragedy," review of *Reinhold Niebuhr: His Religious, Social and Political Thought* ed. by Charles W. Kegley & Robert W. Bretall, in *New York Times Book Review*, January 29, 1956, 6–7, 22.

———. "Social Change and Original Sin: Answer to Niebuhr," *New Leader*, November 11, 1941.

Howell, Ronald F. "Political Philosophy on a Theological Foundation: An Expository Analysis of the Political Thought of Reinhold Niebuhr," *Ethics*, LXIII (1953), 79–96.

Hu Shih. "The Political Philosophy of Instrumentalism," in *The Philosopher of the Common Man*, ed. Sidney Ratner (New York: G. P. Putnam's Sons, 1940), pp. 205–19.

Illinois *ex rel.* McCollum *v.* Board of Education, 333 U.S. 203 (1948).

Jacobson, N. P. "Niebuhr's Philosophy of History," *Harvard Theological Review*, XXXVII (1944), 238–68.

Kegley, Charles W. and Bertall, Robert W. eds. *Reinhold Niebuhr: His Religious, Social, and Political Thought*. New York: The Macmillan Company, 1956.

Kirk, Russell. *A Program for Conservatives*. Chicago: Henry Regnery Company, 1954.

Klausner, Neal W. Review of *Faith and History* by Reinhold Niebuhr, in *Journal of Religion*, XXX (1950), 228–30.

Kuhn, Harold B. "The Problem of Human Self-Transcendence in the Dialectical Theology," *Harvard Theological Review*, XL (1947), 47–68.

Langer, S. K. *Philosophy in a New Key*. New York: Penguin Books, Inc., 1948.

Lewis, H. D. *Morals and Revelation*. London: George Allen & Unwin, 1951.

———. *Morals and the New Theology*. London: Victor Gollancz, 1947.

———. "Revelation and Reason," *Hibbert Journal*, XLVII (1948), 56–64.

Lindeman, Eduard C. "Conference and Compromise," *The New Republic*, LXI (1929), 364–65.

Loomer, Bernard M. "Neo-Naturalism and Neo-Orthodoxy," *Journal of Religion*, XXVIII (1948), 79–91.

Lyman, Eugene W. *The Meaning and Truth of Religion*. New York: Charles Scribner's Sons, 1933.

Macintosh, D. C. "Is Theology Reducible to Mythology?" *Review of Religion*, IV (1940), 140–58.

———. *The Problem of Religious Knowledge*. New York: Harper & Brothers, 1940.

———. "A Rejoinder to Professor Niebuhr's Reply," *Review of Religion*, IV (1940), 435–37.

MacIver, R. M. *Social Causation*. Boston: Ginn & Company, 1942.

Maritain, Jacques. "Christian Humanism," *Fortune*, XXV (April, 1942), 106–07, 160–73.

————. *Christianity and Democracy.* New York: Charles Scribner's Sons, 1944.

————. *Education at the Crossroads.* New Haven: Yale University Press, 1943.

————. *Principes d'une Politique Humaniste.* New York: Maison Française, 1944.

————. *The Rights of Man and Natural Law.* New York: Charles Scribner's Sons, 1943.

McCown, C. C. "In History or Beyond History," *Harvard Theological Review*, XXXVIII (1945), 151–75.

McIntyre, John. "Christ and History," *Reformed Theological Review*, VIII (August, 1949), 9–42.

Meland, Bernard Eugene. *America's Spiritual Culture.* New York: Harper & Brothers, 1948.

Meyer, Agnes E. "The School, the State, and the Church," *The Atlantic Monthly*, CLXXXII (November, 1948), 45–50.

Miller, William Lee. "The Irony of Reinhold Niebuhr," *The Reporter*, XII (January 13, 1955), 11–15.

Morrison, Charles Clayton. "The Liberalism of Neo-Orthodoxy," *Christian Century*, LXVII (1950), 697–99, 731–33, 760–63.

Murphy, Arthur E. *The Uses of Reason.* New York: The Macmillan Company, 1943.

Orlans, Harold. "Democracy and Social Planning," *Dissent*, I (1954), 189–95.

Otto, M. C. "Creative Bargaining," *The Standard*, XXXVII (1951), 263–69.

————. *The Human Enterprise.* New York: F. S. Crofts & Company, 1941.

————. "Intolerance," in *Encyclopedia of Social Sciences* (New York: The Macmillan Company, 1932), VIII, 242–45.

————. "Professional Philosophy and the Public," in *Philosophy in American Education*, by B. Blanchard, C. Ducasse, C. W. Hendel, A. E. Murphy, and M. C. Otto (New York: Harper & Brothers, 1945), pp. 143–67.

————. Review of *The Children of Light and the Children of Darkness* by Reinhold Niebuhr, in *Crozer Quarterly*, XXII (1945), 165–66.

————. *Things and Ideals.* New York: Henry Holt & Company, 1924.

————. "War and Moral Progress," *The Progressive*, XIII (September, 1949), 5–6.

Poston, R. W. *Small Town Renaissance.* New York: Harper & Brothers, 1950.

Ramsberger, A. G. Letter to the editor, *Antioch Review*, V (1945), 156.

Randall, John Herman, Jr. "The Churches and the Liberal Tradition," *Annals of the American Academy of Political and Social Science*, CCLVI (March, 1948), 148–64.

Ratner, Joseph, ed. *Intelligence in the Modern World: John Dewey's Philosophy.* New York: Modern Library, 1939.

Raven, C. E. "Is There a Christian Politics?" *Hibbert Journal*, XLIX
  (1951), 348–54.
Shinn, Roger L. "Must Theologians and Educators Fight?" *Christian
  Century*, LXVI (1949), 12–14.
Simpson, George. *Science as Morality*. Yellow Springs, Ohio: The Ameri-
  can Humanist Association, 1953.
Sperry, Willard L. *Jesus Then and Now*. New York: Harper & Brothers,
  1949.
"Statement on Church and State," *Christianity and Crisis*, VIII (1948), 90.
Stewart, David A. "The Neo-Orthodoxy of Niebuhr," *University of
  Toronto Quarterly*, XVIII (1949), 347–57.
Thelen, M. F. *Man as Sinner in Contemporary American Realistic The-
  ology*. New York: King's Crown Press, 1946.
Thompson, Kenneth W. "Beyond National Interest: A Critical Evalua-
  tion of Reinhold Niebuhr's Theory of International Politics," *Review
  of Politics*, XVII (1955), 167–88.
Tillich, Paul. "Beyond Religious Socialism," *Christian Century*, LXVI
  (1949), 732–33.
Time. "Niebuhr on History," LIII (May 2, 1949), 68–69.
Vlastos, Gregory. "Sin and Anxiety in Niebuhr's Religion," *Christian
  Century*, LVIII (1941), 1202–04.
Waddington, C. H. *The Scientific Attitude*. Revised ed. London: Pen-
  guin Books, 1948.
West, Anthony. "Night and Fog," review of *The Irony of American His-
  tory* by Reinhold Niebuhr, in *The New Yorker*, XXVIII (May 3,
  1952), 114–21.
White, Morton. "Of Moral Predicaments," review of *The Irony of Ameri-
  can History* by Reinhold Niebuhr, in *The New Republic*, CXXVI
  (May 5, 1952), 18–19.
Wieman, H. N., and Meland, B. E. *American Philosophies of Religion*.
  New York: Willett, Clark & Company, 1936.
Wieman, H. N.; Murphy, A. E.; Williams, Gardner; Hudson, Jay W.;
  Otto, M. C.; Pratt, J. B.; Sellars, R. W. *Religious Liberals Reply:
  A Criticism of Neo-Orthodoxy*. Boston: The Beacon Press, 1947.
Williams, Daniel D. Review of *Faith and History* by Reinhold Niebuhr,
  in *Christian Century*, LXVI (1949), 821–22.

Index